Dollarbird

JEOPARDY OF EVERY WIND

A retired senior project manager in the IT industry, Sue Paul is an experienced amateur genealogist, who discovered Captain Thomas Bowrey whilst researching her one-name study. She lives in Cambridgeshire with her husband.

Jeopardy of Every Wind

The Biography of Captain Thomas Bowrey

Sue Paul

Dollarbird

 Dollarbird

First published in 2020
by Dollarbird, an imprint of Monsoon Books Ltd
www.dollarbird.co.uk
www.monsoonbooks.co.uk

No.1 The Lodge, Burrough Court,
Burrough on the Hill, Melton Mowbray LE14 2QS, UK.

ISBN (paperback): 978-1-912049-62-2
ISBN (ebook): 978-1-912049-63-9

Cover design by Cover Kitchen.

All illustrations copyright©Sue Paul unless indicated otherwise.

A Cataloguing-in-Publication data record is available from the British Library.

Printed and bound in Great Britain by Clays Ltd, Elcograf S.p.A.
22 21 20   1 2 3

We bring no store of ingots,

Of spice or precious stones,

But what we have we gathered

With sweat and aching bones:

In flame beneath the Tropics,

In frost upon the floe,

And jeopardy of every wind

That does between them go.

Coastwise – cross-seas – round the world and back again,

Wither flaw shall fail us or the Trades drive down:

Plain-sail – storm-sail – lay your board and tack again –

And all to bring a cargo up to London town.

RUDYARD KIPLING, *The Merchantmen*,

in *The Seven Seas* (1896)

Contents

ACKNOWLEDGEMENTS   xiii

PREFACE   xv

Introduction: The Paper Trail   1

Early Life (1659-1668)   13

Learning His Trade (1669-1679)   36

Branching Out (1680-1685)   65

Moving On (1686-1688)   92

Starting Out Again (1689-1695)   108

The *St George Galley* (1696-1699)   127

The Malay-English Dictionary (1700-1701)   149

The Voyages of the *Prosperous*
       && the *Worcester* (1701-1703)   169

The Fate of the *Worcester* (1704-1705)   192

The Final Projects (1707-1711)   220

Preparing for Mortality (1710-1713)   244

Epilogue: The Story that Refuses to Die   256

NOTES   261

APPENDICES

    I: THE PAPER TRAIL   277

    II: ANALYSIS OF THE JOURNAL AND LOGBOOK   278

III: TIMELINE   279
IV: BOWREY FAMILY TREE   282
V: BUSHELL FAMILY TREE   283
BIBLIOGRAPHY   285
GLOSSARY   305
GAZETTEER   313
INDEX   319

Acknowledgements

This book would not have been written without the Internet and, though he may never be aware of it, I have to express my enormous gratitude to Tim Berners-Lee for imagining the World Wide Web. Without the Internet, I would never have discovered Captain Thomas Bowrey. Without the Internet, I would never have been able to track down all the books, archive holdings and other sources used. Do not misunderstand me. Even today, no research can be carried out exclusively on the Internet but it does make the holdings in the world's wonderful libraries and archives more accessible.

I have received so much generous help from the British Library, London Metropolitan Archives, Essex Record Office, Quaker House Library, The School of Oriental and African Studies Library, Yale University Library and Stuttgart University Library, all of whom made it possible to do the necessary research from home by copying or allowing me to photograph their holdings. Special thanks must go to Dr John Boneham of the British Library, Luitgard Nuss of the Württembergische Landesbibliothek and Darren Cox of Lloyd's of London for patiently responding to my emails.

Along the way, I have been encouraged by many others interested in aspects of Thomas Bowrey's life. I should like to thank all the academics who have kindly engaged with this amateur when she questioned their conclusions especially Anna

Winterbotttom and Simon Dixon. I am just as grateful to my fellow researchers who have contacted me and hope that they find something useful in this book. In particular, I should like to thank Christine Hancock and Andrew Smith of Adelaide.

With no naval knowledge and experience before I started on this venture, I needed to find a way of understanding life in the days of sail as rapidly as possible. Fortunately, I discovered the novels of J. D. Davies and Alexander Kent and I owe them a large debt of gratitude. The fictitious Matthew Quinton and Richard Bolitho may be officers in the Royal Navy and have lived a generation before and after Thomas Bowrey but their stories written by experts provided me with a painless, and even enjoyable, education.

Special thanks must go to Gill Blanchard and my Fierce Friends, fellow students on her *Writing Her Family History* courses, for helping me hone my writing style. In addition, Gill's questions relating to her own research pushed me in my own.

Finally, I am most grateful to my husband, Richard, for his loving support allowing me the time to write this book, for acting as my fiercest friend reviewing my drafts and for his encouragement in everything I do.

Preface

DEFINITIONS

We live, today, in a world of absolutes. The introduction of standard time with the arrival of the railways and the telegraph was so long before living memory that we take Greenwich Mean Time and time zones for granted. Once, time was local and measured by the sundial. In Thomas Bowrey's day, dates, values, and measures, among other things, were not absolute. Often they varied by location, time or even what was being measured. In view of this, some explanation of the conventions used in this book is necessary.

DATES

In 1752, Britain adopted the Gregorian calendar – the one we use today. During the period of this book, the Julian calendar was still used in England but not in much of Europe, especially the Roman Catholic countries. This resulted in the English calendar being ten, later eleven, days behind Europe. Until we adopted the calendar promoted by Pope Gregory XIII, the New Year in England officially started on 25 March but the situation was more complex. 1 January had been celebrated as New Year's Day for centuries.

In view of this, dates between 1 January and 24 March were often, but not always, written in the style 14 March $17^{12}/_{13}$. The English writing in the East Indies tended to use the English form of date but correspondence between England and Europe often used the style $^{25}/_{14}$ March $17^{12}/_{13}$. Where these formats were not used, there can be doubt about the true date.

At the same time, some non-conformist groups, such as the Quakers, refused to use the standard, pagan names, for months used in English. Instead, they numbered months from the official New Year. Thus 9^{br} was the ninth month, counting from March, which is November.

For simplicity, all dates in this book have been converted to the modern calendar for years and months whilst maintaining the English day used in the original document. The New Year will be taken to be 1 January. Thus, the date in my example (that of Thomas Bowrey's burial) will be shown as 14 March 1713. Because of the variety of formats that may have been used, at times the true date is ambiguous in the manuscripts consulted and, in those cases, I have used the most likely in the context.

MONETARY VALUES

Inflation today may be more under control than in the relatively recent past but anyone reading this will have experienced how prices rise year on year. The value of money since the time of Thomas Bowrey has devalued considerably. In order to present monetary values in terms that can be understood, I have used the *measuringworth.com* website to convert them to present day values. This site presents estimates of a value in a target year (the current year) given the price in the year the expenditure was incurred but the calculation made is not that simple. For any cost input, the values returned depend on a large number of factors. Rather than confuse by varying the calculation used in different circumstances and to avoid any risk of exaggeration, I have used the *real price* of *commodities* calculations throughout.

In India in the seventeenth century, the primary currency in use was the pagoda. In his *Bay of Bengal*, Thomas Bowrey sets out the value of a pagoda in different locations. In most of his accounts, he specifies whether the values are expressed in pagodas from Fort St George or elsewhere. In Pulicat, there were twenty-four fantams to the pagoda and twenty-four copper cash to the fantam. This breakdown was not consistent. There were thirty-two fantams to the pagoda and eighty copper cash to a fantam at Fort St George. Alongside the pagoda, trade was also carried out using royals of eight (Spanish silver reales or pieces of eight), rupees and other currencies. Where possible, I have converted these currencies to sterling using Thomas Bowrey's own conversion rates.

The United Kingdom introduced decimal currency in 1971. Prior to that there were twenty shillings to the pound and twelve pence to the shilling. Nine pounds, nineteen shillings and eleven pence was written £9/19/11. A shilling was converted to five pence at decimalisation.

MEASURES

Many different units of weight were used in the East Indies and these, again, varied by location and the goods being measured. Although Thomas Bowrey listed the various units used in his *Bay of Bengal* he did not give as much detail as for monetary values. In view of this, where weights and other measures are involved, it has not always been possible to give modern equivalents.

The United Kingdom today uses metric measures that did not exist in Thomas Bowrey's day. However, imperial measures remain widely understood, and even habitually used by many. To avoid the cumbersome translation of all imperial measures into metric ones, I shall give the conversion rates here:

DISTANCE

1 inch		= 2.54 cm
1 foot	= 12 inches	= 30.48 cm
1 yard	= 3 feet	= 91.44 cm
1 mile	= 1,760 yards	= 1.61 km

WEIGHT

1 ounce		= 28.35 g
1 pound	= 16 ounces	= 453.59 g
1 stone	= 14 pounds	= 6.35 kg
1 hundredweight	= 8 stone	= 50.80 kg
1 ton	= 20 hundredweight	= 1.02 tonne

NAMES AND PLACES

In the days before the first English dictionary, there was no standard accepted spelling of words. The same applied to personal names and geographic locations. The spelling of names of geographic locations was even more problematic for English writers overseas to whom many local names were difficult to understand or pronounce.

Throughout this book I have used modern spellings in most cases and have attempted to standardise personal names. For geographic locations I have chosen, for the most part, to use the name by which they were known by Europeans at this time as they remain more accessible to the majority of readers in English. Where multiple names and/or spelling were used I have opted for a single variant. For example, in the case of what is now known as Chennai, I have used Fort St George, the name of the East India Company fortified factory there. Thomas Bowrey and his correspondents appear to have used Fort St George, Madras (the settlement that grew up around the Fort) and Madraspatam (Madras town) interchangeably. I have included a gazetteer at the back of the book for further clarification.

The majority of the story of Thomas Bowrey's life took place before the political union of England and Scotland. Possibly because of his role in the events that accelerated the union, he was precise in his use of the terms *England* and *Britain* before and after the union. I have maintained this convention in this book.

SHIPS

In the seventeenth and eighteenth centuries, a *ship* was technically a square-rigged, decked vessel with three masts. However, in the papers of Thomas Bowrey, the term *ship* was often used in the same way as in the twenty-first century; that is, with the wider meaning of any large seagoing vessel and it is this definition I have used in this book. Thomas Bowrey was involved with the voyages of many types of ships. Definitions of each of these can be found in the glossary.

POLITICS OF PRE-COLONIAL INDIA

Thomas Bowrey's lifetime long preceded British rule in India. When the Europeans arrived, the sub-continent had been ruled by Muslim Grand Mughals since 1526. Between 1658 and his death in 1707, the sixth and, effectively, last Mughal was Muhi-ud-Din Muhammad, known as Aurangzeb. The Mughal Empire was made up of a large number of semi-autonomous princely states each with their own ruler. Muslim rulers of princely states held titles such as Nawab and Hindu and Sikh rulers were called Maharaja among other titles.

European East India companies negotiated licences to set up their settlements alongside the existing political structure. The opportunities of the region also attracted Europeans independent of the companies such as Bowrey. They joined retired company employees who remained once their contracts ended. These independents had an ambiguous relationship with their national company expecting freedom from their control but looking to them for protection when threatened. As the number of their nationals free of their company increased, European governments sent consuls to the region to look after their interests. Consequently, an individual may have had to answer to the Mughal's and local authorities as well as to their consul and company officials.

EAST INDIA COMPANY

On the final day of 1600, the queen granted *The Governor and Company of Merchants of London Trading into the East Indies* a royal charter with a monopoly of all English trade in all lands washed by the Indian Ocean from the southern tip of Africa to Indonesia in the South Pacific. The East India Company was destined to rule India with its own army but this was over one hundred and fifty years in the future. Initially, it was purely a trading company until, in 1683, it was granted a charter by Charles II giving it the power to establish *courts of judicature* with jurisdiction over European residents.

Over the years, the East India Company's monopoly of the English East Indies trade was challenged and periodically reinforced. In 1694, a group of independent merchants took their case to the House of Commons. Four years later, the *English Company Trading to the East Indies*, commonly known as the *New* or *English East India Company* was created, in return for a £2 million loan to the government. The original company of London merchants became known as the *Old* or *London East India Company*.

The Old Company took a large share of the New, dominating it. There was still a strong rivalry between the two companies for the dominant share of the trade but, as a large part of the profits from the New Company went to the Old, the result was little real commercial competition. Eventually, in 1702, the two companies were amalgamated under a tripartite agreement with Queen Anne. They were allowed a number of years in which to wind up their businesses before the union was ratified.

For simplicity, throughout this book, I have used the single term *East India Company* for the Old, New and United companies unless it is material which company was involved.

INTRODUCTION

The Paper Trail

THE BOWREY PAPERS

It was a great inconvenience. He was extremely busy but now red spots had broken out on his face, forearms and hands, Thomas Bushell could no longer ignore his fever. He needed to find an apothecary. Although the symptoms were relatively mild, was he concerned he had contracted smallpox? He had probably known of cases of the disease where the early symptoms were similar but much more severe.

It was 17 February 1721 and later the same day, he wrote home to his cousin at Cleeve Prior about five and a half miles north of Evesham in Worcestershire saying he hoped his mother would not be concerned because the apothecary had confirmed his was a *very kind sort of pox*. Bushell almost certainly had *variola minor* or ordinary smallpox, which although as highly infectious as the more usual variation was much less common. The rash would soon spread to his trunk and lower limbs but this form was fatal in less than one percent of cases.

Bushell was not greatly debilitated by his illness. On the same day as he saw the apothecary, he despatched an iron chest containing silver and jewellery weighing about two hundredweight home by carrier. He suggested a wheelbarrow would be needed to collect it. For security, he had retained the key so the chest could not be opened until he returned home, presumably once he had fully recovered.

The letter was written from Marine Square in Wapping, the home of his late aunt, Frances Gardiner. Frances had died in mid-January and Bushell, her sole executor, may have organised her funeral at Lee in Kent on 17 January 1721 before staying in London to obtain probate on her estate two weeks later. Frances had recognised her affairs were complex and made provision for her servant, Joseph Noden, to assist Bushell until he became familiar with them. The help was probably much needed. It was a busy time for Bushell. He had buried his father at Cleeve Prior on 6 October 1720 and obtained probate on his estate the day prior to his aunt's.

Cleeve Prior manor house. [From *The Papers of Thomas Bowrey (1699-1713)*, edited by Temple.]

It is not known if the iron chest contained anything in addition to the silver and jewellery or whether Bushell returned to the manor house at Cleeve Prior with another chest because nothing more is heard of Frances Gardiner's legacy for the next two hundred years. It is likely anything other than the valuables mentioned in the letter were considered of little worth. Twenty-three years after Frances' death, Bushell's uncle George Fettiplace died naming his nephew as his heir. Thomas Bushell changed his name to Fettiplace and moved his family to his late uncle's estate at Swinbrook, Oxfordshire.

The house the Bushells vacated at Cleeve Prior had been in continuous occupation by the family since the dissolution of the monasteries under Henry VIII. During the English Civil Wars, the family had Royalist sympathies. Anthony Bushell (born 1611) was a Royalist Lieutenant-Colonel who deserted the king's cause before the Battle of Naseby. The penalty for fighting against Parliament was the confiscation of property but, in 1649, Anthony managed to avoid losing his estates by compounding for his delinquency, paying a fine. According to tradition, in 1650 Thomas Bushell, probably the father of Anthony, hid in a converted disused garderobe, or toilet chute, to evade capture by Parliamentary troops. He later obtained his liberty by giving securities for his good behaviour. After 1744, the house stayed in the ownership of the family but was occupied by tenants.

In August 1913, the then resident of Cleeve Prior decided to have a clear out and discovered an old, wooden chest in a windowless attic room. As one newspaper reported some years later:

How excited most of us would be if we discovered a little

room under the roof that no one knew about before! ... In one corner there was a curious old chest. It was a romantic moment. Would there be Spanish doubloons or emeralds from the newly-discovered land of Peru lying in that ancient coffer? Eagerly the old fastenings were undone, and to everyone's disappointment nothing was seen but a bundle of letters.

The chest. [From *The Papers of Thomas Bowrey (1699-1713)*, edited by Temple.]

The disappointing find was a large collection of late seventeenth- and early eighteenth-century manuscripts which, when examined by John Humphreys the president of the Birmingham Archaeological Society, were found to relate to Captain Thomas Bowrey. When I learned of the papers from a chance Internet search another century later my reaction was very different.

I had recently registered my Bowry surname study with the Guild of One-Name Studies and such a find is like treasure to a genealogist. I immediately set to tracing the present whereabouts of the documents. Over the intervening period, the papers had been purchased by Henry Howard in 1921, examined, sorted and divided between different repositories. The chest was presented to the Victoria and Albert Museum. The documents were donated and sold in a number of tranches and have all moved at least once since but the majority are now held by just two archives.

In the main, documents relating to Thomas Bowrey's life in India and his Malay-English dictionary are at the British Library. Those relating to his life after he returned to England are kept at the London Metropolitan Archives. This split is not as clear cut as it may sound. Smaller groups of manuscripts are now held elsewhere. By 1955 when they were published in Healey's *Letters of Daniel Defoe*, two letters from the author were in the possession of Dr Henry C Hutchins of Connecticut. Hutchins sold them at Sotherby's, New York, in 1984 and they were sold again at Christie's, London, on 3 July 2007 for £15,600. Their present location is unknown. The documents signed by Elihu Yule were donated to Yale University but typed copies were retained. A few receipts issued by Quaker Peter Briggins' were given to his descendant, Lady Ruth Fry, and are now at the Quaker House Library. The whereabouts of many of the family papers, especially those relating to the Bushell family, including the letter quoted at the start of this Introduction, is unknown.

Some of the papers have been published. In 1927, Richard Carnac Temple edited the diary of a six week tour of Holland and Flanders in 1698 together with those connected with the *Mary Galley* into *The Papers of Thomas Bowrey (1669-1713)*. In his General Introduction, he states that the earliest document discovered was dated 1669 and the latest 1751. The earliest manuscript I have tracked down from the papers discovered at

Cleeve Prior is dated 28 September 1671 and the latest 4 June 1715. Disturbingly, in his Introduction to the story of the *Mary Galley* Temple mentioned chemically treating water damaged pages of sailing directions. These have disappeared. How many other manuscripts were treated in such a way, damaged beyond recovery and are no longer available? Later, in 1930, Temple wrote the *New Light on the Mysterious Tragedy of the* Worcester *1704-1705*. Temple's death in 1931 brought to an end his hopes of publishing all of the papers.

THE BAY OF BENGAL MANUSCRIPT

Temple's interest in Thomas Bowrey had begun in the early years of the twentieth century when he was asked to inspect another manuscript in the possession of Eliot Howard, the cousin of Henry Howard. It had been known prior to this date and had been quoted from by Yule (in 1889), Anderson (1890) and the *Oxford English Dictionary*. With permission of the owner, Temple edited the manuscript, publishing *A Geographical Account of Countries Round the Bay of Bengal 1669-1679* in 1905.

Temple was, perhaps, an obvious choice as editor because of his wide knowledge of the region. He was born in 1850 in Allahabad, India, where his father was working as a civil servant. His great-grandfather had been Governor of the Bombay Presidency 1838-1841; a position Temple's father was to hold some forty years later. After his education at Harrow and Cambridge, Temple joined the army transferring in 1877 to the British Indian Army serving in many areas from Bombay to Rangoon. Following his retirement and return to the UK, he became a writer and amateur anthropologist. From shortly after his retirement until his death in 1931, Temple served on the Council of the Hakluyt Society dedicated to publishing the records of voyages, travels and other geographic material.

Howard and Temple proceeded to carry out extensive research and identified the author as the Captain Thomas Bowrey who had written the first Malay-English dictionary. Temple suggested the *Bay of Bengal* manuscript had passed down the Eliot-Howard family from an ancestor, Quaker diarist Peter Briggins. From the two Briggins' diaries, Temple deduced that he was acquainted with Bowrey during the period from 1706 until the captain's death. Subsequently, Briggins helped Bowrey's widow. Temple concluded that it was only reasonable to conjecture that the manuscript was given to Briggins as a token of gratitude.

My reading of Briggins' diaries alongside Thomas Bowrey's papers leads me to conclude their relationship was purely a business one. Bowrey was renting the King's Head Inn in Southwark from Briggins and they met only when the rent was due, when Briggins often had to chase after Bowrey for a number of days. As he usually paid his bills promptly, this suggests Briggins was not in the forefront of Bowrey's mind. In the final days of Bowrey's life and immediately afterwards, Briggins assisted Thomas and then his widow in an insurance matter. This was most likely insurance on the Southwark inn. An incomplete manuscript seems to have been an unlikely thank-you gift for someone, especially for a recipient with no connection to India except for some shares in the East India Company, but there are few other plausible explanations for the manuscript being held by Briggins' descendants. A John Eliot was surgeon on Thomas' ship the *Mary Galley* and it is possible he may also have been a member of the Eliot-Howard family although I have been unable to identify any connection. As ships' doctors had low status compared to other officers, it seems unlikely there was any reason for giving him the manuscript.

Whilst the provenance of the manuscript remains a mystery it undoubtably relates to Thomas Bowrey, the subject of this biography. The original manuscript signed only *TB* is now held at the British Library. To this amateur eye, the handwriting is correct and sufficient of the contents can be cross-referenced to other documents to have confidence in the attribution.

THE ESSEX MANUSCRIPTS

Thomas Bowrey's father-in-law, Phillip Gardiner, died in August 1704 at a property he held in Great Clacton, Essex. A small bundle of his papers, including some in Thomas' hand, are now held in the Essex Record Office but no acquisition record survives. It is possible these were either donated to an unidentified local repository by Henry Howard or, as suggested by the record office, they were a separate batch of documents held by a local firm of solicitors who deposited them locally before they were transferred to the county archives.

THE SLOANE CHARTS

While trying to identify the author of the *Bay of Bengal* manuscript, Temple discovered a set of twelve charts of the islands of the Indian Archipelago, the River Hooghly and the Persian Gulf by Thomas Bowrey at the British Museum Library. The earliest was dated 1681. I was naturally curious about how these charts were acquired by the Library long before the discovery of the Bowrey papers.

Unexpectedly, rather than coming to the British Museum Library from the India Office, the twelve charts form part of the Sloane *Additional Manuscripts*. Although said to be part of Hans Sloane's personal collection that formed the basis of the original British Museum collection, these additional manuscripts were transferred to the Department of Manuscripts after the publication of Samuel Ayscough's *Catalogue of the Manuscripts in the British Museum* created in 1782, nearly thirty years after Sloane's death. Consequentially, the source of these charts is ambiguous.

Sloane was a contemporary of Thomas Bowrey. They were born just seven months apart. Sloane left for Jamaica in 1687 and returned to London in the same year as Bowrey arrived back from India but there is no evidence that they knew each other. However, Sloane and William Dampier, who had also spent time in Jamaica, knew each other later in London. Dampier was believed to have received at least one chart from Bowrey and may have passed others to Sloane. Otherwise, in his will dated 11 March 1712, Bowrey bequeathed his maps to Thomas Studds, the son of his cousin Hannah Middleton, and eventually they may have passed from a Studds descendant to the British Museum sometime between 1783 and 1835.

THE IDENTITY OF THOMAS BOWREY

In his introduction to the *Bay of Bengal*, Temple states that there were *no grounds for doubting that TB* was the same Thomas Bowrey who wrote the Malay-English dictionary. Although, he reached the conclusion purely on the weight of evidence that there was no one else it could be, I agree with him but there are people who question the attribution. He wrote many years before the Bowrey papers were discovered at Cleeve Prior. Has that discovery strengthened his argument?

In the preface of his dictionary, Thomas Bowrey says that he was resident in the East Indies for nineteen years, departing from Fort St George on the *Bengal Merchant* in 1688. From this, it can be concluded he started his residence in the East Indies in 1669. Documents relating to the dictionary were included in the Cleeve Prior papers as was a draft letters dated 1688 stating that he was *being now bound for England on the* Bengal Merchant. At the beginning of the *Bay of Bengal* manuscript, Thomas repeated the claim to have started his time in the East Indies at Fort St George in 1669. Thus, the discovery of the Cleeve Prior papers provided the confirmation that the person responsible for them also wrote both the dictionary and the *Bay of Bengal* manuscript.

THE LIFE OF THOMAS BOWREY

The death of Richard Carnac Temple may have brought to an end his hopes of publishing the remaining papers of Thomas Bowrey but that was not the end of interest in them. For more than a century, his papers have been referenced by academics, writers and students of subjects ranging from the East India Company to the recreational use of cannabis. Yet, in all that time, no one has attempted to write his full biography.

Today there is an enormous amount of material available referencing the man and his writing. I constantly make new discoveries. The more I learned about Thomas Bowrey, the more intrigued I became with his life and character, and determined to write this book. The sheer volume of material available has, at times, seemed overwhelming but my study of it has been rewarded by uncovering a fascinating character who led an extraordinary life.

CHAPTER 1

Early Life
(1659-1668)

THE BEGINNINGS

There was a lot to fear as Elizabeth Bowrey felt the first pangs of labour. Childbirth in the mid-seventeenth century was dangerous and Thomas, her husband, was at sea. The sea was a perilous place at any time but England was at war. Thomas had engaged with the enemy already that year. What Elizabeth could not know was he had done so again the previous day. Would he return to her and their baby in Wapping? If he returned, her worries would not be over.

It was September 1659. The civil war that had raged in England for nine years had ended just eight years earlier. The country had been bitterly divided. The king had been executed. The memory was still fresh. The Parliamentary victory in October 1651 had not brought the peace everyone craved and since then England had been at war first with the Dutch and, now, with the Spanish. These were both naval conflicts impacting on the lives of those living in Wapping. Both sides saw the enemy's merchant shipping as legitimate and lucrative targets. Prize money awarded to crews for the capture of enemy shipping was some compensation for tardy payment of wages. When the focus of the naval war moved from Europe to the West Indies with the change of opponent, the opposing navies still had to protect their own shipping around their coasts.

Following the purge of Royalist naval officers and the execution of Charles I, there had been an unprecedented expansion of the Commonwealth Navy. The opportunities for those sympathetic to Parliament were good. Elizabeth's husband had followed his brothers into the service. By January 1653, shortly before his eighteenth birthday, he had already seen action. Having demonstrated his courage and discretion, the captain of the *Constant Warwick* recommended his promotion to lieutenant. Promotion was rapid in times of war but during the Commonwealth period, officer selection depended on ideology and religious zeal in addition to the traditional criteria. Less than two years later, he was already master of the *Roe* ketch when his officers and crew petitioned the Admiralty over their dissatisfaction with their lack of pay. Thomas' crew were, by now, in dire straits having received neither wages nor prize money.

Although similar to the king in being tardy paying their mariners, Parliament differed from the monarch in recognising the importance of trade. They implemented a convoy system and Thomas' service was primarily spent protecting the country's merchant shipping. Necessary but tedious, it was not a glamorous career. Most of his time was spent on the east coast of England trying to press a crew, fitting his vessels out ready for sailing and overseeing repairs to his ship. In the choppy waters of the North Sea, he had to keep station with his ponderous charges. England's shipping was at risk from the enemy, privateers and pirates. The crew could not always look forward to the reward of a hot meal.

During storms or enemy attack, the galley fire was dowsed to reduce the risk of conflagration. In February 1659 Thomas was involved in an engagement with a Spanish pirate close to the Humber. The *Roe* was a small ship with just eight guns and came off worse. More than a third of her main mast was shot away and her sails destroyed. It was an inglorious engagement. Thomas lost the ships he was escorting and had to head to Harwich for repairs. His ketch repaired, Thomas returned to the tedium of convoy duty interspersed with action against the enemy.

On land civil war was replaced with political and religious infighting, the two inextricably intertwined. Simply to believe the wrong thing brought the risk of condemnation, arrest or even death. In Wapping and the other Thames-side hamlets where the population was constantly exposed to new ideas from travel and immigration, independently minded scepticism was the norm. Education of children was important to equip individuals to decide for themselves. Religious radicalism, anti-Catholicism and Puritanism formed the basis of their beliefs. Such free-thinking had given rise to support for the Levellers during the war. Levellers believed in the equality of all citizens and freedom of conscience in religion. These egalitarian views were seen as dangerous and threatening by the ruling classes.

England as a whole did not seem to know what it wanted. Eight years after beheading their king, Oliver Cromwell was offered the crown. He declined but when he died the following year his son, Richard, inherited the title of Lord Protector just as if he was a royal heir. Richard Cromwell was not much of a leader and had been deposed earlier in the current year. A crisis was building. First Parliament ruled the country and then the army before Parliament took over again. Those who fought for

Parliament questioned if this is what they had risked their lives for. The tension was rising, especially in London. Within months there would be rioting. Some even described it as anarchy.

There were rumours of Charles' son returning as king. Elizabeth wondered if her husband would still have a job. Worse, would his life be at risk on land as well as at sea? Commanding a ship in the Navy was not just a job, it involved taking sides. And London was always a volatile place. Was it all starting again? Would she ever be able to stop worrying for her child?

Thomas, the son of Captain Thomas and Elizabeth Bowrey, was born into this uncertain world on 7 September 1659. The event was recorded three times: in the margins of the pages of the parish register for October 1660 and September 1661 and immediately before his sister Elizabeth's baptism on 17 March 1665. The three records of Thomas' birth are a result of the troubled times. During the republican period baptisms were disrupted. The English Commonwealth government had decreed births should be registered in their place. Baptisms took place where the minister had not fled his church but were often not written up until later. Few birth records survive from this period. None has been found for Thomas but his birth was recorded when he was baptised in the parish church at Wapping on 23 April 1660. Still over a month before the Restoration of the monarchy, the baptism was not written into the parish register at the time. When his sister was taken to be baptised some years later his parents probably thought to check Thomas' was there. It had been missed. The minister wrote it out of order before his sister's and tried to add a note on the correct page as well, as many others had been, but got it wrong the first time. Thomas was later to confirm his birthday in an early draft of his will.

The three baptism records were to form the pattern of Thomas' life. There is nothing unusual about there being two types of record for his marriage – the licence and the parish register – but, more unusually, there are two for his burial – first in the Stepney parish register with the note that the body had been taken to Lee in Kent and again at Lee where he was buried. In between, he left a wealth of documentation much of which shows his mother, Elizabeth, was right to worry.

The day before his first son's birth, Thomas senior had requested permission to put into Harwich to clean his ship's hull and restock with supplies. On east coast convoy duties, his ketch would become foul from worm and weed, and required cleaning every three months. In a navy constantly short of funds, it was probably considered pointless to carry provisions for a much longer period. A week later, he was reduced to six days' provisions and was short of men. He again requested permission to return to port. This time permission was granted and his ship was docked at Harwich for two weeks. Did he have the opportunity to return home to see his son?

If he did, it was not a long visit. By the end of the month, Thomas senior had sailed from Harwich to Plymouth Sound to deliver a package before returning to Harwich and then carrying another package to Sweden. Six weeks later, he was to play a small part in a crucial action during the death throes of the English Commonwealth, one that was recorded on the first page of Samuel Pepys' diary as *Lawson lies still in the Thames*.

Following the overthrow of Richard Cromwell as Lord Protector, the army had closed down the Rump Parliament, the reduced Parliament made up only of anti-royalist members. Vice-admiral John Lawson, a staunch republican with the loyalty of most of his officers and crew, resisted attempts to persuade the navy to join the army in establishing martial law. He, along with much of the country, supported the supremacy of Parliament. During December, riots broke out between soldiers and apprentices in London. This turmoil was mirrored in the rest of the country. On 13 December 1659, Lawson and his fleet, including Thomas senior with the *Roe* ketch, sailed from the Downs to Gravesend in the Thames estuary. Here they anchored, prepared to fight to force the army to reinstate the Parliament. By blockading the river and starving London of precious provisions and trade, Lawson hoped to gain the city's support for his aims.

Thomas senior departed the Thames as Pepys made his note of the blockade in his diary. Lawson had sent his ketch to Dover on an errand. When completed, Thomas returned to the vice-admiral at Gravesend for further orders. The fleet was to remain on the Thames for several weeks but whether Thomas remained with it is not recorded. The army backed down and the Rump Parliament survived for the time being but the disruption was not at an end. The political machinations eventually lead to the return of the monarchy.

Young Thomas cannot have been aware of troubles in the country but his first winter was hard. Pepys recorded in his diary that it snowed hard all morning on 4 January and his nose swelled with the cold. It snowed hard again eleven days later and the next day was cold, frosty and windy. Any disruption to coal supplies from the north of England due to the blockade involving Thomas senior would have had severe consequences for his son's well-being.

FAMILY

Another Commonwealth period regulation replaced marriage in church with civil marriages. Few records survive for the civil marriages of the time but some couples' forthcoming marriages were announced on market days and others had notices called by the cryer. In Wapping, the equivalent of banns were recorded in the parish register. The marriage of Thomas' parents, Thomas Bowrey mariner and Elizabeth Bentham spinster, both of Wapping, was announced on the three Lord's Days up to 27 September 1657 in Wapping Chapel.

In a phrase of the time, Thomas was *born to the sea*. His father, grandfather and other family members were all intimately connected to the sea in one way or another. Thomas senior was the son of Joseph and Hellin Bowrey and was baptised at Wapping on 1 March 1635. Joseph was a shipwright of Queen's Head Alley down by Wapping Dock, close to the river and his work. The footprint of Queen's Head Alley still exists as the path through the middle of Wapping Rose Garden. As was common, his house probably overlooked his shipyard. Here Joseph's family were surrounded by Thames watermen and lightermen, mariners and other shipwrights. It was a rough area crowded with rowdy taverns where children were raised surrounded by those who worked on the water.

Thomas senior had three older siblings: Ellen born in 1624, John in 1626 and Joseph in 1630. The brothers were also baptised at Wapping but Ellen's baptism took place at Deptford, the location of a major naval shipyard and where Joseph senior had married Hellin Wall on 16 June 1623. All three brothers, perhaps entranced by the tales of exotic places they had heard from birth, chose to go to sea rather than follow Joseph's trade. Ellen, married another mariner, William Middleton, and young Thomas' Middleton cousins were to be close to him in later life.

Hellin was still living in Queen's Head Alley when she wrote her will in 1669. There is no surviving record of Joseph senior's death but he probably predeceased his wife as married women had few property rights at the time and she owned her own house, a second in the Alley plus other property at the time of her death.

CHILDHOOD

As for most children at the time, little is known about Thomas junior's childhood except it was short - by 1668 he was on his way to India – and traumatic. With a father and uncle who suffered injury, shipwreck and defeat at sea, life ashore ought to have been more secure but there were greater risks to come.

His father was at sea when Thomas was born in 1659 but, with naval officers laid off at the end of the Anglo-Spanish War and the purge of parliamentarian sympathisers following the Restoration, he may soon have been at home more often. He is only mentioned once in the records after being with Lawson at Gravesend. It is possible he found work within the merchant navy. If work was hard to find, Thomas' parents may have had money worries. The political situation was uncertain for someone who had demonstrated his sympathies by serving in the Commonwealth Navy. In 1662, a little brother, Joseph, was born. He was baptised at Stepney on 25 January 1663. Another brother followed on 17 April 1664 but little Joseph had probably died before then because the new baby was also baptised as Joseph.

Finally, on 2 March 1665, a sister was born and named Elizabeth.

Whilst many institutions suffered during the Protectorate, education of the young was considered important. There was a strong belief the people should be able to read the bible themselves. London was better provided with schools than other areas of the country and, based on the number of adult who could sign their name, the level of literacy in London across all classes and for both sexes was between double and treble the national average. Schools teaching navigation and elementary engineering had been set up in the Elizabethan period because of the importance of sea-power to the country's security. Schooling was not compulsory but started at the age of six or seven. Knowing Thomas' abilities with writing and accounts later in his life, it seems impossible he did not receive schooling or other education whilst living in England. School fees were not high and his parents may have received support from family but, if they found themselves unable to pay, many parishes had their own school offering free tuition to the poor. As well as writing and arithmetic, navigation was seen as a subject suited to prepare pauper students for a career in the Royal or merchant navies but whether this was taught to pupils under the age of ten is not known.

Just as life may have become more settled for Thomas' family, the plague hit London.

PLAGUE

Plague was a periodic hazard throughout the seventeenth century but London had been spared the epidemics of the 1650s and had not experienced a serious outbreak since 1636. There was a small outbreak in the autumn of 1664 but it did not cause alarm among the complacent population because the epidemic was expected to die out before the end of the winter. In the second week of February 1665 the Bills of Mortality recorded just a single death from plague in London. Two further deaths were recorded in the third week of April followed by nine in the week ending 9 May. The City authorities took action but this was all in the west of the City, a long way from Wapping and unlikely to have concerned Thomas' parents. But the actions of the authorities failed to stop the spread. The first plague deaths in Wapping and the nearby parishes of Stepney and Whitechapel occurred in early July. By the first week of August the number of deaths across the whole City had risen to more than four thousand. In the heat of summer, the plague really took hold.

All around Thomas' neighbourhood, homes were closed up with red crosses painted on their doors. The family stayed indoors as much as possible. Nobody wanted contact with others and risk infection. Shut up inside his home to avoid contagion by others, Thomas heard the constant tolling of the passing bells and the drivers of carts crying out for people to *bring out your dead*.

Burying the plague dead. [By unknown, public domain.]

Then, in the peak month of the plague during which 30,000 people died of it in London, what the family had all been dreading happened. Thomas senior contracted the plague. If he was fortunate, he may have dropped dead in the street without warning as happened to a few. More likely, he was shut up with his household in his house for at least forty days as the regulations demanded, dependant on others to deliver food to them. Food was left on their doorstep and, in return, they left the money for it in a dish of vinegar to destroy the contagion. The symptoms experienced were diverse but usually started with a fever. The course of the disease was always painful and accompanied by the swelling of the lymph glands called buboes and known at the time as the *marks* of the plague. Often, towards the end, gangrene set in turning fingers, toes and noses black as the tissue died.

Thomas senior died. By this stage of the epidemic, fear meant that bodies were no longer buried with respect. His was collected by the cart that came round each night collecting the dead and he was buried at Whitechapel on 10 September 1665. The following January his widow, Elizabeth, administered his estate. No further record of Joseph and young Elizabeth has been found and they were not mentioned in their grandmother's will. This last major outbreak of bubonic plague in England killed about a quarter of the population of London. Many plague deaths were not recorded. The two children may well have perished at this time leaving six-year-old Thomas alone with his mother.

UNCLE JOHN

After the death of his father, it was likely Thomas still had a father-figure in his life. His uncle John Bowrey had no children and may have entertained his young nephew with tales of life at sea. John had married Judith Lester of Wapping in the City of London on 12 February 1650. His career in the Commonwealth, and subsequently the Royal, Navy is well documented. If he craved excitement, at least that is how his career started. He had seen action as early as 1652 when he was seriously enough wounded on board the *Unity* to be awarded thirty pounds compensation, worth over £4,000 today. The *Unity* was part of a squadron commanded by Sir George Ayscue when they were defeated by the Dutch at Plymouth. Despite having prevented the fleet defecting to the Royalist cause during the Civil War, Ayscue was relieved of his command, not returning until after the Restoration.

A career in the navy was rarely continuous as officers and crew were laid off when they were not needed in times of peace or when their ship was out of action for repairs. Thus in 1653, although being described as *a raw seaman but civil and stout, fit for a lieutenant* by the Admiralty, John was awarded a privateer's commission for a trading voyage on the *Hope* of London bound for Leghorn, now known as Livorno. However, England was at war for most of the seventeenth century until 1668 and by July John was needed back in the Navy. He was captain of the *Hunter*, a small fire-ship with just ten guns and a crew of thirty which was sunk by the Dutch at the Battle of Scheveningen. He had been an unlucky sailor until then but later he successfully commanded the *Eaglet* and for four years the *Drake*, mostly undertaking convoy duty. In 1656, John was accused of embezzling prize goods but he admitted his error and apologised. That appears to have been the end of the matter because there is an almost continual record of John's naval service beyond the Restoration and until 1663.

On 21 February 1663, with a Captain Taylor he met with Samuel Pepys. Four months earlier, John had been recommended to Pepys as deserving further employment because he had acquitted himself well in two voyages carrying horses. He had just been hired for a voyage to Tangiers and the three walked along Cornhill before going to a tavern together where Pepys had a glass of wine. He did not record what John drank.

By 1666, the Hearth Tax returns for Stepney show John as having six hearths, which probably equated to nine or ten rooms, a sizeable house. The majority of households had only two or three hearths. He was doing well but not for much longer. In February 1667, John was relieved of his command of the *Antelope* at Portsmouth because he was no longer fit enough for a voyage to Gothenburg but, before then, another catastrophic event hit London.

FIRE

When Thomas awoke on Sunday 2 September 1666 there was a tension in the air. In the west, about a mile from where he and his mother were living they could see thick smoke rising. There was a strong easterly wind blowing so the smoke did not immediately trouble Elizabeth and her son. Like most people in London not yet affected, they probably went to church as usual and prayed for salvation from the fire. Fire at sea was the worst fear of every sailor at the time and, after the long dry summer, the risk could not be ignored. The old, poorly maintained, timber-built houses, warehouses and other buildings were tinder-dry. That Sunday morning, the Wapping congregation understanding this probably prayed more fervently than most.

As the day continued, the conflagration grew larger. The warehouses down by the river between the Tower of London and London Bridge exploded as their contents spontaneously combusted in the incredible heat. Thomas had been brought up among people who knew that alongside tar, pitch and oil, wine and brandy, the warehouses held highly flammable hemp, flax and cordage. Fire was an enormous risk at the best of times. Many on ships and in shipyards started when pitch was being heated. The heating of the stored pitch by the conflation could easily start new, spontaneous fires.

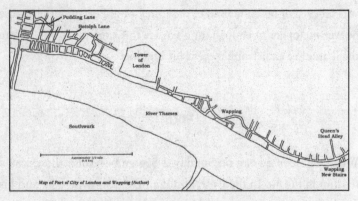

City of London and Wapping river front.

Did Thomas venture down to his grandmother's house by the river and watch the scene from there? Did he watch in horror as the bridge burnt or was his child's mind amused by the sight of people's prized possessions floating by? For Elizabeth and Thomas' watermen and lightermen neighbours, the fire was a mixed blessing. They were making a small fortune rescuing people and their belongings from the river bank. Other neighbours who owned carts, waggons and barrows were also doing well taking goods in the other direction, north to Moorfields. Most refugees headed north but some streamed through Wapping to the fields beyond.

That night the fire had grown so that it stretched about half a mile wide. Eastwards, towards Thomas' home in Wapping, it had only spread to Botolph Lane, the next street along from the source in Pudding Lane, but westwards the wind had carried it as far as Three Cranes Wharf more than five hundred yards west of the bridge. Northwards, it stretched as far as Cannon Lane about three hundred and fifty yards from the river. At night the sky in the west glowed red from the flames.

The people of Wapping woke on Monday morning to find the fire still burning. The easterly gale was still blowing but, if it should turn, the Tower would be at risk. It stood less than half a mile from the Pudding Lane and was used to store 900 barrels of gunpowder, the largest ammunition store in the country. As all mariners knew, gunpowder, stable when left undisturbed, was very unstable when exposed to a flame. Only eighteen months previously, the explosion when fire broke out in the powder room of the ship *London* close to Leigh in the Thames estuary was heard as far away as Holland. If the powder in the Tower was to ignite, a huge area would be devastated. The bridge would be destroyed and so would much of Wapping.

Firefighting teams were set up, led by soldiers and manned by volunteers. Now, even as far as Wapping, the noise was dreadful. The cracking sounds of homes burning or being pulled down to make firebreaks were terrible. The flames roared as it raced before the wind. The shattering of glass windows announced the destruction of each church in in its path. The heat could be felt over a great distance, even when separated by several streets of as yet undamaged buildings. Many of Thomas' mariner neighbours were likely to have volunteered. They were experienced fighting fire at sea and knew what needed to be done.

During the day, clouds of smoke blocked out the sun. By the end of the day, nightfall no longer brought darkness. The fire lit up the sky and had doubled its reach northward and westward but it was still only creeping eastward towards Wapping.

Tuesday morning brought no respite. The conflagration continued to spread but the wind was still blowing from the east, continuing to protect Wapping. As it spread, the stream of refugees was endless. The noise was relentless. Time passes more slowly for children. Had Thomas wondered if it would all end? How would it all end? Was he watching from Wapping later that evening when the unthinkable happened? St Paul's, the soaring landmark built on a hill and visible to all of London, burst into flames. As the fire reached its climax, lightning bolts sparked above the cathedral. This can only have been made more dreadful when around the same time there were explosions much closer to home as the buildings next to the Tower were blown up to create a protective firebreak. Overnight, the wind changed direction increasing the risk to the Tower.

During Wednesday, the people of Wapping grew accustomed to the sound of explosions as more and more firebreaks were created elsewhere in the City. At the same time, the wind eased. The fire was beginning to come under control and some semblance of normality returned. Markets were set up in nearby Mile End Green and Ratcliffe, as well as other places further afield, at the order of the king. Many of the City markets had been destroyed and the population including the estimated 100,000 refugees needed to be fed.

By the evening, most of the fires had been extinguished although there were small outbreaks in places that needed to be dealt with. As everyone relaxed a little, the alarm went up that 50,000 French and Dutch soldiers were invading London. The rumour was false but rioting broke out among the refugees in the fields before it was quashed.

The next day, Thursday, the fire finally burnt itself out possibly as much because the wind had stopped as the belated efforts to create effective firebreaks. Miraculously, it had stopped just before it reached the Tower but it would be a long time before London was to recover. That night, the moon was red.

Thomas woke on the morning of Friday 7 September, his seventh birthday, to a city flattened and blackened by fire. Little rebuilding took place before he left London, bound for India, less than two years later. By the time he returned after twenty years, the city of his childhood would be unrecognisable. He was to remember the threat to Wapping all of his life and, after he had returned to England, was to raise a petition protesting against the Tower still being used as an ammunition store.

THE END OF CHILDHOOD

Thomas wrote in his *Bay of Bengal* manuscript that he started his life in the East Indies at Fort St George, later known as Madras. There is no record of how he travelled to India but the prevailing winds in the South Atlantic dictated a direct voyage needed to leave England some time during the last quarter of 1668 to arrive at India during the late spring or early summer 1669. Thomas was just nine when he left home in London. The following can only be speculation but fits with the known facts.

Thomas' father had died of plague in 1665 and it is likely his siblings also died around this time. The fire the following year made life extremely difficult for all Londoners, even those whose homes had not been destroyed. How much more difficult it was for a young widow with a young son? Only nine months later, the Dutch carried out a devastating raid on the Medway and burnt the English fleet at Chatham. Fearful that their city would be the next target, nervous Londoners fled again. To prevent the Dutch navy sailing up the Thames, merchant ships, still laden with their rich cargos, were sunk at Woolwich Reach and Barking Creek. It would have been understandable for Elizabeth to have been concerned about her son's future.

She would likely have found a new husband as soon as possible and, living where she did, her neighbours were all connected to the sea. A power of attorney for Elizabeth Smith, the *sister* of John Bowrey and wife of Samuel Smith has survived in the Bowrey papers and this Elizabeth may well have been Thomas' mother. The terms *sister* and brother were often used to denote in-law and step relationships at the time. Did the widowed Elizabeth marry Samuel Smith? Her son's grandmother mentioned *my daughter Smith* in her will. Although not conclusive, this was not indicative of a close relationship and may have referred to her widowed daughter-in-law.

It is most likely Thomas sailed with his close relation Samuel Smith to India. It was not unknown for boys as young as eight to be employed on board ships as cabin boys or officers' servants. Many officers in the Royal and Commonwealth Navies started their careers as a captain's servant at the age of nine years. With his family background Thomas was probably always destined for the sea. The insecurity of life in London, may have hastened the start of that career. Being in the care of a relation, stepfather or uncle, put Thomas in a better position than most young lads and his mother knew pay and conditions on East India Company ships were considered better than those in the Royal Navy.

On 28 December 1666, the East India Company in London wrote to their factory at Fort St George advising them they were finding it difficult to charter trading ships and were sending a small ship of their own, the *Charles*, also known as the *Little Charles*, commanded by Captain Samuel Smith. The *Charles* was to take trade goods to Fort St George via the Atlantic island of St Helena and return with a cargo of saltpetre to be used to preserve food and make gunpowder. It is not clear if the difficulty chartering ships was connected to the Fire but Smith was to carry with him a copper plate of a map showing the devastation of the capital. This was likely to be a copy of Wenceslaus Hollar's famous map.

The *Charles* departed from the Thames in January 1667 but in the middle of this month disturbing news of Fort St George arrived from Surat causing the Company to delay the voyage. Eventually, new orders were issued on 16 April and delivered to Walter Clavell who was to travel on the ship as a newly appointed factor at the Fort. As it was now too late to beat the monsoon in the Bay of Bengal, the *Charles* was to be diverted to Surat. Once they arrived, if there was more positive news, Clavell was to proceed from there to Fort St George. In the event, the *Charles* did not arrive in Surat on the far north-west coast of India until May 1668.

Surat, on the banks of the Tapi River and close to the Arabian Sea, was a natural hub for the trade of the region when Thomas first arrived in India. It was the reason it existed. Despite this, the river was heavily silted and heavy ships such as the *Charles*, anchored at Swally Hole close to the Hazira Mangroves at Suvali and about fifteen miles downriver. Here the ships were protected by a sandbar. In May, it was approaching the end of the dry season when the heat and humidity reached their peaks and was almost intolerable, especially to Europeans. Within a month, the monsoon season was expected to begin bringing heavy rains and stormy seas. This was why Smith had been diverted to Surat despite the imperative to get to Fort St George and it is likely that he decided to sit out the wet months at Bombay about one hundred and eighty-five miles south of Swally.

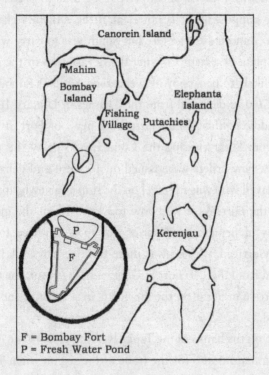

F = Bombay Fort
P = Fresh Water Pond

Bombay.

The East India Company was planning to move its western headquarters from Surat to Bombay to avoid the increasingly frequent Maratha raids. The Company was already encouraging the production of quality cloth on the island that had been ceded to England in the dowry of Catherine of Braganza in 1661. At that time, there was a Portuguese manor house there, close to where the Gateway of India stands today. Seven years later, Bombay was leased to the East India Company who immediately built a quay, customs house and warehouses. The manor house was renamed Bombay Castle. It was surrounded by a pleasant garden but defended by just four guns. It was a matter of urgency to build fortifications to protect it.

The January following the *Charles'* arrival at Surat the Deputy Governor of Bombay wrote to Company officials at Surat informing them Smith had been appointed Chief Engineer and Master Controller of the Ordnance following the death of the previous holder of the post. He was to take charge of constructing the fortification of Bombay, being described as extremely well qualified and experienced both for the building of the fortifications and artillery. He drew up plans and the work started immediately.

The island of Bombay had already been reclaimed from six islands by the time the English took over. More reclamation has taken place since and it is no longer an island. At the time, it was approximately seven miles long by three and a half miles wide. The English town only covered about one mile of the south-east tip. Beyond it were fields of buffalo, an orchard and coconut grove, the Portuguese settlement and a fishing village. There was no fresh water on the island other than one spring near the fishing village. A reservoir for collecting rain water was build next to the fort. It was an unhealthy place and miserable during the monsoon rains. In October 1669 Smith died of the flux as dysentery was known.

If Thomas had stayed with the *Charles* he would no longer have his relation to watch over him but the newly settled Bombay was no place for a young child. The East India Company was already experiencing difficulties with widows of deceased Company servants there. Thomas had travelled with Clavell during their long voyage from England and may have accompanied him, perhaps as a servant, when he proceeded to Fort St George. Clavell departed from Bombay on the *Charles* but illness forced him to go ashore at Goa from where he travelled overland to Masuliputam before finishing his journey to Fort St George on the *Loyal Merchant* that had departed England a year after the *Charles*. Clavell arrived there, weak from illness, in January 1669. He recovered but died in August 1677.

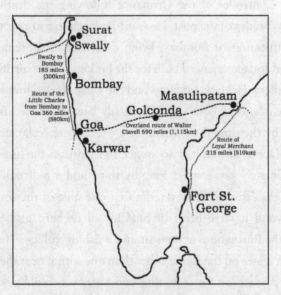

India showing journey of William Clavell.

However Thomas had travelled, a young child had arrived alone in the East Indies where he was to spend the next nineteen years of his life before returning to Wapping, his childhood home. Despite the distance, the insecurities of his early life would never be forgotten.

CHAPTER 2

Learning His Trade (1669-1679)

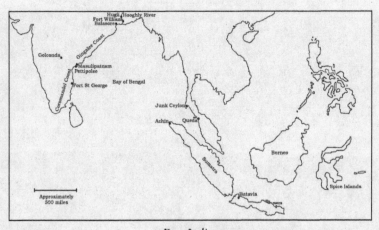

East Indies.

1669

One wave carried the flimsy boat crashing onto the sandbar. It sat there a short while until the next wave carried it up and over the bar, into smoother water. More paddling by the ten men brought the boat up onto the beach. With a bump, nine-year-old Thomas had arrived at Fort St George.

His first sight of his new home was a huge white and red flag of St George flying over the massive walls of the fort. His ship had anchored off shore in what he would come to know as the Roads. To a child used to the sturdy wherries and lighters of the Thames, the flexible *masula* surf-boats used to ferry passengers and cargo ashore were equally scary and exciting. Made of planks sewn together with coir twine and caulked with coconut fibre, they had no rudder and were steered by the front two rowers. Ten local men paddled the boat slowly towards the shore until the breakers marked the sand bar that made it impossible for larger, less flexible vessels to come ashore.

As Thomas walked up the beach, the sand was scalding hot through the thin leather soles of his shoes. Perhaps it brought back memories of walking across the ruins of London after the Fire. It forced most of those arriving to hurry to the Watergate in the centre of the wall. The gate was defended by a semicircle of five battery guns. Once through the outer gate, a path of smooth stones led through an inner one. Through that and the old fort dominated his view. A longer look showed there were other public buildings including an exchange. A couple of months before his arrival, the fort had been hit by a severe cyclone reported to have ruined buildings and left almost no trees standing. It is possible the reports were exaggerated or repairs carried out at great speed because Thomas described his arrival and made no mention of the damage.

Thatched huts provided warehouses, known as *godowns*, to the north of the old fort and shelter for the workers. In the spaces between the huts the more robust merchandise was stored and leather tanners, carpenters and wheelwrights worked. Most of the activity was comfortingly familiar to him from his home in Wapping. Cattle foraged in the remaining spaces.

As Thomas continued walking towards the river he arrived at houses surrounded by gardens ranged alongside the shore. The streets were clean, and lined with beautiful, fine, brick and stone mansions low enough to be protected by the walls. The houses had battlements and terraces, and trees lined the paths up to doors framed with Italian-style porticoes.

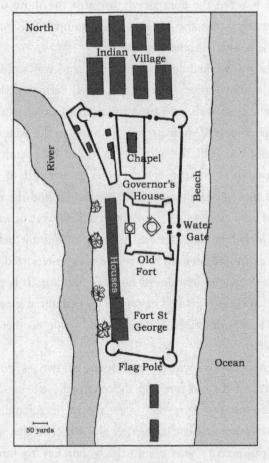

Fort St George.

Having travelled from Bombay, Thomas would find it more comfortable here. The fort's proximity to the equator and coast ensured it experienced no extreme variations in temperature which rarely exceeded 37°C. Sea breezes for ten months of the year and humidity levels similar to those in England resulted in a climate more tolerable than other areas of the East Indies for Englishmen wearing their rough woollen breeches and coats. The main discomfort for Europeans was caused by the monsoon rains. The average annual rainfall was only about fifty percent greater than that in London but most of this fell in a two-month period from mid-October each year. Although the occasional portraits of a European in oriental dress exist, the majority of scenes show that most continued to wear the same clothes as at home during the period Thomas lived in the East. Cargo lists survive of woollen clothing sent out presumably for sale to Europeans. A gentleman was expected to wear a good cloth silver-laced jacket. Most wore their hair short. Only those who were concerned to demonstrate their importance wore the heavy, full wigs fashionable at home.

As he settled in and explored further, Thomas found a large village with an Indian population had grown up outside the north walls. In return for the fort's protection, they paid duty to the Company for all goods bought and sold. The area immediately outside the wall housed a market during daylight hours and shops were to grow up in the houses facing this area. This is where the European women would do their shopping and socialise each morning. Carried on palanquins by servants and led by two other servants, the women were protected from the sun and undesirables. The Indian village had a pagoda or temple but the English did not have their own church until St Mary, funded by voluntary contributions, was consecrated in 1680. Until then both the Protestant English and Catholic Portuguese used the same small chapel for worship. The recent hostilities between the two religions meant this was unheard of at the time in Europe and points to the pragmatism required to survive so far from home. Outside the walls there were also the Europeans' burial ground and market gardens producing food for the town.

Fort St George c.1850. [Postcard published by Taj Coromandel.]

Contemporary estimates of the population at this time were approximately three hundred English, three thousand Portuguese and tens of thousands, possibly as many as forty thousand or more, Indians including women and children. This was larger than Norwich, the second largest town in England at the time. Thomas noted that although the East India Company pay rates were low, the cost of living was also low and their employees lived well. Despite being the minority population, the fort was governed by the English. In India, the Company used pomp and ceremony to help maintain their authority. It would not be long before Thomas witnessed this for himself. Whenever the governor went out he was accompanied by fifes, drums, trumpets and a flag, his personal guard of three or four hundred Indians, and his council and factors on horseback with their ladies in palanquins.

If Thomas Bowrey had a home in the East Indies, it was this place, Fort St George. It was here he learned the business of a country trader, independent of the East India Company, and it was here he was recorded as being a Freeman during the last few years of his nineteen-year stay in India. Four decades before he arrived at the settlement, the area was an uninhabited sandy strip of land six miles long and one mile wide between the Cooum River and the sea a little to the south of the Dutch factory at Pulicat. Known as Madras until 1996, three centuries after Thomas' death Chennai would be India's fourth largest city, home to six and a half million people and the gateway to the south for millions of overseas visitors each year.

In 1639, Francis Day, an East India Company factor or factory head, at Masulipatnam negotiated with a local *naik*, or Indian district officer, to purchase the land about eight miles from San Thome, where legend claimed St Thomas, known as *Doubting Thomas*, was martyred in 72 A.D. The purchase came with a licence to build a fortress on the land and it was to become the first East India Company territory anywhere. The Company was anxious for a base from which they could take advantage of the production of textiles on the Coromandel Coast. By 1653, the initial small settlement inside a palisade fence of pointed stakes had developed into a small fort measuring approximately one hundred and sixty-five yards by one hundred and ten yards and named Fort St George. The walls of stone, earth and brick enclosed living quarters, public buildings and warehouses. A few buildings had been erected outside the walls to the north of the fort. All around were low, sandy dunes. Fishing huts and a few palm trees were seen in the distance.

Over the years the Company business attracted other traders and settlers and, by the time Thomas arrived, the original fort now contained just the governor's house set diagonally in the centre of a much larger fortified area with gun batteries. These later walls enclosed an area approximately six hundred yards wide and three hundred yards deep on three sides. They were sufficiently thick to stop a cannonball and had palisades towards the sea with a deep, wide ditch on the landward side. It was well defended. The guns were directed both towards the sea and inland.

1670

Thomas was still at Fort St George in 1670 when yet again events around him took a turn for the worse and may have caused him to recall his father's stories of his part in the blockade of the Thames shortly after his birth. The fort was besieged by a local naik, whose native army of thousands of cavalry and foot soldiers camped within two miles of the walls stopping both incoming provisions and the Company's ships leaving for England. The naik took things much further than Vice-Admiral Lawson had done in London. Rather than simply trying to starve the fort into submission he threatened to attack and torture the inhabitants unless a ransom of ten or twenty thousand pagodas, a coin worth about eight English shillings, was paid. The ransom was worth between £600,000 and £1.2 million in today's values. It was paid but Thomas later commented they would have accepted much less. He may well have been correct but I have been unable to find any corroboration of this element of the story. Richard Carnac Temple, in his notes to the *Bay of Bengal*, reported that the siege came to an end on the orders of the naik's superior.

Thomas Bowrey started his life in the East Indies at Fort St George but little else is known about his first decade in the region. Other than the incidents he described in his *Bay of Bengal* manuscript, there is nothing in his papers and, not being one of their apprentices or employees, he does not appear in the records of the East India Company at this time.

Long after Thomas' death, the Company would become extremely powerful in India but the British were relatively late arriving in the region and, initially, were not greatly interested in India itself. Prior to the sixteenth century, all trade between Europe and Asia was Asian-led and its growth was constrained by the capacity of the overland transport. At the end of the fifteenth century there was a revolutionary change in the market when the Portuguese Vasco da Gama first sailed around the Cape of Good Hope. This discovery of an all-water route to the East enabled the Portuguese to become involved in the procurement of spices and other luxury goods in the region.

The Portuguese, granted a monopoly by a Papal Bull, remained the only Europeans trading in the East Indies by sea for almost a century but, at the end of the sixteenth century, rival Dutch companies were set up. In 1602, these companies were merged into the Dutch United East India Company, known as the VOC. They understood very early they needed to dominate the fine spice trade and secured a monopoly on cloves from Amboina, now in the Maluku province of Indonesia, nutmeg and mace from the Banda Islands, and cinnamon from Ceylon, now Sri Lanka.

In the seventeenth and eighteenth centuries, France, Denmark, Scotland, Spain, Austria and Sweden also established their own East Indies trading companies. None of these provided any threat to the Dutch who maintained that they had sole rights to the trade. As a Protestant country, the Dutch refused to recognise the prior rights granted by the Catholic Church to the Portuguese. The long process of globalisation had begun.

It was not until 1593, when a Portuguese ship returning from the East was captured and forced into an English port that the English became aware of just how much they were losing out. It was the largest vessel that had ever been seen in England and the hull was packed with an immensely valuable cargo of gold, spices, textiles, pearls, porcelain and ivory. A few years later, London merchants engaged in the Levant spice trade seeing that the first Dutch voyage made a four hundred percent profit, petitioned Elizabeth I to set up their own company. On the final day of 1600, the English East India Company was established.

The Company was destined to become the world's first multinational company and to rule India with its own army but this was over one hundred and fifty years in the future. Initially, it was purely a trading company primarily interested in the Spice Islands centred on Banda. The Company's first two voyages were directed at Bantam where they established a factory in 1602 hoping to break the Dutch dominance of the spice trade. They were not well funded and it failed. In 1623, the Dutch governor at Amboina beheaded ten Englishmen alongside ten Japanese mercenaries and a Portuguese merchant on a charge of conspiring to seize the port. Rather than retaliating, the English withdrew from the Spice Islands, moved to Batavia, present day Jakarta, sourced their pepper from Sumatra and concentrated their operations in India.

For the majority of the Company's employees in Asia, life was communal within the confines of the settlements. On average, it took five years for Europeans to acclimatise to life in the East Indies but most were lucky if they survived two monsoons. Alcohol, diet and the heat took their toll. Cholera, typhoid and malaria all contributed to the death rate and as many as a third of the Company's overseas personnel died each year. Despite the risks, the opportunity to return to England with a personal fortune for those lucky enough to survive for a number of years ensured the Company had little difficulty recruiting staff and they were able to pay low wages. One of the perks of working for the East India Company overseas was the opportunity to trade in diamonds which were not covered by the Company's monopoly. Diamonds were to be found in Borneo and in Golconda. The main advantages of diamonds were they were inexpensive to ship home when the employee returned to England where the readmission of Jews by Oliver Cromwell in 1655 had resulted in London becoming the main European market for uncut stones.

Having escaped the tumultuous events back home what had Thomas expected from his new life? No doubt, he was looking for some security. Making his fortune was part of this plan. He set about learning to be both a mariner and merchant. It is possible that he was apprenticed to someone unconnected to the East India Company but, if this had not been planned before he left England, how did he acquire the necessary premium? When his grandmother died following his departure, she left houses to her other grandchildren but just five pounds to Thomas. It is probable she had already provided him with sufficient funds to cover his apprenticeship premium which usually ranged from ten to one hundred pounds, the equivalent of between £1500 and £15,000 today.

Later in life, Thomas was to show a paternal interest in two young men and their experience may show us how he spent his early years in India. Robin Lesly, the nephew of Thomas' future business partner, was apprenticed to a country trader for five years and learned astronomy, surveying, mathematics and merchants' accounts. Thomas sent him three blank notebooks and a copy of his Malay dictionary. He paid for his cousin, Thomas Studds to be tutored in navigation and mathematics before he started his career as a midshipman on the *Mary Galley*. He also provided him with the clothing and equipment he would need. When the ship sailed, Thomas issued instructions to the captain that Studds' education in mathematics should continue under the tutorage of the second mate. The captain was to ensure that Studds was allowed to observe all trade negotiations ashore and all discussions on board that concerned the ship or cargo. This was considerably more than the average midshipman could expect and points to the type of practical training Thomas himself may have received.

1672

In the distance, Thomas could see a large fire. It was about half a mile away. He was on horseback, following a large group of adults and children leaving the town. A man's corpse was burning. As he got closer, he could see a young woman beside another fire surrounded by a crowd. Without hesitating, the widow *salaamed* to her friends, handed Thomas some flowers from her hair and sprang into the fire.

Thomas had broken his journey at a village for dinner. Before continuing on his way, his interpreter asked if he wanted to witness the burning of a widow. During his first year in India, he had heard a story about a case in which twenty-seven wives and concubines were burned. He had been told not all widows went to their death willingly but, when he rode up to her, the young woman standing by the fire seemed unexpectedly cheerful. He had questioned her, asking why she allowed herself to be so deluded by the Brahmins. They overheard and appeared angry but, before they were able to react, the widow smiled and said it was her happiest hour. Thomas suspected she was intoxicated.

Sati, widow burning, seen as abhorrent by the thirteen-year-old Thomas, was not always condemned by Europeans in the late seventeenth century. Some admired the act. In the West generally, sati has never been properly understood but was a religious ritual that conferred a status similar to Christian sainthood on the deceased widow. The rite of sati was, in theory at least, voluntary and practiced only in Bengal and Rajasthan. It was not until 1829 when the East India Company passed the Abolition of Sati Act that any attempt was made to ban the ritual.

Despite Thomas' horror, he was to voluntarily witness such sati again in the future. He described two further widow burnings in Bengal. At one, the woman was unwilling but resigned. She stood courageously by the fire but, when the time came, refused to leap into the flames. The Brahmins moved to force her but she took hold of one and threw herself with him headlong onto the pyre, where they both died. Thomas demonstrated some sympathy with the widow's defiance of the males in authority over her. Although it is not possible to ascribe modern-day feminist beliefs to him, it is an enlightened attitude at a time when within his own culture women were legally the possession of their fathers until married and, after, belonged to their husbands. Only widows had any autonomy.

North of Fort St George, the summers were hotter with peak temperatures between April and June. Monsoon rains fell between June and October. The winters were more moderate. The coast was frequently affected by the cyclones in the Bay of Bengal, bringing tidal surges year round. For many months of the year, the weather made it impossible to sail from port to port on the east coast of India. It was during one such period in 1672 that Thomas witnessed the widow burning while on his overland journey from Fort St George to Masulipatnam, a centre of maritime trade especially for diamonds and textiles. The town stood on the Coromandel Coast of India at the mouth of the River Krishna.

Spices may have been the primary reason for the creation of the East India Company but its first profitable business was in exotic cloth. The serious rivalry in the spice trade with the Dutch and Portuguese, as well as the risk of piracy, resulted in each voyage requiring a minimum number of ships in order to enable the fleet to defend itself. The first Company voyage returned with so much pepper the market was flooded with a consequential detrimental effect on prices. On subsequent voyages only sufficient spices were purchased to fill just one ship. Other trade goods were required to fill the others and the Company began importing both painted and printed cotton fabric into England as early as 1620 when they brought fifty thousand pieces back from India. A piece was about a yard wide and between ten and twenty yards long. Even as late as the mid-eighteenth century, Indian textiles provided sixty percent of the Company's profits. The muslins and hand block-printed fabrics of Masulipatnam were an important part of this trade in textiles.

This was the opposite of what the government had wanted when the East India Company was established. At the time, England's main manufactured product was high-quality, heavy woollen broadcloth and the East Indies was seen as a huge new market for this. Otherwise, all the country had to export was silver. The Company's charter obliged them to include a substantial proportion of broadcloth in its exports. Thomas' papers at the British Library include two sheets with woollen fabric samples showing the colours considered suitable for export. This objective had one huge flaw: heavy woollen broadcloth was unsuitable for the Asian climate. The result was that rather than supporting English industry, the Company damaged it by importing Indian fabrics into England.

The climate was not the only impediment to selling English cloth. The centuries-old Indian textile industry was sophisticated. They produced products in great demand throughout the Malay Archipelago. These cloths were an important element of the established trade routes of the Indian Ocean long before the arrival of the Europeans. Indian production ranged from plain, functional, hand-woven cotton cloth and garments to exquisite, luxury hand-printed or embroidered silks and the finest, sheer muslins. They were experts in dying cloth. Chintz and *kalamkari*, for example, went through a complex, multi-stage, multi-colour dying process that remains valued today. Alongside the broadcloth samples, the British Library holds a textile colour chart resembling a modern paint chart showing the range of colours that could be obtained. Before he returned home, Thomas would spend some time in Porto Novo having cloth dyed to his specifications.

The printed fabrics from western India, which were among

the first imported into England, were of inferior quality and very quickly the Company switched to the Gujarat cottons embroidered in coloured silks. These textiles were a luxury fashion item. Wealthy customers were looking for exclusivity and novelty. The earliest imports were in the styles made for local use in Asia but soon European designs were copied. New designs, patterns and colours were wanted each year. Thomas developed a good commercial understanding of the textile market and his education may have started during his visit to Masulipatnam.

Thomas' destination at the end of this eventful journey was the East India Company factory there. This factory was subordinate to Fort St George but the population was wealthy because of their fine textiles and inlaid ebony furniture, goods popular in other parts of the East Indies as well as in Europe. The harbour was good and the river navigable up to the town. It was here Thomas described a novel way of smoking tobacco by simply rolling the leaf, lighting one end and holding the other end between the lips. He said the Portuguese called these rolled tobacco leafs *cheroota*. According to the *Oxford English Dictionary*, this account was the first use of the word *cheroot* in the English language.

Before he reached his destination, at the village of Pettipolee, he visited Ambrose Salisbury, the East India Company's Chief of Affairs. They had probably met three years earlier when Thomas was on his way to Fort St George and he was pressed to stay the night. The next morning Thomas spent some time looking round the town. The village had been a Company factory since their earliest days in the country. Having investigated the food market and been impressed with both the variety of food available and the reasonable prices, he was attracted to a clamour at the factory gates. Hearing there was a young English visitor, a number of snake charmers had come to perform for him in the hope of receiving some payment. It was his first such experience and Thomas was fascinated by the display of venomous cobras dancing, enchanted by the music and verbal commands of their keepers but he was also aware the same snakes were often used to execute criminals.

1674

It was eleven o'clock at night and Thomas was holding court with a group of Brahmins when they rose up in haste, raising their hands to heaven and muttering prayers. They rushed to a large water tank and sprinkled themselves with water. As the Brahmins prostrated themselves, women brought lamps and offerings of flowers. The cause of this excitement was a full eclipse of the moon and the rituals continued for two hours until the moon reappeared.

By this time, he had learned enough of the local language and gestures to understand when the Brahmin explained the eclipse was believed to be a venomous snake biting the moon. With the arrogance of youth, Thomas lectured them on astronomy. The motion of the planets had been understood since the time of Johannes Kepler (died 1630) and astronomy was an essential part of the education of navigation. Yet again, Thomas only succeeded in angering the Hindu priests. By this time, he had moved from Fort St George and was living at Balasore, 885 miles to the north-west.

Thomas' father had been a captain in the Commonwealth Navy and it is likely his son was raised as a low-church Protestant before leaving England. In the East Indies, he was exposed to many religions new to him. He commented on the Hindus and Muslims he encountered in his *Bay of Bengal* manuscript. In awe of the courage shown by those who threw themselves under the wheels of Jagannath's chariot and, perhaps surprisingly having recently left Puritan Wapping, he admired Hindu ceremony and was appreciative of the dancing at religious festivals but he believed their worship of many gods to be idolatrous, in his opinion making Hinduism inferior to Christianity, Judaism and Islam. Thomas made few comments about the Muslim religion except that he considered it *irreligious*. He approved of their reverence of God and the Prophet but was disparaging of the Koran. Although impressed by the fair application of Islamic justice and the offer of sanctuary to widows under threat of sati, he found Muslims insolent and superior. This attitude was to get him into trouble many years in the future.

Balasore had been a major port from the time of the Mughals and was associated with the nearby centres of textile production and sugar. Situated on the River Haraspore, about four miles from the sea, shipbuilding was an important industry. The Danes had a settlement there, fortified by a natural moat, before the English established their factory in 1633. The area around the town was rich agricultural land. The primary crop was rice but sugar cane, wheat and barley were also grown. Cows, sheep and goats were raised. During the months of May to August, the local poor living in cottages close to the sea produced salt. The region supplied the East India Company with arrack, the spirit made from the fermented sap of coconut flowers, sugarcane, grain or fruit, and it may have been here that Thomas developed his taste for this alcoholic beverage. Balasore was also a source of diamonds. They were found following the rains in the river at Sambalpur but the

Mughal Emperor attempted to control the trade with Europeans.

Thomas complained the river a Balasore was not deep enough for any ship over two hundred tons to navigate and it was too dangerous to ride out in the open bay due to the tidal waves caused by cyclones in the Bay of Bengal. Even small ships could not cross the bar into the river except on the flood tide. Pilots were essential at the port and it became the centre for river pilot services for the Hooghly River. Despite the navigational difficulties, the port was used because large quantities of calico, muslin, plain cotton longcloth and chintz fabric were made in Odisha and transported to there for sale to the Dutch and English factories.

1675

By 1675, Thomas Bowrey had moved on again to Junk Ceylon, present day Phuket Island, Thailand. He was employed there by William Jearsey who was a long-time resident in the East Indies. Jearsey had become a factor at Sirian, the East India Company's Burma factory at Pegu, at the beginning of 1650 and married Catarina Hemsink, the eldest daughter of a Dutch East India Company employee. Between 1652 and 1655, he was the chief at Pegu but refused to return to Fort St George at the end of this period when the factory was closed and he was dismissed. Alongside his employment by the Company, Jearsey undertook extensive private trade and may have been reluctant to abandon a lucrative situation. He eventually returned to the fort where he lived as a freeman until, in 1662, he was re-employed by the Company as the chief at Masulipatam and diamond commissioner. At the same time, in defiance of London, he was operating up to nine country ships of his own trading with Pegu, Junk Ceylon, Achin, Kedah and Persia. By December 1669, the East India Company directors had had enough of Jearsey's conduct suspecting him of working against their interests. Two of his ships, the *Nonsuch* and the *Adventure*, both richly laden, had been taken by the Dutch. There were rumours in London that Jearsey's port to port activities had ruined him and he had defrauded the Company. He had not presented his accounts for some time. They dismissed him for the second and final time demanding he return to England with his accounts so that they could recover what they were sure he owed. Locally, Jearsey was popular and continued his defiance of the directors in London, living in Charles Street, Fort St George, for a further sixteen years before finally producing his accounts in return for the Company withdrawing their claims against him. Thomas and Jearsey arrived in Fort St George around the same time. As one of the biggest employers in the country trade, Thomas may have been employed on Jearsey's ships from the beginning. Catarina died in 1688 and Jearsey in 1690.

At this time Jearsey was an independent merchant operating without a licence, a so called interloper. In the beginning, the East India Company ships sailed from London to the East Indies and then from port to port, picking up cargos before returning home. They would unload their outward cargo at Surat and call at one port for the finest textiles, another for the best pepper and so on, picking up goods close to where they were produced. In this they were following long established Asian trading routes. However, it was a slow process. Navigation in the region was restricted by the seasons. It was only possible to sail from India to the Red Sea or Persian Gulf between November and March. Voyages to Malacca from India were not able start until March. A voyage from the Philippines to Surat required two changes of wind and ships often had to take shelter in the Strait of Malacca when winds were unfavourable. The Company captains also lacked the long-term relationships with the merchant communities that the local traders had.

Very quickly, this system gave way to the country trade by which smaller ships carried out regional trade in Asia and ferried goods to one of the major factories for transhipment to England. Although some of these country ships were operated by, or contracted to, the Company most were privately owned and outside their supervision. In 1661, the Company decided to withdraw from the intra-Asian trade completely and from the mid-seventeenth century, there was a growing community of Englishmen settled in the ports of the East Indies willing to take employment wherever offered. Some of these may have been licenced by the Company but many were not. It was possible for the successful country ship's captain to amass a large personal fortune. Elihu Yule, governor of Fort St George, later free merchant and benefactor of Yale University in America, retired with a fortune estimated to have been £200,000, or nearly £27 million at today's values.

The arrival of the European country trade stimulated and changed the patterns of trade in the region. Textiles from India were taken to the Indonesian archipelago to pay for pepper and spice, to Persia for raw silk and the Red Sea for silver. In addition to supplying the East India Company ships returning to England, the free merchants dealt in certain types of goods to ship home on their own account provided they could find a ship to carry them. These were most commonly precious stones, the valuable waxy substance excreted by sperm whales and used in perfume production called ambergris, certain spices, carpets and textiles incorporating gold or silver threads. Working for Jearsey, Thomas had entered the world of the free merchants.

There were other employment opportunities for someone like Thomas. Indian-owned ships often employed European gunners and officers. They were in great demand. Ships' commanders, whether Asian or European, were usually also merchants and had a substantial financial stake in their cargos. They required a good knowledge of the markets. Even if they were acting on behalf of someone else, they were also likely to be undertaking their own private trade.

Thomas described Junk Ceylon as being the shape of the island of Ceylon but only a sixth of the size. It belonged to the kingdom of Siam and was ruled by a rajah. Although most of the inhabitants were Siamese, those in the ports were primarily Malays. He considered the Malay population to be rogues who were sullen and ill-natured. It was here he first recorded his encounters with pirates. They were to be of concern to him for the rest of his life. Thomas claimed the Malays carried out acts of piracy on most ships visiting the island for trade by posing as Javanese settled at Malacca. Junk Ceylon was a rich source of tin but, during the sixteenth century, trade was affected by the prevalence of these pirates, called *salateers*. Thomas described the island as mountainous and heavily wooded so that only ten percent was usable except by elephants, tigers and monkeys.

Thomas recounted the story of how a tiger that had been killing the rajah's goats was caught in a trap. It was brought, alive, to the rajah's house and Thomas was summoned to look at it. Although he had seen many before, this tiger was special because it was completely black with very large teeth and claws.

Seeing his fascination at this rarity, the rajah ordered a soldier to knock out the teeth and claws and give them to a grateful Thomas. The tiger was likely to be a black panther. However horrendously this episode reads today, the rajah clearly wished to impress the sixteen-year-old Thomas by presenting him with a rare gift.

Thomas continued to say the only trade goods the island produced other than tin were elephants. Tin was plentiful and was traded for Indian textiles, iron, steel, knives, scissors, sugar and carpet-covered floor cushions. Few elephants were shipped from the island because of the high export duties charged although the logistics of getting an elephant on and off a ship at anchor in such difficult ports was surely a contributory factor.

The three sea ports on the island were excellent but had very shallow entrances restricting the size of ship that could enter. For some time before he arrived, the Dutch had blockaded the safest anchorage on the island and, whilst there, he witnessed the event which broke this blockade. At the time there was a great deal of friction between the Dutch and the people of Achin in Sumatra. The Dutch, keen to protect the monopoly of trade in the region they believed to be theirs by right, seized a ship from Achin. The Malay inhabitants, believing the ship to be under the protection of their rajah, forcefully freed it before blocking the entrance to the bay with felled trees. Thomas explained the Malays had squashed the Dutch plans so effectively they left and never molested them again. The Dutch complained to the Thai king but he issued orders to the rajah to build a fleet of ships to guard the island's three ports and to attack the Dutch if they should return. Thomas was with the rajah when this order was received. He put the order into effect immediately. Despite this, not long after the king replaced the rajah with two military brothers. Thomas was to meet up with these brothers a few years later.

From Junk Ceylon, Thomas Bowrey moved on to Achin on the northern tip of Sumatra. From the sixteenth century, it had been a major supplier of pepper to the Mediterranean via the Red Sea. The East India Company had first established a factory there in 1615 but suffered continuous opposition from the Dutch. It was abandoned by the English in 1646 and they had not returned until 1668 when they built a grand building for their chief and his factors. By the time Thomas was there, this building had burnt down and had not been rebuilt. Very few English wanted to live there. He described how the houses were built many feet above ground on stilts because of the heavy rains each September or October when the town flooded. Europeans found these conditions undesirable yet many years later Thomas would live there for some time.

He was at Achin when the old sultana died on 23 October 1675 and had been there since at least July. Sultana Taj ul-Alam Safiatuddin Syal had reigned for thirty-four years. Thomas described the three months of mourning when the men wore old clothes, fasted and refrained from both gambling and sport. The women were forced to cut their hair. The sultana was succeeded by another female monarch but the population outside of the town was not happy, preferring to be ruled by a king. Thomas was still in the town when it was attacked by seven hundred of these *insolent highlanders* but the revolt did not succeed. The majority of the rebels were executed but one mullah was reprieved on the intervention of his superior. His punishment instead was the same as for theft, that is to have his hands and feet cut off plus his possessions confiscated so he had to resort to begging for sustenance. In Thomas' opinion, forcing him to steal to survive by maiming him and condemning him to a slow death was the more severe sentence.

1676

Thomas sighed with relief. He had found calm water. It had been a close shave but the *Sancta Cruz* was safe. As they were carried violently down the Hooghly towards the sandbanks he thought he was going to have to tell the ship's Portuguese trader owners that he had lost it and her cargo. Having anchored on long cables he settled down to wait out the tidal bore. His complacency was shattered half an hour later when they were hit by the incoming tide and caught in an eddy that spun the ship round and round incapacitating everyone on board. A cable broke. The situation looked dire. Then a wind came up. He cut his remaining cable and was able to sail into a small creek and safety. Unwilling to take any further risks, Thomas remained there until the wind abated completely fourteen days later.

At the same time, two East India Company ketches, the *Arrivall* and *Ganges*, rode out the tidal bore at anchor in a safer place on the same reach as the *Sancta Cruz*. On board the *Arrivall* was Streynsham Master who had recently arrived in India. William Callaway, Thomas' very good friend, was taken seriously ill on the *Ganges*. A surgeon was sent but, expecting the worse, Master also sent the *Arrivall*'s captain, George Herron, the chaplain and a young man to the *Ganges* to pray for Callaway and secure his belongings. On returning to their vessel, the boat overturned and both the chaplain and the young man were drowned. The captain and four seamen were swept away on the upturned hull of their boat. Thomas' purser happened to arrive at this point on a small *ulak* or cargo boat and managed to rescue the five. The purser, Clement Jordan, was a free merchant trading on country ships at the time of the incident. Like Thomas, he was known to have been at Balasore in 1674 and they may have been friends since then.

It was September and Thomas had moved from Achin to Bengal. The Hooghly River, an arm of the River Ganges, flowed southwards into the Bay of Bengal. The strong tides on the Hooghly produced tidal bores when the head-wave of the incoming tide became restricted by the narrowing of the estuary and rose up over seven feet high as far up river as Fort William, Calcutta. The variation in the height of the tide between low-water in the dry season and high-water in the monsoon was almost twenty-one feet resulting in difficult conditions for navigation. All ships heading for Hugli and Fort William needed the services of an experienced pilot.

River Hooghly. [By unknown, public domain.]

Thomas blamed his Ganges pilot for the incident claiming that he did not having sufficient knowledge of the conditions on the river. The East India Company had been training pilots on the

Hooghly for seven years but there were only two experienced men at the time. Determined not to put himself at the same risk again, Thomas ensured he that educated himself. Many years later in 1687, whilst at Fort St George, he demonstrated this by drawing a chart of the river.

Another episode involving Thomas in Bengal has long fascinated modern writers. It has been claimed he wrote the earliest first-hand account of the recreational use of cannabis. Robert Knox did not publish his account of the medicinal use of cannabis in Ceylon until 1681.

A group of nine or ten young Englishmen were kicking their heels one afternoon when their conversation turned to the *bangha* the locals used. Each in turn denied having tried it but all were curious. They went to the bazaar where they purchased enough for each to have a pint. Returning to his house, Thomas called his servant and ordered him to fetch a *fakīr* to instruct them on its use. The ascetic made them an infusion and each drank his share. Determined to maintain their dignity, the *fakīr* was ordered to leave and they locked all the doors and windows. Certain no one could run into the street and no outsider could enter to witness their behaviour they settled down to wait. Very soon, one of the youths started weeping bitterly and continued to do so all afternoon. Another, terrified, put his head into a large earthenware jar, staying like that for over four hours. The third, angry, hit a door posts until his knuckles were raw. Whilst Thomas and a friend simply sat, sweating, the remaining young men lay on the carpets believing themselves to be emperors. He reflected that the use of cannabis exaggerated the participant's existing mood.

Thomas was familiar enough with the market for cannabis to differentiate between bangha, grown locally, and *gangah*, a stronger version imported to India from Sumatra and five times more expensive. Gangah was more enjoyable at the expense of being much more addictive, taking only a couple of months to become dependent. Both forms were taken in a number of ways, all equally intoxicating: smoked mixed with tobacco, chewed or, as Thomas tried, as an infusion in water.

1677

The palace doors had been barred by the Siamese troops but, as the huge angry crowd continued to approach, the guards decided their loyalty was to their king and not the unpopular Indian Muslin brothers. They fled their posts. While the rebels hammered on the doors, the two servants of William Jearsey feared for their lives and ran for their ship. Only Thomas, his fellow trader, the women and children escaped brutal massacre by the mob.

Thomas had returned to Junk Ceylon as the guest of Mohammed and Ismail Beg, appointed to represent the Siamese King Narai on the island. The brothers were unpopular with the majority Thai and Malay population, treating the local residents badly and making them work too hard for too little reward. The Begs' commercial ambitions were at odds with those of the local population of nine thousand. When the brothers brought in almost one hundred fellow Muslims from India to help control the island and its trade, displacing those who traditionally held these positions, the discontent increased to dangerous levels.

Following their escape, Thomas and his associate fled to Queda about three hundred and fifty miles to the east, a Malay kingdom with the largest and most navigable river in the region. On the spring tide, the river was deep enough for a ship of two hundred and fifty tons to sail upstream for sixty miles. The kingdom was sparsely populated because the land near the sea was low, swampy and wooded. Houses were built on stilts because of flooding each autumn. Further upcountry was mountainous. Despite the country producing sufficient for its population and their rulers being benign, Thomas claimed they had taken to piracy, robbing English and Portuguese shipping. Regardless of the risks, one East India Company ship a year went to Queda for oud, a wood with an aromatic resin used for incense and perfumes, and elephants which were exported to Bengal and Masulipatnam. The ruler here was more reasonable in the custom duties demanded than those at Junk Ceylon and this, combined with the ability to bring ships further in, was clearly sufficient incentive to overcome the difficulties of transporting elephants. The best pepper in the East Indies was grown on an island off the Queda coast.

The uprising against the rajah may have affected Thomas badly. His memories of piracy and political unrest stayed with him and may have affected his actions in the future. For now, he was moving into the next phase of his career in the East Indies where he would start to build his fortune. At the start of Thomas Bowrey's *Bay of Bengal* manuscript he explained it was the account of his experience in Asia between 1669 and 1679. There is nothing in the manuscript beyond the stated end date of 1679 although Thomas is known to have stayed on in the East Indies for another nine years. Very much is unknown and unlikely ever to be known. Why did Thomas choose to end his account in 1679? When did he write it? There are sections of the manuscript with only headings, no text. Why did he never compete and publish his manuscript?

Whatever the answers, our knowledge of Thomas' life in the East Indies from 1680 onwards must rely on other sources. Fortunately, the records of the East India Company in the region are more informative during this period and a greater volume of material for the period has survived in his papers. The Company recorded the comings and goings of Thomas' ships while his letters and business papers add details. Combined, the two sources not only provide a comprehensive picture of his life in the East Indies but also corroborate each other, confirming they relate to the same person. Other, independent, contemporary accounts such as those of William Dampier and Streynsham Master complete the validation.

CHAPTER 3

Branching Out
(1680-1685)

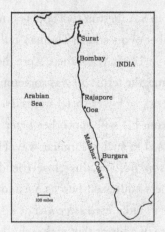

West coast of India.

LETTER OF S ADDERTON DECEMBER 1680

Loving Son ... many thanks for the piece of Tonkin silk you sent my wife ... I do not want you to think that I have anything but the same love & kindness for you as ever ... Captain Smith speaks out against you ... but I know Captain Smith very well, & give him no credit ... because I do not believe that you neglect me ... I and my

wife send our love & ... should be as glad to see you here
... as the father was when the prodigal son came home in
the Scriptures ...I am in the Hunter *frigate now but, if my*
plans work out, I intend to acquire a ship of about 150
tons and intend to come your way and for you to have a
share in her ... I am your ever loving father ... S Adderton

[Paraphrased British Library manuscript IOR Mss Eur D1076
folio 014]

This letter from S Adderton to Thomas Bowrey in December
1680 poses a number of questions. Thomas' father had died of the
plague in London in 1665. Who, then, were the letter writer and
his wife? At the time, the term *son* was sometimes used to address
a younger man or one of lower social status. However, other than
correspondence from his wife, no other letter survives in which
Thomas is addressed in such a familiar way. His future parents-
in-law wrote to *son Bowrey*, his close friends who were also
his business partners addressed him as *Sir* and senior East India
Company officials in India used *esteemed* or *respected friend*. It is
the *loving son* form of address that makes this letter so intriguing.

As the letter was delivered to Thomas by his friend and
business partner, Robert Masfen, it was likely to have been written
from somewhere in the East Indies but where exactly? It was
likely Captain Smith was Henry who many years later would act
as Thomas' agent in Edinburgh. Henry Smith was known to have
spent some time in Bombay; did he cross paths with Adderton
there? The answers to these questions can be found in the records
of the East India Company and the Bowrey papers.

According to a list of officers and soldiers under the command
of the Governor of Bombay in April 1672 held in Thomas'

papers, Stephen Adderton had been an ensign, the lowest rank of commissioned officer in the infantry. Two years earlier, he had written to the East India Company at Bombay from Mahim in the north of the island. He had probably already been in the area for some time. In January 1672, Ensign Adderton was sent from Bombay with two armed sloops to act against the pirates menacing Company shipping on the Malabar Coast and succeeded in capturing one of their vessels. A month later, he encountered the pirates again off Rajapore and sank one of their vessels, captured another and succeeded in killing about one hundred of their men. It may seem strange that an infantry officer was commanding a naval force but it is clear from Company records this was not unusual at the time.

Later in the year, Captains Longford and Adderton were put in command of the Bombay militia. Based on the militia bands of London, the Bombay militia was formed from Company servants and other civilian residents of the settlement under the command of professional soldiers. It is unlikely Adderton had risen from ensign in just a few months and may have held the honorary higher rank only whilst in command of the militia. In October, Adderton was sent with ten columns of muskets to prevent problems during the annual pilgrimage to Mahim about eight miles north of the fort of Bombay. Eighteen months later, Adderton was one of the three captains sent to quell a mutiny among between sixty and eighty soldiers under Captain Shaxton who had joined the Company from England in 1672. The men's complaint was that their pay was too low compared to the local cost of living and, because they were not paid in the local currency, they lost further when they exchanged it.

Although the mutineers complied with the orders brought

by the three captains, the rebellion flared up again the next day. This time, Adderton was sent accompanied by the Bombay chaplain with a written offer to regulate prices but the mutineers turned them away. As the cost of living was an issue for all the inhabitants of Bombay, the mutineers may not have believed enough concessions were being made specifically for them. Their demands about the currency in which they were paid had not been addressed. While the unrest appears to have died down at this stage, it would flare up again and affect Adderton more severely in the future.

When it did in August 1674 even their captain, Shaxton, became involved. The men demanded a contribution from the Company towards the costs of a feast those who had gone out to India together were planning. This time it was taken more seriously by the Company's Council. Shaxton and the other officers of the garrison were replaced. Adderton was believed to be involved and placed under arrest. The Council decided to bring the men to trial. Shaxton was found guilty and sent home to England although he was allowed to do it in style by being allocated the ship's great cabin. The three ring leaders were sentenced to death, the Company took mutiny as seriously as the government in England, but only one was actually executed by firing squad. Despite being implicated, Adderton did not stand trial as he was able to convince the Council he had simply been lax in his duties. He did not get off without punishment. His commission was suspended.

Adderton's career did not appear to have suffered long from this ruling because, subsequently, he was appointed to a committee of five charged with setting fixed prices for provisions and to monitor the prices charged by the local merchants. The committee's duties were an attempt to balance the needs of the locals with those of the Europeans and included the establishment of English weights and measures all over the island alongside the prevention of the theft of hens by soldiers and sailors. The theft of poultry had discouraged breeding, resulting in shortages and consequent higher prices.

Adderton continued to appear in the records for some years and was still based in Bombay in March 1677 when Henry Smith, who had been dismissed from his post at Bantam, was sent by the Council in Surat to Bombay. Despite having been dismissed, Smith was known to be an efficient accountant and was to assist in the accounts office while he awaited a ship home. The exact nature of Smith's misdemeanours are not known but in February 1677 East India Company officials in London wrote to the Council at Bantam requesting clarification about reports of embezzlement there. In late summer 1678, Bantam had replied to London naming two employees, not including Smith, in respect of the suspected financial misdealing and also mentioned the scandalous behaviour of their factors delaying their accounts hiding the financial fraud. It is likely Smith was one of those involved because he owed the Company a little over one hundred and fifty-seven pounds at the time his employment was terminated.

As an outsider without any knowledge of the island or its inhabitants, Smith was unable to put the factory's disorganised accounts into any order and was forced to continue on his homeward journey in 1678 but he refused to submit. Having arrived back in England he appears to have convinced the East India Company in London that he deserved another chance and departed again at the earliest opportunity. He returned to Bombay on board the *Williamson* in August 1679. The next month, he was sworn in as a member of the Council but without any specific duties.

Unlike his masters at home, the president at Surat who was still, at this time, in charge of Bombay continued to have a poor opinion of Smith and refused his suggestion he should be put in charge of the island's accounts. He was expected to simply assist in the work. Around the same time, Adderton was given temporary command of the *Hunter* frigate charged with the defence of Bombay. At the end of the year, Adderton's wife died and he spent the first nine days of 1680 ashore. According to the evidence of his letter, he quickly remarried. It is the pirates Adderton encountered off the Malabar Coast and the arrival of Smith at Bombay in August 1679 that provide the links to Thomas and the letter.

Bombay harbour fishing boats in the monsoon.
[Drawn by Clarkson Stansfield RA, engraved by E Goodall.]

Leaving Bombay on the *Dispatch* in late 1680, with a cargo of rice for Muscat a storm blew up and Thomas was blown further from the shore than planned. The small ketch was crippled when the main mast was damaged. Vulnerable, he hoped to return to the safety of Bombay but the winds were against him. He headed to Goa instead. Just off shore he was attacked by the pirates and was unable to put up any resistance because his powder was wet following the storm. The attack started thirty minutes before sunset and the pirates stayed with the ketch through the night. Fearing for the lives of the Europeans on board Thomas, John Dunaway, a Portuguese boy and three lascars, local native seamen, stealthily slipped into their boat at 3 a.m. and silently rowed towards the shore. They left eleven more lascars on board. When the sun rose the six witnessed the pirates board the *Dispatch*. Thomas and the others successfully made their escape but it took five days of rowing to reach Goa. Forty days later, several of the lascars left on board the *Dispatch* arrived in Goa from the port of Burgara where they had been stranded by the pirates. The lascars confirmed the pirates had intended to kill Thomas and Dunaway had they remained on board.

Piecing together the available evidence, it would appear that Thomas had visited Smith in Bombay whilst purchasing rice and Adderton was at sea, leaving the silk for Mrs Adderton with him. If the earlier supposition that the widowed Elizabeth Bowrey had married Samuel Smith, believed to be Henry's brother, was correct, Thomas' mother boarded a ship for Bombay in February 1670 and arrived later that year to discover her second husband had died and her son moved on. The East India Company at Surat and Bombay at this time strongly discouraged the wives, widows and children of their employees from returning home despite there being a grave shortage of accommodation. The reasons for this are not obvious from the records but perhaps they were seen as necessary for the settlements to become established. As the only transport available was controlled by the Company, it was impossible to leave without its permission. In these circumstances, it is likely Elizabeth married for a third time. If Mrs Adderton was Thomas' mother, he may also have had personal reasons for his visit to Bombay on the *Dispatch*. He is not recorded as visiting the island again before Stephen Adderton was wounded in action with pirates in September 1685 dying of his wounds. None of this can be proved because no records of Elizabeth's life in India survive but there is a tantalising glimpse of what may once have been. On 13 August 1686 the Company officials at Bombay wrote to their superiors in Surat enclosing an attestation from the attorney for Captain Adderton deceased. The declaration explained the absence of documentation needed for the administration of Adderton's estate in favour of a Mrs Bentam. At the time, Bentam was a common variant of Bentham, Elizabeth's maiden name.

Before his death, Adderton was to meet up with Henry Smith again. In the intervening period, Smith's reprehensible behaviour had continued. In December 1682, Smith was sent to Sombaji on a failed trade mission. Relations between Smith and his superior at Bombay were strained. Possibly to put distance between the two men, Smith was sent off again on his embassy to Sombaji. Negotiations were said to have gone well but he failed to secure a deal. It was claimed that the negotiation had been finalised but, as Smith had spent the money entrusted to him as gifts, he was not in a position to complete the deal. There were suggestions that Smith should be charged the full cost of the failed mission. Smith's reputation deteriorated further. It was claimed his behaviour was outrageous and he incited unrest among the island's soldiers. The officials at Bombay claimed Smith had conspired with a ship's captain to leave Bombay surreptitiously with the objective of becoming head of another, unnamed, factory elsewhere in the East Indies. By March, matters came to head during a Council meeting when, during a heated altercation, Smith drew his sword. He was ordered to apologise publicly and refrain from wearing his sword for four months.

Then, on Saturday 30 June 1683, the commander of the Company ship *Berkeley Castle*, recently arrived from England, invited a number of people on board including Smith, Adderton and a Captain Richard Keigwin of the Bombay militia. After dinner, Smith spoke about the recent prohibition on Company employees purchasing slaves. He announced that he would not give a farthing for the proclamation and to prove it would by purchasing two or three slaves within the next few days. The *Berkeley Castle*'s commander said that, if he did, he should like a girl to take home to England to which Smith retorted he should just take one from the slave ship in port. The dinner probably included a great deal of wine because the commander and his chief mate immediately tried to carry out Smith's suggestion. The result was the captain being thrown, wounded, overboard from the slave ship. His mate stripped naked and dived in to save him and the *Berkeley Castle* fired on the slave ship wounding twenty-four of the crew. This was the last reported meeting between Adderton and Smith.

Keigwin, one of the parties on board, was also a member of the Council at Bombay who had an equally bad relationship with the Company. In December 1683, he was excluded from the Council and led a revolt against the Company. He took the fort by force and, for nearly a year, ruled Bombay allegedly in the name of the king. Adderton joined the rebels and was appointed admiral of their fleet. The following March, Adderton was sent by Keigwin to obtain supplies from a sympathiser at Surat. Whilst there, he was put under pressure by Company officials. Despite claiming that he and his crew would die rather than submit, two days later they all surrendered in return for a free pardon. Keigwin was furious and, to make an example of him, seized all Adderton's possessions and burnt his house. The rebels damaged no other private property during the rebellion but the loss of Adderton's papers at this time was to have the consequences for the administration of his estate following his death referred to previously.

These incidents may explain why nothing more is heard of Adderton's plans to purchase a ship mentioned in his 1680 letter. Despite this, Thomas was soon to become an owner of his own. Perhaps this is why he believed 1679 to be the end of a phase of his life and why the *Bay of Bengal* manuscript ends at this date. Having spent a decade learning navigation and trade in the region he was planning to work for himself, in partnership with others. This theory is reinforced by Thomas' trade papers starting from this date. Any earlier documents within his papers relate only to members of his family and their business.

1682

On 25 October 1682, Thomas Bowrey with a group of other free merchants, including James Wheeler and Henry Alford, purchased a small ship or ketch from the shipbuilder, Sancho Narsa, at Madapollam about three hundred and ninety miles from Fort St George. Having a burden of just twenty tons, the ketch named *Adventure*, was much smaller than usual for such a ship, perfect for navigating the ports and rivers described in the *Bay of Bengal* manuscript. Thomas would do business with Narsa again in the future.

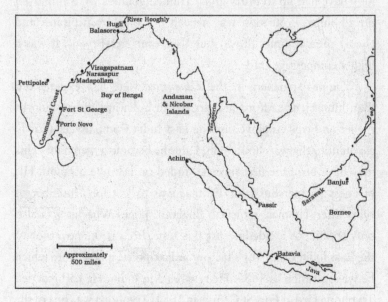

East Indies showing Vizagapatnam and Madapollan.

The ships of the country trade were locally built regardless of whether they were owned by Asians, the Company or free merchants. Ships to be commanded by Europeans were built of teak but to European designs. Teak was exceedingly durable and hulls made from it would typically last ten times longer than a European-built ship. This was the reason Indian-built ships were favoured. The traditional rigging of Indo-Arab vessels was based on the lateen sail, a triangular sail that permitted sailing only before the wind, unlike the square-rigged ship on which most Europeans were trained but the shipyards of the East Indies were able to copy any English vessel. Most locally built ships intended for a European captain were square-rigged. Regardless of design, all ships used in the country trade were heavily armed. Larger ships may have had up to thirty guns. Trained gunners were employed on all ships. Protection was needed not only from pirates and enemy ships in times of war but also commercial rivals. It was a highly competitive trade.

Thomas' partners in the *Adventure* were less experienced than him. Henry Alford had arrived in India just fifteen months earlier and was employed by the East India Company as a lowly assistant to the warehouseman. Later he became a merchant. This may have been the first time he traded on his own account. His business partnership with Thomas was to last for a number of years after Thomas' return to England. James Wheeler was also only trading as a side-line. At this time, he was the governor of the East India Company's factory at Pettipolee, a post from which he was to resign in 1685. He remained in India. He had married Tryphona Ord at Fort St George in 1681. Tryphona was one of the bridesmaids at the marriage of the son of Elihu Yule the previous year. When Wheeler died in 1693 aged only thirty-seven, having been accidentally poisoned by his surgeon, he was described as a merchant and councillor of Fort St George.

At the beginning of September before the ketch had been completed, Wheeler had written from Madapollam to Thomas with instructions for his voyage to Bengal. These instructions demonstrate the complex nature of the country trade. He was to go first to Vizagapatam with some goods for a Mr Ramsden who may have had some textiles suitable for sale in Borneo. From there he was to go Hugli in Bengal where he should dispose of the lead and salt in the *Adventure*'s cargo and purchase silk and long pepper. Long pepper was not for human consumption but used for medicines in India and to feed elephants in Siam. On his return, Thomas should call in at Madapollam so Wheeler could advise him how to dispose his cargo at either Porto Novo or Fort St George.

How was Thomas, at the age of 23 years, able to afford to purchase a share in a ship and her cargo? The cost of the *Adventure*, fully fitted out including provisions and the first two months' wages for the crew of nine but excluding the cargo, amounted to the equivalent of £24,000 today. Typically, the smallest share was one sixteenth but, from later evidence, Thomas may have had as much as a half share. In addition to this, there were running costs to add before any profit came in. He received only ten pagodas a month as master of the *Adventure*. This was the equivalent of just a little more than £7,000 per annum today. He is unlikely to have earned more working for others. It is inconceivable he would have been able to save enough from his wages and he had probably started trading on his own behalf as soon as he was able. That Thomas was paid a wage as the master of the *Adventure* is significant. This does not happen in his future ventures indicating that perhaps he did not have much spare cash after the purchase of his share of the ship.

As master, Thomas was expected to stay at Madapollam for some time overseeing the fitting out of the ketch. It was no hardship. He described the town and river as pleasant and healthy. The river reached as far as the town which had attractive gardens almost surrounding it. The town was cooled by the sea breezes and the climate was so attractive that the senior Company officials from elsewhere stayed there for a few months each year.

At the end of November, the East India Company at Fort

St George issued a pass to Thomas Bowrey to trade. A few days later, Thomas copied a chart of the coast of Tenasserim with the Andaman and Nicobar Islands, in preparation for his upcoming voyages. Before the end of the year, Thomas had loaded a cargo of textiles costing over six-hundred and eighty-eight pagodas, worth over £11,000 today, onto the *Adventure* at Fort St George. This was not destined for the fashionable English market but for Borneo and Java, where they were equally sought after, and both pepper and copper could be purchased. The textiles included in Thomas' first cargo ranged from plain longcloth and other plain cottons through ginghams, originally a striped cloth of mixed cotton and Bengal silk; chambrays of silk, chintz or gold stuff; and betilles or muslins, to various completed garments. Thomas was ready for his first voyage as his own master.

1683

Having loaded the cargo on board the *Adventure*, at the beginning of the New Year, Thomas Bowrey and his crew set sail. It may have been Thomas' first trading venture on his own behalf and he may have been excited at the prospect but he maintained a calm head and did not neglect the administration. He kept a set of accounts from which the details of the voyage can be reconstructed. Their first destinations were Passir followed by Banjar, both in Indonesia. Here they sold their cargo from Madapollam. At Banjar, according to his orders, Thomas purchased pepper. By May, the *Adventure* had reached Batavia where the ketch was refitted and provisioned ready for the return voyage. Provisions included a four and a half gallon cask of arrack.

The Castle Batavia. [Andries Beeckman (c.1656-1661)]

Two months later, Thomas had returned to Fort St George and already set sail again for his business partner, Alford, in Madapollam. Here, on 28 July, Wheeler purchased a quarter share of the *Adventure*. Wheeler now owned half of the ketch. Thomas had released funds for his next venture, a share in another vessel being built by Narsa. On 1 August, Wheeler paid the first 250 pagodas, over £15,000 today, towards the cost of building the *Borneo Merchant*. In the meantime, Thomas still had commitments on the *Adventure* and Wheeler gave him written instructions for a voyage to Bengal. In addition, he was carrying gunpowder and a bale of goods for the East India Company.

By October, the *Adventure* was riding at anchor on the River Hooghly. In his *Bay of Bengal* manuscript, Thomas described the town of Hugli as a sumptuous place, with many fine buildings and beautiful gardens. There was a large population and, consequently, a good-sized bazaar. Altogether it made a pleasant place, which was inhabited by some of the richest merchants in the kingdom. Both the Dutch and English had factories in the town, on the side of the river and about a mile apart. Opposite the Dutch factory was the Hugli Hole, where the depth of the river was sixteen fathoms. Hugli was the main port for Bengal, a region rich in a wide range of produce. Of particular interest to the Europeans were the textiles ranging from calico to wrought-silk. In Thomas' time, Bengal textiles were both traded in the East Indies and exported to England. Opium, said by him to be the best in India, musk and long pepper were also purchased here for the European country trade. Musk is a greasy secretion with a powerful odour produced in a gland of the male musk deer and other animals. Unlikely as it may seem, this highly valued substance was used in the production of perfume and a recognised way of sending wealth to England.

A cargo of silk and long pepper, purchased with the proceeds of selling the Borneo lead, copper and salt, was laden on the *Adventure* at Hugli. They also took on board goods consigned for Borneo for third party customers and while here, the Reverend John Evans added to the *Adventure*'s cargo. Evans had gone to India as an East India Company chaplain in 1678. He was based in Hugli and, later, at Fort St George but he was censured by the Company for his association with free merchants such as Thomas and for trading on his own account. The Company discussed stopping his salary at the beginning of 1692 and he returned to his homeland of Wales via London six years later. Reputed to one of the most successful independent merchants in Bengal at the time, he returned home with a fortune worth about £2.5 million today. Evans would be made Bishop of Bangor in 1702 and, later, of Meath and was not afraid of courting political controversy. He was to keep in touch with Thomas once they were both home.

By 28 November, Thomas had returned to Madapollam where Wheeler reimbursed him for what he had spent in Bengal. The *Adventure* continued on her voyage but, a few days later, was forced into the river of Naraspore by the weather. The friendship between the two men was demonstrated by a letter and generous gift Wheeler sent to Thomas at this time. Understanding that the ship was detained, Wheeler sent his condolences and stressed that safety was the first priority. He continued by saying he had sent Thomas four bottles of claret and another of brandy to cheer his spirits. In the same letter Wheeler provides a testimonial for Thomas, telling him he had so far found him careful, industrious and someone who acted on honest principles but perhaps, in view of the gift, not too sober. As the unexpectedly bad weather did not last long it has to be hoped Thomas remained sober and did not consume the whole gift before he departed from Naraspore. He arrived in Fort St George only a few days later and would have had a massive hangover if he had.

Wheeler wrote to him again, from Madapollam, complaining Narsa had delayed fitting out their vessel. He had visited twice each day to try to hurry him along and they had quarrelled. The letter was written over a period of ten days up to 23 December and was intended to be delivered by the *Borneo Merchant* when Narsa had finally finished her. In the end, the ship was still not ready and was not likely to be for another three days. Wheeler appears to have been put into a foul mood by the delays and his instructions were accompanied by many complaints about trade. Each time Wheeler added to the letter there were further, similar complaints. However, he had been told there was the possibility of one hundred bales of fabric suitable for Borneo being available at Porto Novo. The letter ended with Wheeler noting that a Mr Prickman had been engaged to command the *Adventure* and he hoped it was not the mad Prickman who was once a servant to Captain Bays. There were a number of Prickmans in the East Indies at the time including Samuel, a mariner married to an English woman, recorded at Fort St George in the 1680s. There were no further complaints from Wheeler so it is likely that a sane man had been appointed.

Notably, this letter contains the first reference to Thomas being ill. Wheeler wrote he was sorry he was not yet rid of his fever and ague, the name for malaria at the time, wishing him fully recovered by the time he received the letter. Despite what Wheeler believed, the *Borneo Merchant* was delivered before Christmas Day because, on that day, he and John Beavis of Fort St George loaded cargos of textiles onto the ship in readiness for a voyage to Borneo. Thomas' health was still uncertain. The instructions noted that the ship was to be commanded by Thomas Bowrey or, in the case of his death *which God forbid,* by Robert Masfen.

Thomas and Wheeler each had a half share in the new ship and there is an interesting account of stores required for a voyage to Borneo ranging from weapons through navigational instruments to domestic items. Domestic items were needed for everyday life on board and included plates and dishes; tallow and lamps; spoons and knives; and a gong. Very few food items were included in the list, the exceptions being water, butter, a bag of sugar and a thirty-five gallon cask of the essential arrack. Understandably, there were many navigational instruments. Not only did they carry a meridian compass but also a spare glass and card for the instrument plus another small compass for the service boat. They also had on board two log lines, three buoys and a seven hundredweight anchor plus both red and white fabric for signalling flags. It was important to be able to carry out repairs during a voyage and the ship carried a comprehensive collection of woodworking and other tools. Finally, for defence, the ships armaments comprised four firelock and five matchlock muskets, two brass blunderbusses and a barrel of gunpowder. The masts, yards and rigging were supplied with the hull by Narsa for a total of 1,400 pagodas. Some of the items needed to outfit the ship were purchased in Madapollam, possibly also from Narsa. The remaining items were taken from their previous ship, the *Adventure*, or purchased in Bengal. The total spent on the additional items and services was 350 pagodas, the equivalent of over £100,000 today. Thomas had started to build his fortune.

The *Borneo Merchant* was ready to sail but was Thomas fit to command her?

1684

Thomas Bowrey's pain, weariness, vomiting and fever continued into January. As others loaded their goods onto the *Borneo Merchant*, they repeated the contingency that Masfen would command the ship in the event of Thomas' death. There were no effective remedies for malaria in India although Robert Knox reported the medicinal use of cannabis on Ceylon around the same time. Sickness was expected. Most Englishmen in India were lucky to survive more than two years. Thomas had already lasted fifteen years and did recover before the end of the month as Wheeler again wrote to him from Madapollam. After the *Borneo Merchant* had departed, he had managed to persuade Mr Freeman to let Thomas have his dog, Tiger. In return, Freeman wished Thomas to bring him an *orum mutan*. Wheeler added he thought that he meant the kind of monkey he had brought previously. What he referred to was probably a lesser orang-utan, a smaller form native to Borneo but Thomas did not include the word in his Malay dictionary published after his return to England. Freeman was reluctant to part with his dog and Wheeler only persisted because Thomas had begged him to find him one.

It is not known when the *Borneo Merchant* departed from Fort St George. Thomas was next heard of at Banjar where he was trading by March. On 26 June, Thomas purchased the sloop, *Pearl*, for five hundred Spanish dollars, over £18,000 in today's values. Nothing more is heard of the *Pearl* and, being described as a sloop, it is likely that this was purchased as the *Borneo Merchant*'s service boat to be used for transferring people and goods between ship and shore.

On 19 July, Thomas wrote to John Evans at Hugli. He had commissioned him to carry goods for him and Thomas explained why he was unable to return to him this year. The letter gave Evans a detailed account of the business he had done on his behalf. It was not one-sided. Evans had purchased some musk on Thomas' behalf. Thomas arrived back in Fort St George from Batavia on 14 August with his cargo of Borneo pepper. The East India Company wished to buy the pepper to send to England if the price was acceptable and had a ship ready to leave. They were unable to agree a price as Thomas was holding out for what he believed he could get in Bengal and he sailed north. By 7 September he was in the road at Vizagapatam. At this time the East India Company had a factory here but within five years the factory was seized by Aurangzeb's forces and the English residents murdered.

For Thomas, it was neither illness nor attack that foiled his plans to sell his pepper in Bengal. The *Borneo Merchant* with the pepper still on board returned to Fort St George having been forced back when the monsoon changed. Monsoons are the changes in atmospheric circulation and precipitation associated with the asymmetric heating of the land and sea. In the Bay of Bengal, the monsoon flows from the Nicobar and Andaman Islands towards northeast India and Bengal in the early summer picking up more moisture as it goes. During the other half of the year, there is a counter clockwise southwest current. The monsoon is important for the rains it brings but the currents and winds associated with it restricted where and when ships could sail. However, even with today's modern technology, the monsoons are notoriously difficult to predict.

On 19 September, Thomas wrote again to the Reverend John Evans at Hugli apologising for not being able to reach Bengal that year. He claimed Wheeler had delayed him at Vizagapatam resulting in the weather prevented him sailing further north. He was stuck at Fort St George until the end of the monsoon but he would resume his voyage to Bengal once the weather permitted, hopefully the following February. He had sold Evan's textiles to another consignee in Borneo for a good price except for the longcloth which he had brought back. Thomas clearly had to leave Vizagapatam in a hurry because he explained he could not let Evans have any details of his account because he had to leave his escritoire, writing desk, behind and it had not yet caught up with him. In this letter, Thomas said he had sold the ketch, *Adventure*. There is no record of what she was sold for but a month later, Wheeler sold his half share of the *Borneo Merchant* to Thomas for 750 pagodas, the equivalent of over £45,000 today. He was now the sole owner the ship. It would appear he was making a financial success of his business only part way through his second trading voyage.

Fort St George squall. [William Daniell RA (1769–1837)]

Thomas Bowrey's good fortune did not continue. On 26 September, the East India Company at Fort St George determined to take advantage of his misfortune and bought his pepper at fifteen percent less than the price they originally offered. To compound his problems, his relations with Wheeler may have become strained. On 18 October, Masfen together with two others swore a statement that it was not possible for the *Borneo Merchant* to carry a larger cargo of pepper than she had. Presumably Wheeler believed Thomas should have purchased a greater quantity. Thomas was learning from experience the difficulties of trading in the East Indies. A few months later he left the *Borneo Merchant* to ride out the monsoon in the Ennore Creek, a Fort St George backwater, whilst he was carried on a *palanquin* overland to Porto Novo. He left Fort St George at 9:30 p.m. on a Monday and arrived at his destination at 6 p.m. the following Friday. It was a journey of about one hundred and forty miles mainly walking during the late afternoon and at night, sleeping during the day. On 26 December, the *Borneo Merchant* arrived back at Fort St George. The cargo of Borneo peppers that had been destined for Bengal was still on board.

1685

In January, the Company's officials at Fort St George relented a little over the issue of the pepper and agreed to purchase it at a higher price than that originally offered but still lower than Thomas had wanted. On 11 January, Thomas sold Henry Alford ambergris, baleen and some Bengal textiles. Perhaps Thomas had a cashflow problem after buying the sloop because Alford also loaned him fifty pagodas and Thomas left six canisters of tea and thirty-four bundles of gangah with him. A fortnight later, Alford sold a quantity of china bowls and tea cups on Thomas' behalf. Previously, on 8 January, Thomas had finalised his account with his late partner, Wheeler. He was recovering from his aborted voyage to Bengal and preparing for his next trading venture.

On 27 January, the Council of Fort St George issued a pass for the *Borneo Merchant* commanded by Thomas to trade for one year. In mid-February, he transferred goods to the *Boa Vista* commanded by Masfen for him to take them to Evans in Hugli. The *Boa Vista* was at anchor in the Naraspore Road. Thomas was on route for Achin and had offloaded the last of the *Borneo Merchant*'s cargo. Eleven days later, the *Borneo Merchant* with Thomas on board arrived at Madapollam. Here, he asked the Company's Council if they would sell him their sloop, *Conimeer*, for forty pagodas, the equivalent of over £2,000 today. He probably wanted it as the *Borneo Merchant*'s service boat. It had been unused for a considerable time, was in a terrible condition and had been beached. The Council cannot have believed their luck. They wrote in their diary, if it had remained where it was any longer, it would have fallen to pieces. The sale was agreed on 10 February and Fort St George allowed the Madapollam factory to retain seventeen pagodas of the selling price.

By 25 May, Thomas was at Achin. He spent a few days in difficult negotiations with the local officials in order to receive the necessary permission to land his goods. Having done so, he was frustrated by the weather. The wind was against him all day stopping him from returning to his ship. As soon as he was able, Thomas collected his personal possessions and ten bales of textiles he was selling on his own account. His priority was his own interests rather than the goods he owned in partnership with Masfen. Thomas' earlier frustrations melted away when his chests were passed by the Customs House without being opened. This was a privilege granted to the English. He took everything to the house he had rented close to the catacombs and bazaar. He would have preferred to live by the river from where he could keep an eye on his ship but there had been no house available there. The next day, events turned against him again. Thomas wrote that the local chief officer sent for him and told him no Christian merchant was permitted to stay in the house he had rented. None ever had lived above the English factory. He was shown an alternative which he took although it was not as satisfactory and the next day he moved his goods to his new house.

For the next two months whilst at Achin, he sold Indian textiles: *hamomes*, perhaps ginghams; ornate waist sashes; cotton and silk sarongs; painted cotton; *mulmuls*, fine, soft, Indian cotton; and *sarassa*, a patterned cloth used as a waist-cloth. In return, Thomas purchased a mixed return cargo of gold ingots, copper, tea, baleen and mace but not as much as he would have liked. He complained about the low prices he was paid for the goods he had sold.

Thomas returned to India. At the end of July he arrived at Balasore where he learned that there was unspecified trouble at Hugli, his intended destination. Consequentially, Thomas stayed in Balasore, keeping in touch with Masfen by letter. Life for independent traders in the East Indies was becoming increasingly difficult and risky as the Company tightened up on what they were permitted to trade. By 20 August, Thomas was still detained by business at Balasore. Two weeks later he was being pursued for the money lost by an Englishman he was with in Achin, John Blaswell, who had been robbed by five of the *lascars* Thomas employed and had loaned to him. Blaswell was claiming Thomas had promised to recompense him but Thomas counterclaimed that he had loaned the *lascars* but was still paying them. He was owed one month's pay. There is nothing more in Thomas' papers about this incident. It was simply yet another difficulty he had to negotiate.

By the 6 September, in between other business exchanges with Masfen, Thomas was discussing purchasing another ship. He left the final decision with Masfen but Thomas reminded him of his plans to return to England. In September 1685, he received the news of Charles II's death six months previously. Despite the time news took to reach him, Thomas was clearly aware of the feeling in England about the new king taking the throne. James's Catholic leanings were not generally welcome and there was a strong likelihood of unrest. He concluded it was not the right time to return home but nevertheless he continued his preparations. Then he discovered a new order prohibiting independent traders shipping musk on Company's ships. He needed to sell the musk Evans had purchased on his behalf the previous year or find an independent ship to transport it.

Two days later, Thomas sent a package of gold wrapped in a cloth marked R.M. and sealed with his seal which he had requested Mr Fitzhews to send to Masfen by the first safe conveyance. Borneo had been known to have gold deposits as early as the fourth century A. D. and gold had been discovered on Sarawak earlier in the seventeenth century. It seems incredible today that it was considered safe to leave gold to be sent on some unknown vessel wrapped only in a sealed cloth but this was a time when there was mutual interest in upholding the sanctity of consignments. During periods of war, letters home were often carried by enemy vessels. On the same day as he wrote to Masfen, Thomas also purchased gold on behalf of a Madam Kiddells. No doubt he had also made purchases for himself.

On 11 September, Thomas left Balasore on the *Borneo Merchant* destined for Fort St George where he arrived sixteen days later having detoured via Hugli. He departed again on 30 September and, four days later, Thomas wrote to Masfen from Porto Novo. He had left behind the cannabis bought in Achin and goods he purchased in Balasore for Alford to sell their behalf. He contracted with Ahmad Marcar to freight as much cargo as the

Borneo Merchant could hold from Porto Novo to Achin. Trade with the East India Company had clearly been difficult recently. Thomas reported to Masfen he had been kindly treated in Porto Novo by the Company president there who was now speaking to Thomas in a more sympathetic manner. He hoped they would not meet any further obstructions at Fort St George.

From Porto Novo, Thomas Bowrey and the *Borneo Merchant*, loaded with Marcar's cargo, headed for Achin again but, on 2 November, he met with a storm which was so violent that he had been forced to cut down his mast to save the ship. He changed course for the Coromandel Coast. On 17 December, he arrived back at the fort laden with paddy before heading to Narsa at Madapollam for repairs. Despite his careful plans, Thomas had missed his prime trading opportunity in Achin.

Thomas' plans in the East Indies were becoming clear. He would work for others garnering knowledge and capital before branching out on his own account, accumulating a personal fortune with which to return home to England. He had suffered a number of misfortunes and taken great risks but would be set up for the rest of his life. He had had enough but was unwilling to risk everything by arriving home during turbulent times.

CHAPTER 4

Moving On
(1686-1688)

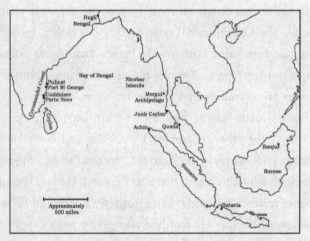

East Indies showing the Coromandel coast.

On 18 May 1687, the Council at Fort St George received a number of letters from Cuddalore all dated four days earlier. The first of these letters, which ended *Sirs Your Most humble Servant ... at present weighed down with Irons*, had been written by Thomas Bowrey from the cookhouse of the havildar, or military commander, of Porto Novo. In a second letter, written the same day, Thomas added he feared he would be killed, and signed off melodramatically *Your Most humble Servant in Affliction*. What had happened that his fortunes had changed so dramatically?

1686

When Thomas Bowrey arrived back in Fort St George, the *Borneo Merchant* was carrying a large amount of opium, both on his own account and on behalf of others, in addition to other goods for Masfen and himself. He remained at Fort St George until 14 January when he sailed for Cuddalore and nearby Porto Novo on the *Borneo Merchant*. He had been hoping to see Masfen before he left and was uncertain how things stood between them. They had not met for almost a year. Unsettled as he was, Thomas' judgement was failing him. Against the accepted practice, he had taken on three new crew members from the East India Company ship, the *Defence*. The Council at Fort St George wrote ahead to Cuddalore, instructing them to detain Thomas while his ship was searched. If the three were found, they were to be returned under guard. If not, Thomas was to provide a bond of £1,000 in case it was later proved that he did have them. This was a stiff penalty. £1,000 was the equivalent of over one and a half million pounds today. Ten days later, the Council received confirmation Thomas had returned the crew members.

Thomas was philosophical about the loss of crew. He had replaced them with an Englishman who had worked for him previously and a careful Portuguese man with a wife at Fort St George. His remaining crew of lascars were the best he ever had: many were previously soldiers at Fort St George. It appears that Thomas may have poached the crew members because he was concerned about his own security. He claimed they were strong enough to deal with any enemies they may encounter. Reaching Porto Novo, Thomas sold the paddy, or unhusked rice, he had on board since he failed to reach Achin, but the remaining goods were still intended for Borneo to where he was heading next.

Before departing from Porto Novo at the end of the month, Thomas wrote again to Masfen. He was no longer certain if they were still in partnership. Was Masfen happy about the planned voyage to Borneo? He left instructions with Henry Alford to buy Masfen out from money in his account at Fort St George if that is what Masfen wanted. He had heard that Masfen was planning to join the crew of a ship destined for China. Alford would also take over the sale of Thomas' goods held by Masfen if necessary. He had left the accounts for the ship, probably the *Borneo Merchant*, with Alford for Masfen to inspect. Nothing survives to explain this possible estrangement between the two men. Thomas continued to address Masfen as *loving friend* and stressed the respect and kindness he felt for him in his correspondence so, perhaps, he was unhappy about Thomas' plan to return home. Thomas assured him that he had no wish to finish their business partnerships despite his plans.

Nothing is known about Thomas' stay in Borneo on this voyage. His papers contain only one short draft of a letter dated Banjar 24 July saying he was leaving for Fort St George that day. He arrived at the fort where he sold his pepper seven weeks later. The Company complained they had to negotiate hard with Thomas for the pepper and, in consequence, forced him to wait almost a month for payment.

At Fort St George, Thomas was soon to take his leave of the *Borneo Merchant* which sailed for Porto Novo and Junk Ceylon with Thomas Flemming as captain on 25 September. The ship would not return to Fort St George for four months. Thomas probably travelled as passenger for the first leg of the voyage because on 6 October he drafted a letter from Porto Novo to Arthur Richards about a small boat he had left at Achin in July 1675. He also gave Flemming written orders for the voyage. On 24 October, back at Fort St George, Thomas again wrote to Flemming, who was at Achin by then, requesting he leave there by 10 December and return directly to the fort.

The last report of Thomas for this year was on 30 November confirming he had arrived back at Fort St George having been pilot on the boat that had taken Señor Axel Juel to Tranquambar where Juel was imprisoned by the commissary. Tranquambar was a Danish settlement on the Coromandel Coast and Juel had been governor there since 1681. After leading a force that attacked Porto Novo, his men mutinied and he returned home after executing the two ringleaders. There he was court martialled and sent back to Denmark in January 1687. He was eventually acquitted at the end of 1690. It appears it was Thomas who delivered the unwitting Juel to his fate.

1687

On 10 January 1687, Thomas Bowrey was given permission to sail for England on the East India Company's ship, the *Shrewsbury*. He needed to keep in favour with the Company because their permission was required to travel home on their ships. However, in doing so he would only be allowed to carry his essential items and no trade goods. These would need to be sent home separately, probably on an independent ship, or converted into easily portable valuables such as diamonds. The *Shrewsbury* sailed for England on 2 February but Thomas was not on board. During February he was recorded as a freeman of Fort St George. He spent January and February tidying up his business loose ends. The voyage of the *Borneo Merchant* under Flemming had not gone to plan so Thomas tried to make as much as he was able from the goods he owned, especially his stock at Porto Novo.

On 8 February, Thomas wrote home to Phillip Gardiner from Fort St George. He had purchased a quantity of Chinese musk only to discover he was now prohibited from shipping it home on a Company ship. This was, in part, the reason for the delay in his leaving India. He was now planning another voyage and had left the musk with Henry Alford to be sold or sent to Gardiner when he was able. He still expected to be home shortly. He finished his letter by sending his regards to Gardiner's wife, daughter and friends, signing himself *his loving kinsman and humble servant*. Gardiner was to be Thomas' future father-in-law and the signature implies they were related. The familiarities in the greetings imply that the kinsmen were well acquainted yet no earlier correspondence between them survives.

The previous day Thomas had been issued a new licence by the East India Company at Fort St George for a further year's trading voyages. According to this licence, he was taking charge of the *Borneo Merchant* again and presumably heading for Porto Novo because, on 7 February, Henry Alford wrote to Thomas there in anticipation of his arrival. Alford had deposited Thomas' gold at the Mint where it was awaiting him but had not been able to send on the musk because he had been unable to find a ship leaving for England that was not already full. Thomas left for Porto Novo on 11 February and remained there for the next three and a half months.

This may not have been Thomas' original intention. It was three months later that the Council at Fort St George received the two desperate letters from Porto Novo. Following a voyage in which he carried a cargo of cloth and slaves for two of the brothers of Ahmad Marcar, he was in dispute with Marcar who refused to hand over fabrics he had purchased on Thomas' behalf. In the argument that followed, Thomas physically assaulted Marcar's assistant on East India Company premises. Thomas was arrested and held in leg-irons in the cookhouse of the havildar. From his makeshift cell he wrote his letters to the Company. The first claimed the havildar's superior had ordered his release but to no avail. In the second letter, written the same day, Thomas added he feared he would be killed.

The events leading up to this began when Thomas sailed from Porto Novo without the customs duties due on the slaves being paid. The brother of Marcar who was responsible for them had disappeared and Thomas became liable for them by default. Then he stopped at Junk Ceylon, selling the brothers' goods there rather than at Queda and Achin as contracted. Following his brush with Malabar pirates at the end of 1680, he is unlikely to have wanted to risk those based at Queda. On his return to Porto Novo, Marcar claimed that Thomas had sold the goods in a bad market. As he received less than he expected, Marcar withheld Thomas' textiles in compensation. Having been arrested for the assault and failure to pay the customs duties, Thomas believed his dignity, and even his life, had been threatened.

The Company's officers at Cuddalore were torn between the slight against a fellow countryman under their protection and their annoyance at Thomas' actions. They were concerned

Thomas' future conduct may risk the factory's security and their own lives. The Council at Fort St George was less sympathetic and demanded a bond for 10,000 pagodas, nearly £660,000 today, to indemnify the Company from any legal demands that may be made against them. In their opinion, Thomas should not have taken matters into his own hands, the officers at Cuddalore would have been justified in doing nothing and they intended to demand he accounted for his actions when he returned to Fort St George. For reasons which are unclear, Thomas was released by 24 May when he wrote in a calmer fashion to Fort St George setting out what happened. He confirmed he had given his bond to the Company and requested it be returned once the matter had been resolved.

At around the time Thomas was released, Christopher Wilson consigned two bales of cloth on the *Borneo Merchant*. Wilson, a member of the East India Company Council at Cuddalore, grudgingly handled the issue of Thomas' imprisonment showing distain for an independent trader yet was perfectly happy to carry out his own private business using Thomas' ship to carry his goods.

Meanwhile, on 31 May, Thomas wrote again to his *loving cousin*, Phillip Gardiner explaining why he did not return home when expected. Surprisingly, he made no mention of being imprisoned at Porto Novo still claiming the East India Company prohibition of the carriage of musk on the Company's ships as being the main reason. Perhaps he felt guilty, recognising his own responsibility for the incident. He now hoped Alford would send the musk to Gardiner in England on the *Loyall Adventure*. His latest plans were to embark on a small voyage before returning home. He expected to be back in England in just a few months.

Two days later, Thomas sailed from Fort St George for Achin on the *Borneo Merchant*. There is no extant record about this voyage except his purchase of gold and, on 31 August, he wrote from Hugli in Bengal to Captain George Herron of the *Shapir* with instructions for a bale containing gold he had requested Captain Nicholson to deliver to Herron. The reason for this is unclear but Thomas wrote he was indebted to Herron so it may have been in recognition of this gratitude. Thomas reminded Herron not to forget to send him two quilts, one large and one small, of the quality suitable for England.

At the end of September, Thomas arrived back at Fort St George from Bengal on the *Borneo Merchant* with correspondence from Hugli for the Company. His association with the ship was shortly to end. In yet another unfortunate incident, the *Borneo Merchant* and the East India Company ship, the *Loyall Adventure,* were both lost in a storm at Fort St George on 4 October. Thomas' ship was driven ashore and broken up, presumably before Thomas' musk had been loaded because this appears on a later bill of lading. He continued to make arrangements for his return to England. On 3 December, he wrote to Alford from Fort St George saying he was leaving him a lacquered, tortoiseshell escritoire or writing desk plus another in black lacquer containing a number of boxes, five Chinese fans, a quantity of porcelain tableware, several journals and papers, silk tassels and fringe, a quantity of jewellery and coins, and some Japanese toys, small decorative items. Mr Rodrigues was to deliver a bale of diamonds. The escritoires were to be sent to Gardiner in Wapping by the *Royal James* and the diamonds by the next available ship. Thomas wanted the bills of lading to be sent separately for security.

Despite his experience there earlier in the year, a week later

Thomas was back at Porto Novo where, according to his account books, he stayed for a further three months. Called Porto Novo, or New Port, by the Portuguese, who were the first Europeans to settle in the area, the English established a factory there in 1683 because its good harbour in the mouth of its river was sheltered by the Coleroon Shoal, making it the safest on the Coromandel Coast. However, the river was only navigable by small country ships such as the *Borneo Merchant*. In Tamil, the present-day name of the port town, Parangipettai, means Europeans' Town reflecting the European influence in the area but it was a trading centre with strong links to Achin and Ceylon even before the Portuguese arrived. A further attraction was the excellent local iron ore deposits.

1688

At Porto Novo, Thomas Bowrey continued to deliver the gold he had obtained in Sumatra. At the same time, he was trading in cloth and preparing it for the English market. By this time, he had gained an expertise in the textiles of India that he would use to his advantage after his return home. The East India Company did not restrict its textile trade to painted chintz that imitated the fashionable but expensive woven silks from Spitalfields. Prior to the arrival of the Huguenot weavers from France, English cloth production was based on woollen broadcloths. In contrast, the trade in Indian fabrics had been known to the Egyptians as early as the first century A.D. Thomas fully understood the full range of textiles available and the best markets for them. Cotton and silk, sometimes combined, sometimes wrapped in metals including silver and gold, were woven in different ways to produce various types and weights of fabric. Pre-dyed threads were woven into striped, checked or plain cloth. Plain cloth was often embellished with embroidery. At Porto Novo, Thomas was to supervise the dying of his cloth. This may have been plain cloth but was more likely the complex, multi-stage, multi-colour process that created chintz patterns.

Thomas kept a dyer's account book covering the period 19 December 1687 to 28 February 1688 and separate trading accounts but the most interesting record whilst at Porto Novo was his household expenses book. Some entries were generic, with provisions listed almost every day, but there was still great detail. There is no note of the size of his household but over the three months he bought two quarters of pork, eight pigs and eleven hogs. The hogs, at least, were alive because on two occasions rice was purchased specifically for the hogs. In addition, there were fifty chickens, one hundred and forty hens, two ducks, two hundred and forty-nine fowl and twenty-four non-specific birds. Some of the hens may have been kept for eggs because over the eighty-two days, only fifty-six eggs were bought. Compared to pork and poultry, very little fish was purchased – six mullet, seventeen small flat fish called pomfrets and seven non-specific fish, three of which were to be salted, plus one turtle.

The accounts include eight hundred and eighty-three limes. As a mariner, Thomas understood these were essential to avoid scurvy. This equates to more than ten limes per day. However, unless provisions included other fruit and vegetables, very few of these were consumed. In addition to the limes, there were only fifteen oranges, two coconuts, a small quantity of plantains, a large quantity of onions, one papaya and one guava. A single cheese was purchased a few days before the end of Thomas' stay in Porto Novo and may have been to take back to Fort St George for use on board ship. Also purchased at the end of the stay was a large volume of spices in quantities ranging from about ten ounces to about two and a quarter pounds. Perhaps he had acquired a taste for spice over the past twenty years and purchased these for his use back home.

It is difficult to be specific about the quantities of the other items in the accounts. Most were given in non-specific measures or in *seers*. A seer was the equivalent of between ten and thirty ounces, which varied both by location and according to the item being weighed. A number of measures of rice were bought each day but bread was not purchased as often. There is no indication whether the bread was European, Indian or, even, hard tack as was used on board ship. Some fine rice and some paddy were used but most was of ordinary grade. Both oil and butter were consumed regularly as well as about twenty-two pounds of sugar. Other consumables purchased included salt, sugar candy, milk and rose water. The only beverages in the accounts were arrack, toddy and a bottle of what Thomas called *server* but there was also five bags of malt and the household may have brewed its own beer.

In addition to food items, a quantity of china root, a natural medicine, and a few household items were purchased: four knives, six plates, three dishes, ten candles plus quantities of wax, pots and pans for the cook, some mats and two muskets. A considerable portion of the expenditure was on services including a fulltime cook paid monthly, a baker, a washer-man, a water woman, tailor, barber, plasterer, a Dutch servant, someone to grind wheat into flour, and local labourers, including those to carry the palanquin.

A charitable donation was given to a poor Armenian. Thomas also employed a *batta peon*, an armed guard, each time he travelled. Perhaps after his earlier experience in the town he felt the need for more security. The total spent maintaining the household at Porto Novo over the three month period was almost seventy-four pagodas, the equivalent of over £5,000 today.

Towards the back of the book, Thomas kept an account of slaves at Pulicat, a little north of Fort St George. During most of the sixteenth and seventeenth centuries, Europeans traded in slaves from the Coromandel Coast sending them to Ceylon and the West Indies. Pulicat was one of the main ports involved in this trade. Between 1621 and 1665, the Dutch sent one hundred and thirty-one ships with a total of over 38,000 captured Indian slaves to their plantation at Batavia from Pulicat. Thomas' account of rice purchased for slaves recorded purchases almost every day between 3 and 17 February. The total spent during that period amounted to the equivalent of nearly £3,000 today. Fifteen percent of this rice was sent to Fort St George and the remaining kept for his voyage. The *Slaves Acco^t kept in Palicatt* covered the period 10 January to 1 March. Separately, in Thomas' trading account, he records the spending the equivalent of £650 today on fifteen hundred and fifty-five dried fish. It can be assumed the slaves' diet consisted of dried fish and rice. The only entry relating to the purchase of a slave was crossed through but was twelve *fantams* or four shillings for a boy slave, equivalent to thirty-four pounds today. A hog cost the same.

Meanwhile, Thomas was still planning to return to England. On 5 February, he wrote again to Gardiner that he was intending to sail for England by the next ship, which he hoped would be within the next six months. He had arranged for the goods he had previously left with Alford to be sent to Gardiner on the *Beaufort* and included instructions about what to do with them. Thomas sent two copies of the letter by different routes in case one failed to arrive. On 1 March, Thomas wrote to the Council of the East India Company at Fort St George thanking them for their kindness in helping to resolve his dispute with Ahmad Marcar and at other times, saying he was always ready to be of service to them. As this was some months after their intervention, was Thomas attempting to smooth the way to the Company allowing him to travel home on one of their ships?

Soon after writing this letter, Thomas left Porto Novo. He arrived back in Fort St George as commander of the *Francis* on 4 March. His account book contained entries that indicated Thomas was fitting out another ship but there had been no previous mention of the *Francis*, which was presumably the replacement for the *Borneo Merchant*. Within a few days, the ship was being loaded for a voyage to Achin. However, before leaving, Thomas wrote again to Gardiner saying he was planning to travel home overland. Despite the dangers from piracy, enemy ships and shipwreck, an overland journey was more dangerous than a sea voyage home. Was he still in disgrace with Company officials?

On 10 March, Thomas left Fort St George for Achin as commander of the *Francis* and arrived on 15 April. The next day he wrote to Alford saying his plans were unclear. It was possible he would not return to Fort St George before setting off for England. Between 20 April and 16 May, he kept a journal. For the first time, Thomas was using double-entry bookkeeping. Although invented in Italy in the middle ages, what was known in Thomas' time as *merchants' accounts* were not practiced by most merchants in England but were by East India Company clerks. Perhaps learning this skill was another stage of Thomas' preparation for his return home. This is especially likely as he did not keep it up for the whole of his stay in Achin. On 4 June, Anthony Weltdon entrusted him with three bales of gold to deliver to Alford at Fort St George.

Whilst Thomas was at Achin, East India Company's frigate, the *Pearl*, and her crew arrived there having escaped detention by the Siamese for some months. He learned from them that almost one hundred other Englishmen were still being detained at Mergui, an archipelago in what is now southern Myanmar. They were being ill-treated. Nearly eighty others had been massacred. Thomas was to break this news to the Company when he arrived back at Fort St George later this year. The incident unsettled Thomas further.

Around this time, he met William Dampier, a disillusioned pirate who had recently determined to complete his voyage around the world and had arrived at Achin with two accomplices. Impressed with Thomas' kindness, the three decided to visit his home first. The invitation may not have been the altruistic act it initially appeared. As so often, Thomas kept his long-term objectives in mind. By the time Thomas met Dampier, he was in a nervous state. More than anything, he wanted to get his fortune home safely. Was Dampier a means to this end? He proposed that Dampier accompany him on a voyage to Persia. He was not honest about this, withholding his plans to sell his ship there and take the overland caravan to Aleppo from whence he intended to make his way home. If he did this, Thomas would not need to entrust his valuables to others or risk them being taken by pirates.

Thomas needed to spend longer in Achin to complete his business but was nervous about his ship being attacked whilst he was there. At the time, England was at war with Siam. When the heavily armed ship of the Siamese ambassador arrived in the port, Thomas set off on the *Francis* to the Nicobar Islands taking along Dampier and his friends as crew members. They were forced back after a few days by the weather but, by that time, a number of English ships had arrived in port and Thomas felt secure enough to remain. Throughout the short voyage, Dampier and his friends were too sick to do any work yet Thomas paid them well giving each man twelve gold coins. The amount paid to each man was the equivalent of fifteen English shillings, worth nearly one-hundred and thirty pounds today but approximately a month's wage for a sailor at the time. Still hoping to talk Dampier into sailing with him to Persia, Thomas again invited him to his house and entertained him with *wine and good cheer*.

Despite Thomas' generosity Dampier chose to sign onto the crew of one of the other English ships. Thomas returned to Fort St George. By the time he arrived back there his plans had changed again, for the final time. He wrote he would sail for England on the *Bengal Merchant*. Masfen was taking over the command of the *Francis*, presumably the ship he had intended to sell in Persia. His partnership with Masfen was to continue, at a distance, and Alford was to have his power of attorney for his business in the East Indies. Thomas had left goods with Alford, requesting him to sell them and invest the proceeds in goods from China or Bengal or diamonds, if possible, or if all else failed to send his money home by ship. Everything was now in place for his return to England after nineteen years. He was now twenty-nine years old and ready to marry.

His fortune secured, on 20 October 1688 Thomas left Fort St George for the last time as a passenger on board the *Bengal*

Merchant. An undated bill of lading shows his musk and a quantity of fabrics accompanied him. A fellow passenger was Mrs Lucy Francis, the widow of Captain Francis who had been killed the previous year in the Company's service. She had been sent to Fort St George in a very poor and weak condition. As she had no income and did not consider the Company's charity sufficient she had petitioned to be allowed to return home. Described as being of a *turbulent* and *clamorous* nature, she had a bad reputation. The Company readily agreed to her leaving for England. As Thomas recounted in the introduction to his Malay-English Dictionary, the voyage home was a long one and he, for the first time in his life, had leisure time. He used it to write down all he could remember of the Malay language. Was it also possible he was trying to avoid his disruptive and annoying fellow passenger?

CHAPTER 5

Starting Out Again
(1689-1695)

When Thomas Bowrey boarded the *Bengal Merchant* in Fort St George in October 1688, he was returning to a London unrecognisable from that he left two decades earlier. As a young child, he was unlikely to have picked up anything more than the tensions caused by the political atmosphere around him but he had kept abreast of events in what he still considered home whilst in the East Indies. He had already delayed his return once when he learned James II had acceded to the throne a few years earlier. What he could not know was that during his voyage to England there was to be further turmoil.

Religion remained the source of conflict in England but now the protagonists were Parliament and the country against the Crown. As Thomas had understood, James was known to have Catholic beliefs and this was only emphasised by his marriage to the Catholic Mary of Modena in 1673, an event that was greeted by the Protestant population with concern mitigated only slightly by their understanding of the powers of Parliament and his Protestant heirs, his daughters Mary and Anne. The country had suffered much strife since the Church in England had split from Rome. A bitter civil war, with its undertone of religious divide, had been fought within living memory.

At the time of James' coronation, none of his children by his present queen had survived. The news the queen was pregnant again was greeted with dismay and many hoped, believed or claimed it was not true. The reasons varied. The queen was not really pregnant. The child had been still born. The child was a girl. Whatever the reason, when James Francis Edward was born in June 1688, despite witness statements to the contrary, it was claimed the infant was an impostor smuggled into the queen's bedchamber in a warming pan. Princess Anne's support for the rumours gave them certain credibility. The masses wanted to believe anything but that there was a male Catholic heir to the throne.

Across the North Sea, King James' son-in-law William of Orange saw an opportunity. He wanted to secure Protestant England as an ally against his Catholic enemies. Having been assured of support within England for an armed intervention, he landed at Torbay with an army less than a month after Thomas set sail from Bombay. William then proceeded towards London without any opposition in what came to be known as the *Glorious Revolution*. Everything was going William's way. Within a few weeks, James had given up any semblance of resistance and retreated to London where he was greeted by an angry mob at Whitehall threatening the queen. He discovered his daughter Anne had deserted his cause for that of her brother-in-law. The mood in the country was against James and he saw no future there. On 11 December he made an attempt to flee, throwing the Great Seal of State into the Thames as he crossed to Lambeth. Stranded by the tide at the Isle of Sheppey, James was apprehended by priest-codders searching for Catholics escaping from a hostile country. William, who had been unable to conceal his delight at the news of James' escape, is unlikely to have been pleased at the news of his subsequent detention.

A period of negotiation between William and Parliament concluded with him and his wife, James' daughter Mary, being declared joint monarchs on 13 February 1689. How much Thomas was aware of these events depended on which ships the *Bengal Merchant* met on their voyage home. Outbound ships probably carried news of the birth of James Francis Edward and the unease in the country but most would have left before the momentous events that followed. His ship arrived some months after the coronation of William and Mary at Westminster Abbey.

Having left a London that was essentially an enormous building site, Thomas returned to a city with a completely different atmosphere. It was to be many years before the new St Paul's Cathedral would be ready for its first service but its rebuilding was well underway. It again dominated the City but this was a new city built of brick with a uniformity of design. Only four sizes of houses were permitted. They were not as tall as before the Fire: just four storeys for the grander houses and only three for the smaller ones.

Closer to home, in Wapping, what were fields twenty years before were now built over including Well Close Square where Thomas was to live, on and off, until his death. Well Close Square, also known as Marine Square, along with Prince's Square next door were the only planned developments in an area thrown together over the years. The primary developer of the Square was the son of Puritan Praisegod Barebone, Nicholas If-Jesus-Christ-Had-Not-Died-For-Thee-Thou-Hadst-Been-Damned Barbon. Barbon purchased the freehold of Well Close Square for £3,200. In about 1683, he designed a haven for wealthy sea captains and merchants who wanted to live close to docks and wharves essential for their trade. With the aim of protecting the inhabitants from the nuisances of the surrounding area, the houses faced inwards towards a central green with only narrow passageways leading from the square. A Danish church was built on the site of the original well in the centre of the square in 1694 to serve the Scandinavian timber merchants who lived there. The earliest houses, probably timber-framed and timber-clad, were on the south side and had two storeys plus an attic. They were spacious and had staircases with barley-twist balusters. The houses on the north side were later and larger.

Wapping was not Barbon's first development. He had previously taken advantage of the opportunities following the Great Fire, building houses for prosperous merchants in the West End. In 1680, he opened a fire insurance office and one of his first schemes was in Well Close Square where a permanent fire engine was maintained on the north side. There is little doubt that this was reassuring for someone one of whose last memories of home had been the Great Fire.

Outside the control of the City and untouched by the Fire, old Wapping had none of the uniformity of the rebuilt city. Away from Well Close Square, it was a jumble of two- and three-storey houses, workshops, inns and warehouses. Dark, narrow alleyways ran down to the wharves lining the river. The roads and lanes were filled with horses, donkeys and carts laden with goods. More than anything, the smell of the place had not changed over the years. It is hard to imagine Thomas' wonder at this after so long. Having made his fortune, a man not yet thirty years old returned to a confident new city in which he believed he could make his mark.

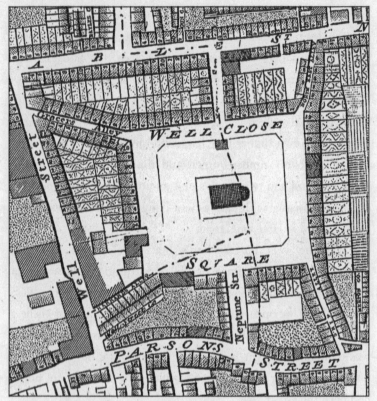

Well Close Square. A detail from John Rocque's 1742 map of London.

1689

After a traumatic childhood and a time in the East Indies that was both exciting and increasingly dangerous, no one would have blamed Thomas Bowrey for looking forward to a peaceful, even boring, life back in England. There had been signs of periods of sickness leading up to his return. Perhaps he believed his health would improve. Certainly his new life started calmly enough.

Little is known of Thomas' return voyage except that the *Bengal Merchant* stopped at the East India Company island of

St Helena. Here, Captain Poach requested Thomas to take eight pounds ten shillings in respect of *a black boy* he had purchased from Gabriell Powell. The *Bengal Merchant* docked at Portsmouth on 23 July 1689 but the date of Thomas' arrival back in London is unknown. In September 1689 he attended the auction there of goods brought back on the ship. It had been a difficult voyage home. A copy of the sale catalogue, which has survived in Thomas' papers, shows much of the cargo was damaged in transit.

Some of the cargo belonging to Thomas was sold in the same sale. Most Englishmen who went to the East Indies to work were hoping to make their fortune. The conditions were such that many did not even survive a year. Having survived nineteen years, was he a wealthy man? Thomas had shown the prudence that was to characterise the rest of his life and spread the risk by sending his fortune home over thirteen years. He started in December 1687 using two separate ships, sent more later and left funds in India for Henry Alford and Robert Masfen to trade on his behalf. Goods purchased were sent to him in London until the remaining funds were returned in cash by Masfen's executor after his death. A summary with an estimate of the value is set out in the table overleaf.

This is possibly an underestimate as some of the goods may have been sold for a good profit but it was to be more than a decade before Thomas realised everything. For the time, a fortune of over £2,000 was considered well-off but not wealthy. It was worth the equivalent of nearly £350,000 today. Thomas could have lived well but £10,000, five times the value of the goods he repatriated, was only moderate for a London merchant.

Back in India, in February 1689 his friend, business partner and attorney, Henry Alford, wrote a letter to Thomas that arrived

Date	Item	Pagodas	Estimated Sterling Value
Dec 1687	Bale of gold consigned on the *Beaufort*. (Probably the bag of 600 Pulicatt pagodas purchased by Thomas.)	60/0/0	£255/0/0
Dec 1687	2 escritoires containing boxes, fans, porcelain tableware, journals and papers, silk tassels and fringe, jewellery and coins and some Japanese toys consigned on the *Royal James*. (Probably personal rather than trade items)		£0
Oct 1688	Quantity of fabric consigned on the *Bengal Merchant* and sold in London 1689.		£665/8/6
Oct 1688	915½ ounces China musk consigned on the *Bengal Merchant*.	56/0/0	£6/8/4
Feb 1689	7 chests and 2 bales of Chinese silk plus 2 canisters of tea purchased on Thomas' account by Alford, consigned on the *Rochester* and sold by the East India Company May 1690.		£956/1/10
Feb 1692	Chest containing 29 Chine images, quantity of fine large and small tea cups, 22 diamond rings, small box and small jar (of tea?) from Masfen and send by Allen on the *Orang*. (Value not recorded, the value estimated from other items sent home.)		£80/0/0
Feb 1695	Golconda book and 2 China books sent by the *Princess Anne* purchased from funds left with Masfen.	14/0/0	£5/12/0
Apr 1695	Box of china ware sent by the *Fame* Oct 1698 purchased from funds lef with Masfen.	25/0/0	£10/0/0
Feb 1696	4 pieces Chintz sent by the *Mary* purchased from funds left with Masfen.	20/18/0	£8/4/0
Sep 1696	Parcel of mango and other seeds sent by the *King William* purchased from funds left with Masfen	3/0/0	£1/4/0
Jan 1698	Diamond ring sent by the *Sidney* purchased from funds left with Masfen. (Value estimated as a 4 carat Indian diamond.)	45/0/0	£18/0/0
Oct 1698	China ware and fans sent by the *Fame* purchased from funds left with Masfen.	4/0/0	£1/12/0
Jan 1699	Diamonds sent by the *Martha* purchased from funds left with Masfen. (Value estimated as a 4 carat Indian diamond.)	71/24/40	£28/14/1½
Feb 1700	Cash balance from funds left with Masfen.	4/35/40	£1/19/10¾
			£2,038/4/7¼

Wealth repatriated.

on the same ship as some of his goods. The letter provided an update of Thomas' affaires in India including the dreadful news that all his goods in Bengal had been seized by the *moores*. All the English had abandoned the area, including Thomas' friend Robert Masfen, and he reported all had lost everything. On 22 February, Masfen wrote a graphic letter describing these events, his usual eccentric spelling and grammar presumably worsened by the stress he had suffered. After a difficult six-week voyage to Bengal, he arrived at Balasore to discover the situation. He had his ship commandeered by the English commander to land one hundred and twenty soldiers and sailors. They were part of a force of about five hundred and twenty landed under the cover of the toddy trees. After ten hours, one of the forts had been retaken. It took another ten days for the town and the other fort to be secured. Still on board, he gave no details how this was achieved. Reading between the lines, the objective of the offensive was simply to rescue the English remaining in the town because, by the time of writing, everyone had left Bengal. Masfen's only consolation for having his trading voyage interrupted was, he hoped, that his part in the action would ensure he was treated more favourably by the Company in future. Others at Balasore were less fortunate than him. The ship, *Dragon*, belonging to James Wheeler was burnt and the sloop, *George*, was sunk although Masfen had rescued most of her cargo. He had been advised by Mr Herron that all their goods in Bengal had been left behind and lost.

The finale of Masfen's letter referred to the earlier disagreement between them when Thomas was upset that his business partner planned to sail for China. He reflected that they had not parted well but he was writing in the spirit of friendship. However, it was addressed to Mr Thomas Bowrey and signed *your humble servant* – none of the usual mention of friendship. On 16 October, Masfen wrote again to Thomas and this letter gives us an insight into the plans Thomas had shared with his friend. He wrote that he hoped, by this time, Thomas would be well married to a good lady. As many Europeans, including Masfen and his sister, found a marriage partner in India, this is unlikely to be the sole reason for Thomas' return. The letter ended *pray let me hear from you.* Thomas had not replied to the earlier letter and Masfen was still trying to smooth their relationship. Masfen reminded Thomas of his beautiful son, Thomas' godson named after him, and told him the harbour master of Achin had enquired after him and was looked forward to seeing him back there in the future. Surprisingly, after some of Thomas' experiences in the port, he had left a gift for Masfen to pass on to the harbour master.

This letter, addressed to Thomas at Philip Gardiner's house in Wapping, gives the only clue to his intentions when he left India. Had plans been made for him to marry one of Gardiner's daughters? They had never met. The elder, Elizabeth, was a baby at most when Thomas left and he had been in the East Indies for over two years when Mary was born. For Masfen to think he may have been married within a few months of arriving back, he surely had someone specific in mind. Elizabeth was aged twenty, when Thomas returned. Perhaps she was his intended but there is no evidence for this. Although Thomas had been in contact with Gardiner in recent years, there is no surviving letter from him mentioning marriage.

1690

Thomas Bowrey was wealthy enough on his return home to treat himself to a yacht he named *Duck*. He commissioned her to be built at a boatyard on the Thames at Wapping for ninety pounds. The yacht was twenty-nine foot long, nine foot wide and had a burden of fourteen tons. Thomas ordered her in February, work started in the middle of July and she was due to be launched onto the river by mid-September. No doubt Thomas was an exacting customer. The initial agreement included an extremely detailed specification. We can imagine him watching progress closely over the two months until she was his. He was to keep the *Duck* for seventeen years until he sold her in March 1707, keeping her in storage when not being used and having her maintained annually.

Having left England as a child, one of Thomas' priorities on arrival home were clothes. In early January and feeling the cold he had his tailor, William Killingworth, line his striped jacket with flannel and make him two flannel waistcoats. This was needed because he was still wearing his clothes from India. In the first five months of the year he had a coat and waistcoat altered, and a coat, waistcoat and breeches mended. It was not until the end of May that he had a new black coat made. Then Thomas became more extravagant. He purchased three and a half yards of rich gold and silver lace for three pound ten shillings before having Killingworth make a new nightgown and a silk suit of coat and breeches trimmed with gold thread. A nightgown, worn for warmth, was a similar garment to a Victorian smoking jacket or a modern dressing gown. A nightshirt to sleep in was an extravagance when most men slept in the same shirt as they wore during the day. Killingworth's discounted bill amounted to five pounds. In total, Thomas had spent the equivalent of about £1,400 today. Before the next winter, he had more mending done and two more flannel waistcoats made plus another black suit.

This year Thomas started renting the King's Head Inn at Southwark, initially from Thomas Lowfield, for thirty-eight pounds per year. The Kings Head was an old coaching inn situated in what is now Borough High Street close to London Bridge. By the end of the year, Thomas is likely to have received the letter Robert Masfen wrote in March informing him of the death of his wife, Frances Fellows. Masfen was still asking if Thomas had married yet implying he had not yet received any reply from him but, in his grief, it appears Masfen had decided he could no longer maintain his earlier coldness. He signed the letter *Your Reale Friend* and had arranged for his mother to give a mourning ring to his old friend.

1691

By the beginning of 1691, there were signs Thomas Bowrey was beginning to look to the future. He purchased four shares in the Linen Manufacture of England. It is not known what he paid but the shares were worth one hundred pounds each when he was ready to sell them a few years later. This Linen Manufacture is a little of a mystery. The British Linen Company was set up to promoted the linen trade in Scotland and morphed into the British Linen Bank, a Scottish bank that merged with the Bank of Scotland in 1971 but this linen company was not set up until 1746. It can only be assumed the Linen Manufacture in which Thomas held shares was a similar organization to promote the English linen trade. In August Thomas may have purchase £3,000 of shares in a lottery but, the agreement is only a draft in Thomas' hand and, again, I can find no trace of any such lottery before 1694. When they were issued, the lottery purchase was essentially a loan to the government in return for an annuity over a number of years. The 1694 lottery paid sixteen pounds a year for ten years for a ten pounds ticket. In addition, there was a draw for additional annuities of between ten pounds and £1,000.

In May, Thomas Bowrey of Wapping, master seaman, was appointed as a Younger Brother of Trinity House. Trinity House was incorporated by Royal Charter in 1514 charged with ensuring the safety of shipping and the well-being of seafarers. Known today for the provision and upkeep of lighthouses, prior to July 1732, all persons licensed as pilots were required to become Younger Brethren. Under its charter, there is no specific qualification for a Younger Brother, although during the reign of James II its board made an order that only mariners who had served a certain number of years at sea were qualified for admission. There is no evidence Thomas ever worked as a pilot in England. Perhaps he had unfulfilled plans to or simply wanted the status of membership and recognition of his service in the East.

During this year, Thomas had two more suits of clothing made, one in a drab or dull, light brown fabric and another of silk with gold and silver buttons and thread. Then on 11 September he drew up a marriage settlement with Philip Gardiner in advance of his marriage to Gardiner's daughter, Mary. He had been preparing for his marriage since his return.

Gardiner, probably a cousin of Thomas' mother, was an apothecary living in Well Close Square, Wapping. He owned property in Essex and may have been born in the county. As a sideline, in the 1670s, he had invested in shares in at least two trading voyages. Whilst he was still in the East Indies, Gardiner was Thomas' point of contact in London and he addressed him as his kinsman and cousin in letters home but no documentary evidence of their relationship has been found. Gardiner was to give Thomas three hundred pounds at the time of the marriage and pledged to bequeath him at least another £500 on his death. Although deferred payments such as this were not unusual, it was common for a bride's portion to more or less equal the groom's fortune. This marriage settlement would appear to undervalue Thomas' wealth. To ensure his daughter was not to be destitute if she was widowed, Gardiner required Thomas to leave Mary £1,200 or goods to that value in his will. In London at the time, it was custom for a widow to receive one third of the value of her deceased husband's estate. This provision ensured Mary would receive a minimum amount. When the time came, Thomas met this condition by leaving the residue of his estate, after a few small bequests, to Mary.

Three days after agreeing the marriage settlement, Thomas and Gardiner were together again. This time they were applying for a marriage licence. This required Thomas to sign an allegation swearing that there was no impediment to the marriage. According to this statement, Thomas Bowrey, merchant, and Mary Gardiner, both of Greenwich, were to marry at St Mary Magdalen, Old Fish Street, London. Mary was said to be aged about twenty years when she was only eighteen. Thomas had reduced his age by one year closing the apparent age gap between them. The average age for a girl of Thomas' class in London to marry in the late seventeenth century was twenty years, younger than similar girls in the rest of the country. Typically, a man such as Thomas married a girl ten years his junior. Mary was very young. Her sister Elizabeth was the more obvious choice. There is some evidence Elizabeth was more literate and business-minded than her younger sister and she was four years older. It seems Thomas' marriage to Mary was a love match.

Whether there was any real intention of marrying in the City of London will never be known but on 17 September Thomas arrived at the parish church of St Margaret at Lee in Kent, probably wearing his new silk suit with its gold buttons and gold thread trim. He had little time to make friends in England and had few close relatives other than his Middleton cousins. Were they there to support him? Most likely it was a quiet wedding, tucked away in Kent. A marriage by licence avoided the perceived tasteless calling of bans in church and the publicity requiring the expense of catering for a large number of guests. Thomas had started yet another stage of his life.

1692-1695

Following their marriage Thomas and Mary Bowrey settled down at Greenwich in another house belonging to Mary's father. A few letters were addressed to Thomas at Greenwich Crescent and, later, one letter was addressed to East Greenwich, what we would know as Greenwich proper today. Deptford was sometimes called West Greenwich at the time. Despite these clues, it has not been possible to identify where Greenwich Crescent was. The only other clue is a letter addressed to Thomas at his country house at Greenwich. A painting of the Royal Observatory from about 1680 shows the town in the distance. At this time, it was a small settlement of buildings clustered on the side of the Thames to the east of the Queen's House. Another, painted after the new parish church of St Alfege was built in 1714, shows the old town to the west of the King's House. Neither area of the town is far from the river but a house in either area was unlikely to be described as a country house.

Thomas and Mary may have spent the first four years of their marriage getting to know each other better in an extended honeymoon at Greenwich. It is not known how long they stayed there but, by 1695, they were living at Philip Gardiner's house in Wapping and paying nineteen pounds and ten shillings, probably for three months, in respect of rent and board for the couple and their maid. Thomas was also getting to know the few relatives he had in England. In February 1695, he drew up a detailed breakdown of the debts owed by his uncle, William Middleton amounting to over £1,626, the equivalent of around £235,000 today. Below the breakdown of his debts is a statement, signed by Middleton but in Thomas' hand, setting out how he proposed to repay his them. As the document names twenty-five creditors, the schedule of debts and repayments is complex and demonstrated Thomas' accounting skills.

For relaxation, Thomas familiarised himself with the Thames estuary in his *Duck* yacht, writing sailing directions and drawing charts. As well as maintaining his navigation, he also kept an interest in the East Indies trade. On 14 February 1693, Thomas signed a three-year bottomry agreement with Captain Edward Say of Mile End for £900 for a three-year voyage on the *Nassau*. Bottomry, or bottomage, was an arrangement in which the master of a ship used the keel, or bottom, of the ship as security against a loan to finance a voyage. The lender lost their money if the ship sank. The master forfeited the ship if the money with interest was not paid at the time appointed following the ship's safe return. Later in the month, Thomas signed another bottomry agreement with William Gifford of the *Seamour* bound for the Bay of Bengal. Thomas business investments were diverse. In the same year, he invested a small sum, less than fifty pounds, in a trading voyage undertaken by Captain Robinson on the *Hungerford*. At an unknown date, he shipped a ton of Nottingham beer to India on the *Maynard* captained by John Hill. In order to spread his risks, Thomas had granted a mortgage of £700 to a Mr Hendry Downton on his estate close to Tunbridge Wells in return for interest of fifty pounds per annum.

During his time in the East Indies, Thomas learned that both nautical skills and market knowledge were essential for the success of a trading voyage. In October 1693, Thomas supplied Richard Etherington with charts and expertise for a voyage he was planning to Borneo on the *Redbridge*. In return, Thomas would receive five percent of the value of Etherington's return cargo and two and a half percent of his profits. Two years later, Thomas gave Allen Catchpole a silver bowl with cover to be sold plus a further five hundred dollars, worth one hundred and twenty-five pounds at the time, to purchase lead in Borneo. The proceeds from selling the lead in Bengal were to be used to purchase such a specific list of textiles and clothing that they were probably for Thomas and Mary's own use. He wanted a fine set of white calico curtains and valence for a bed wrought with coloured silks and lined with the best striped muslin. He also requested a quilt, two small pillows and six cushions to match the bed set. The final two items were a similarly wrought petticoat and the finest white-striped neck cloth. Any remaining funds were to be invested in striped muslin to be sold in England. The profit from the muslin was to be shared between Thomas and Catchpole, who had been a writer at Cossimbazar from June 1673. He was promoted to factor in 1678 and is likely to have known Thomas from this time.

Thomas continued to visit his tailor during this period, and for the rest of his life, having more clothes made but we do not know what else he spent his money on because the surviving receipts are nonspecific. Perhaps learning from his uncle's difficulties, Thomas was not extravagant and squirreled away most of his money in investments in the East India Company, Linen Manufacture, Royal African Company and Bank of England. The East India Company had become a joint stock company in 1657. Prior to that date, shares were sold in each individual voyage. If that venture failed, investors lost everything. By the time of Thomas' investment, investors were no longer gambling on the success of a single voyage. Knowing the East Indies trade as well as he did, Thomas was confident in the investment he was making. He may not have been as confident in some of his others but he cautiously spread his money across a number of different ventures.

A 1694 Act of Parliament established the Bank of England. The Act had imposed a tax on beer, ale and other alcohol as well as on tonnage of ships to raise funds for the war against France. The same Act had also made provision for individuals to voluntarily advance the sum of £15,000 in the same cause. Why would people pay a tax voluntarily? What subscribers were actually doing was purchasing a government bond attracting eight percent per annum interest. These low-risk bonds funded the war.

The Royal African Company was established in 1672, the successor to the Company of Royal Adventurers Trading to Africa. It had a monopoly over English trade with West Africa but was a significantly riskier investment. Although other goods were traded, by the 1680s it was transporting 5,000 African slaves a year across the Atlantic. This was the start of the notorious slave and sugar trade triangle by which the manpower to work the sugar plantations was taken from Africa to the Americas and sugar grown there sold in England to raise funds to buy more African slaves.

Thomas was not to hold the shares for long. On 16 June 1693, William Bowen, a London merchant, made a statement that Thomas had asked Henry Million of the Linen Manufacturer to sell four shares he owned at one hundred pounds per share. Today's value of the four shares would be nearly £55,000. Thomas claimed that Million *pretended* to sell the shares but had *suspicions* and would not complete the transfer until Million took an oath before a Justice of the Peace. William Bowen's statement appears to be a form of indemnity given to Thomas in return for a fee of ten pounds and sixteen shillings or nearly £1,500 today. On the reverse is a statement made by Richard Sweet that Francis Burdett, to whom Million had claimed to sell the shares, denied having purchased them. There is no record of any resolution to this dispute. Thomas sold the rest of his shares between July and September.

The answer to why Thomas was cashing in his investments is to be found in his correspondence with India. During the four years up until 1695, he continued to receive letters from Robert Masfen. These rambling letters kept Thomas up to date with business in the East but more importantly with news about the people he knew whilst there. Henry Alford, to whom Thomas had assigned his power of attorney, had died in 1692 and was buried alongside his wives at Fort St George. Masfen's sister, Philadelphia, a widow with three children had married Charles Sherer, an independent merchant and mariner. Philadelphia's children had been sent home to live with her mother and sister in England. Thomas kept a friendly eye on the children. Sherer made purchases on Thomas' behalf and, in return, Thomas paid Masfen's mother for looking after the children. Following his sister's remarriage, Masfen needed help looking after his son and remarried himself although he had no real desire to do so. Despite his reluctance, he considered himself lucky to have found another good wife in Ann Hicks. He had been very ill and wrote frequently of returning home. Whatever had caused the rift between them was now well healed and Thomas sent out a number of personal items to his friend including a hat, periwig, cravat, ruffles and stockings. Although why a man would wish to wear a periwig, cravat and ruffles in the tropics is a mystery.

By 1694, Masfen had requested a mutual friend, Samuel Glover, to send advice about Thomas' plans to undertake a trading voyage from England direct to Borneo. He could not recommend going to Borneo at all because they were no longer happy to trade with the English. English goods would not sell well there. If Thomas must go, his recommendation was that it would be better to go via Fort St George where his cargo could be traded for silver dollars. Thomas was not deterred by this news. He continued his planning for a new trading voyage, one that he would command himself.

CHAPTER 6

The *St George Galley* (1696-1699)

Thomas and Mary Bowrey's extended honeymoon in Greenwich was drawing to an end as life continued much in the same vein into the New Year. As his thoughts turned back to living in Wapping, Thomas remembered his childhood and the fears of his neighbours during the Great Fire. His surviving papers include an unfinished draft petition dated March 1696 to the Mayor and Aldermen of the City of London raising concerns about the amount of ammunition stored at the Tower of London, not far from Well Close Square.

At around the same time as the newlyweds' life was changing, the East India Company was facing a change in its fortune. Over the years, the Company's monopoly of the English trade with the East Indies had been challenged and periodically reinforced. In 1694, a group of independent merchants took their case to the House of Commons which declared that they had a right to a share of the market. This led, four years later, to the creation of the *English Company Trading to the East Indies*, commonly known as the *New* or *English East India Company*, in return for a £2 million loan to the government. The original company of London merchants became known as the *Old* or *London East India Company*.

The Old Company took a large share of the New and dominated it but a strong rivalry between the two companies for the dominant share of the trade was maintained. However, as a large part of the profits from the New Company went to the Old, the result was little real commercial competition. In 1702 the two companies were amalgamated under a tripartite agreement with Queen Anne. They were allowed a number of years in which to wind up their businesses before the union was ratified in 1708. The resulting *United East India Company* was given exclusive privileges to the English trade for three years in return for a £3.2 million loan to the Treasury. The government saw time-limited renewals of the monopoly as a way of milking the Company of funds. This, however, impacted on the Company's influence in the East. There was a constant battle with Parliament and from 1712 the monopoly was made more permanent. It was against this background that Thomas commenced a more active involvement in the trade.

1696

One reason for returning to Wapping may have been that Thomas was growing restless. After seven years, he wanted to return to the East Indies. It may not have been his intention when he arrived home but the letters from the friends he left behind had kept the possibility open. When he heard the *St George Galley* was for sale, the urge became impossible to resist and he purchased her. A low, flat-hulled vessel with a single deck, a galley could be rowed in addition to sailed. It was particularly suitable for accessing places with no harbour and for navigating shallow rivers. With such a vessel, Thomas could reach the more inaccessible markets he knew well. Needing to spread the risk, he turned to his friend Nathaniel Long. As a merchant and a member of a wealthy London family, Long had the necessary funds and contacts. Thomas persuaded him to invest £2,000, before pressuring him to convince others to join them in the venture. Having been focused on his marriage and the business he left behind in the East, Thomas was yet to build his own reputation as a merchant in London. Among those persuaded was William Walton, who invested £500 and was a neighbour from Well Close Square. Thomas' father-in-law Phillip Gardiner's share was £400. He had known another of the partners, Robert Harbin who ventured £200, since he lent him a boat at Achin in 1675. There is no record of Thomas previously knowing the other investors and Long's reputation was needed to convince these to join his undertaking. They were each to pay a quarter of their subscription to Thomas on signing the agreement and the remainder by 20 November 1696.

On 29 August, Thomas Bowrey of Well Close master of the *St George Galley* signed an indenture with his fellow investors led by William Walton. Thomas was to act as master and supercargo on a voyage on their behalf and was given considerable freedom to trade as his experience dictated although other documents direct him to go via Cadiz where silver dollars would be waiting for him and he was to deliver a letter to Long's brother-in-law. The agreement was extremely favourable to Thomas. He would be paid a wage as master plus a six percent commission on all the goods he brought back to England for his duties as supercargo. In addition to his share of the profits, Thomas was permitted to take out five tons of cargo and return with 50,000 Malacca canes on his own account. He would also be permitted one quarter of any ambergris he purchased. The total subscribed by the eleven merchants, was £5,400 of which Thomas' share was £400, worth nearly £53,000 today.

By the time the agreement was signed, work had already started on preparing the galley for the voyage. On 27 November, Thomas assigned his power of attorney to his wife, Mary, for the duration of his voyage to the East Indies. In reality, Phillip Gardiner took charge of Thomas' affairs whilst he was away. Prior to this, he had written a summary of all his ongoing business ventures and investments. This document has survived and provides a valuable insight into everything with which he was involved.

The notes for Gardiner included details of Thomas' agreement with Allen Catchpole, who was still to return with the Bengal textiles, and his share of Captain Robinson's *Hungerford*. It seems his total investment in the latter had increased from the initial five pounds. He was expecting John Hill of the *Maynard* to return with goods for him purchased from the proceeds of the sale of the one ton of Nottingham beer Thomas had entrusted him with.

In addition to an update on investments of which we were already aware, one of the outstanding issues for which Thomas left instructions was the estate of John Jackson, who died in the East Indies having left a wife in England. Thomas and William Bowen, another of the subscribers to the voyage of the *St George*, had seen this as an unusual business opportunity. They came to an agreement with Mrs Ann Jackson whose daughter, Mary, married the deceased before he sailed for India where he went into partnership with Robert Masfen and James Luckings. Between them they owned Thomas' old ship, the *Francis*. Before leaving England, Jackson wrote a will leaving his estate to his wife but, once in India, he wrote a new one. Jackson died whilst in the East and his second will was proved in Fort St George. His executors were named as Masfen and Luckings. Back in England, Mary Jackson had also died. Ann was her daughter's executrix. When she heard of Jackson's death Ann believed she had a claim on his full estate and gave Thomas and Bowen her power of attorney to obtain this from India on her behalf. In return they were to receive half of the value of the estate plus any fees paid and other costs. They sent copies of the earlier will, Ann Jackson's letters of administration and their power of attorney to the Governor of Fort St George. Despite Jackson being an independent trader, the East India Company in London made an order for the Governor of Fort St George to receive his full estate and pay it into the Company in India. Bills of exchange would then be drawn on the Company made payable to Thomas or Bowen. In preparation for his voyage, Thomas gave instruction that if the bill arrived while he was away, it should be taken straight to Bowen and his receipt obtained. Once news of Ann Jackson's claim reached India, Masfen's attorney Thomas Wigmore wrote to Thomas Bowrey to point out that according to the later will Jackson bequeathed one hundred pounds to the poor of the parish of Cree Church if his wife had not travelled to India by a certain date. He added that Jackson's later will made no provision for what should happen to the estate if Mary died before it was settled. In Wigmore's opinion this would be more easily decided in England than in India. The unexpectedly complexity of the affair meant that Thomas and Bowen would certainly earn their commission.

Thomas' state of mind returning to a region where he had lived and worked for so long but had also encountered many dangers was unsettled. Dealing with Jackson's estate will have reminded him of the high mortality rates of Europeans there.

He had never previously commanded a voyage such as he was now contemplating. Sailing from England to the East Indies was a different proposition to voyages around the Bay of Bengal. England was at war with France at the time and, just to reach the East, Thomas would risk attack and capture by the French, privateers and pirates. He insisted the other subscribers sign two agreements: one to ransom the ship and the other the cargo if either were captured. His crew had already proved difficult. They were more likely to mutiny if they believed their captain was nervous. If the *St George Galley* evaded mutiny and hostile shipping, she still risked shipwreck. All this played on Thomas' mind. Whilst he pondered on the risks to himself of the voyage, the business side of the venture was not running smoothly. The partners were all required to pay a quarter of their subscription at the time they signed the indenture in August. John Rolls signed but did not pay his promised one hundred pounds. The only funds he had available were at Cadiz. All the others paid on time. As a result, Rolls was required to sign two notes agreeing to cover his share of any losses incurred before the galley reached Cadiz and to guarantee to pay his full subscription of four hundred pounds to another of the subscribers, George Cole. It would appear Cole, who had already pledged £1,000, had generously stood guarantor for Rolls to ensure the voyage went ahead.

At the beginning of the year, Charles Sherer had written from Hugli asking a favour of Thomas. Would he be able to secure a good passage for his stepson Robin Lesly on a ship to India as the captain's servant? Thomas had known Robin as Robert Masfen's nephew. Sherer's intention was Robin should be discharged once he arrived in India so Sherer could train him to become a merchant and teach him arithmetic and geometry. His plan for

Dick, his other stepson, was for him to become a mariner like his father. This would give him the best opportunity for advancement. Thomas had maintained a paternal interest in the brothers and may have offered passage to Robin on the *St George Galley*. There is no record of this but when he did reach India, Robin was apprenticed in Calcutta, initially doing well. Later, Thomas would be disappointed to know the Robin fell in with bad characters at Malacca, gambled and embezzled money entrusted to him in order to pay his debts.

Thomas departed from the Thames on the *St George Galley* around the end of November although the exact date is unknown. He had already experienced problems with a fractious crew at Gravesend. Forced to wait in the Downs for some days for a favourable wind, Thomas had little to do but worry about what was to come. He received a number of letters, including from his wife and father-in-law, reminding him of the cosy domestic life he had left behind. Another letter contained the disappointing news that it had not yet been possible to obtain a letter of marque for the ship from the Admiralty. This was surprising. A letter of marque was a privateering commission that would have permitted the *St George* to take any enemy ship as a prize. These were usually awarded to large merchant ships of several hundred tons. The *St George* was much smaller at only one hundred and seventy-one tons. Thomas persisted and requested Long to petition Parliament on his behalf. Long went further and attended Parliament himself. There is no letter of marque in Thomas' papers and it is likely he was unsuccessful.

As they proceeded from the Downs towards Portsmouth, the *St George* sprung a number of leaks. The weather was dreadful. Thomas' grew more nervous still. He managed to convince his officers to agree it was necessary to head into Portsmouth harbour for repairs. Thomas had no experience of the complex tidal patterns in the Solent, between Portsmouth and the Isle of Wight. It was treacherous to navigate here without the aid of a local pilot but it seems, in his haste to get into safe waters, this is what Thomas chose to do. Entering the harbour and encountering a strong tide, the *St George* hit a large Swedish ship sustaining considerable damage. The Swedish ship was also damaged but not nearly as badly. The cost for repairing it amounted to five pounds and seven shillings, the equivalent of just about £705 today. There was no excuse. Thomas was aware of the dangers in unknown waters from his days in the East.

Thomas immediately wrote to his partners from Portsmouth, advising them of the situation. They responded that he should have the galley repaired as he thought best. Long added an encouraging letter suggesting the *St George* was probably not as badly damaged as Thomas thought. Despite everything, Thomas appears to have complained that he was not carrying as much cargo a he would have liked with the implication that the voyage would not be as profitable as he had hoped. Long was not inclined to be sympathetic and responded that not being overloaded was probably the saving of both Thomas and the *St George*. With a bigger load, they may have sunk. In addition, they would have been unable to use their guns if attacked and been slower, unable to run from attackers. Long reasoned that, once repaired, the galley might be better than before. He reminded Thomas that he had said there was a problem with the galley he had selected from the start. There was one piece of more cheering news. Thomas' wife and sister-in-law would be setting off with William Walton to visit him on 27 December. In addition to his other excuses,

Thomas had complained of being unwell. Long hoped he would be restored to his former health but if not fit to proceed he would not try to persuade him. The best way to recover his health would be for Thomas to accept what had happened and not dwell on what he could not change. Thomas had been putting forward every excuse he could not to proceed with the voyage but Long was far from convinced. There was also the implication that he may have considered Thomas' illness to be brought on by stress. Perhaps Thomas' health would improve with the welcome visit of Mary and Elizabeth. It had been the first time the couple had been separated since their marriage and missing Mary cannot have helped Thomas' frame of mind. Whilst Walton was in Portsmouth inspecting the galley, a number of the partners wrote authorising repairs to be carried out. Rather than accepting this as good news, Thomas summoned the carpenter and other officers to support him in his opinion that the damage was too major be repaired at Portsmouth especially as most of the facilities there were reserved for Royal Navy ships.

1697

Thomas was still in Portsmouth at the start of the New Year but, by this time, had admitted to the other subscribers that he did not wish to continue with the voyage. Walton replied on their behalf, expressing their displeasure. Long and Cole did not believe the galley was unfit to continue. Faced with Thomas' obstinacy, five days later, they reluctantly authorised his return to London. To improve their chances of returning safely, Thomas obtained special agreement from the customs officers to unload some of the cargo before leaving Portsmouth. On 6 January, Long wrote to

Thomas advising him to join two men of war heading to London for protection. Thomas' crew had already made difficulties at Gravesend. Now, with the prospect of their employment being cut short, Thomas was concerned they would abscond. Long made the unlikely suggestion that they could be taken on board one of the men of war in exchange for some of their men. Despite Thomas' continual excuses, Long remained friendly. He had entertained Thomas' parents-in-law for dinner and they had drunk his health. Eventually, when Thomas headed back towards the Thames, it is notable he employed a pilot to leave the harbour.

Thomas' account of the incident stops at this point. Nowhere does he provide his own explanation as to why the venture was aborted. On 26 January the subscribers issued an order to unload the cargo and provisions, and to warehouse them. Had Thomas not fallen out with Nathaniel Long some years later, very little of this story would be known. Long, however, was clearly still annoyed about the incident and, in his anger, wrote at that later date that Thomas had begged him not to force him to go to India because he feared he would not return alive. Captain Heath in particular claimed that, in Thomas' position, most ships' masters would have died rather than return home simply because they were frightened by a little bad weather.

Rather than being contrite about his part in the failure of the voyage he himself had proposed, once back in London, Thomas persuaded the majority of the partners to sell all the cargo and provisions in the way he wanted. Instead of trying to get the best price for every single item, he suggested they sell the goods in a single lot by candle with a £1,200 starting bid and five pound increments. In such a sale prospective purchasers would make increasing bids for the goods until the candle blew out. Whoever had made the last, and highest, bid bought the goods. The sale was to take place at Lloyds Coffee House in Lombard Street on 24 February. Thomas made it clear that he would make the starting bid, no doubt hoping to purchase everything at a knock down price. The sale details stated the value of the goods was £1,405. There was one lone dissenter among the subscribers. This was Rolls. He wanted the goods to be split into several lots for a better return. Thomas was persuasive. The objections were overridden and the goods purchased by a London merchant for £1,205. When the accounts were drawn up, the subscribers made a loss of nineteen pounds and eleven shillings on each hundred pounds invested. John Rolls, who had paid nothing, now owed seventy-eight pounds and four shillings which he refused to pay. Similarly to Thomas, many of the other partners had loaded their own goods onto the galley. Their losses were much greater. They had little sympathy with Rolls who had failed to turn up to any of the subscribers meetings. Thomas started a court action against him. Rolls' defence was, having been encouraged to join the venture, he made it clear that his lack of funds in London meant he could not pay his subscription until the galley reached Cadiz. When the ship did not proceed beyond Portsmouth, he considered his contract to be null and void. He objected to how the cargo and provisions were sold believing the others wanted to profit by buying and selling the goods among themselves at whatever rate was to their own advantage.

Thomas entrusted the *St George* to the care of William Charlton who kept her in his boatyard alongside the *Duck* yacht for sixty-four days. He drew up a complete inventory of the galley, her rigging, stores and equipment. On 30 March, the partners wrote to Thomas with orders to deliver the galley to Captain

Philip Gammon. He had paid three hundred pounds and given security for the balance of the price agreed. The incident was over and could have been forgotten if it was not for Rolls' outstanding debt and the court case to attempt to recover it. The case was to drag on for a number of years but, like many lawsuits of the period, there is no evidence of the conclusion.

His nerve gone, Thomas was never again to undertake a long-distance voyage but his appetite for the East Indies trade never waned. Within a month he was signing an agreement with Captain James Jenifer of the *Duke of Gloucester* who was to take some of Thomas' goods to sell in the East Indies and invest the proceeds in textiles suitable for the English market. Thomas also took the opportunity to send letters to friends and colleagues in India and made a special request for Jenifer to bring him a particular type of arrack. It seems he was missing a favourite beverage from his time in the East. The value of the cargo Thomas sent at one hundred and five pounds, three shillings and eight pence, equivalent to over £13,000 today, was much less than his investment in the *St George* but was, perhaps, the private cargo he had planned to carry on the galley. He was back in business again with a much lower risk to his well-being. At the same time, Thomas entered into a similar arrangement with Captain Richard Etherington, master of the *Resolution* frigate who departed in autumn 1697 and returned to England in 1699. There are few surviving documents relating to this voyage and the accounts Thomas kept are difficult to understand but his overall turnover appears to have been 42,898 silver dollars for which Etherington only received about one percent freight commission. Four silver dollars, according to Thomas' own description in his *Bay of Bengal* manuscript, were worth one pound sterling. By this calculation, the value of this voyage was much greater than his venture on the *Duke of Gloucester* and worth the equivalent of nearly £1.4 million today. This represented an incredible change in Thomas' fortunes.

1698

The complexity of Thomas Bowrey's business affairs continued into the New Year but his experience on the *St George Galley* did not seem to have a permanent effect on his health nor, it would seem, his friendship with Nathaniel Long. During the early summer of 1698, the pair took a trip across the Channel on the *Duck* yacht. For six weeks beginning 28 May they combined business and pleasure in a tour of France, Flanders and Holland. Thomas' full diary and accounts of this trip were published in 1927 in *The Papers of Thomas Bowrey 1669-1713*. The journey took advantage of the only short period of peace during Thomas' life in London. The accession of William of Orange to the throne ensured that England was now allied with their old rival, the Dutch, and the Nine Years' War against the French had ended the previous year. Within a few years, the War of Spanish succession would make the French enemies again and a similar tour impossible.

The friends, together with William Charlton who usually cared for the yacht, his son and John Powell as crew, set off from Greenwich on the Saturday afternoon, sailing the *Duck* to Calais where they arrived two days later. They took provisions with them and purchased more as they went along. At only twenty-nine foot long and nine foot wide, the *Duck* must have been a tight squeeze for five men, supplies and trade goods.

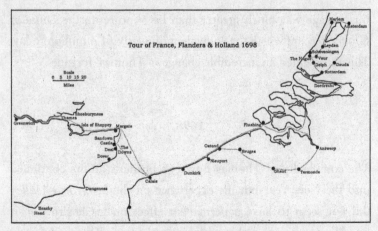

Tour of France, Flanders and Holland.

When Thomas purchased his yacht, he was following a recent fashion. The first yacht was built in England for the Royal Navy shortly before the Restoration of Charles II. In the early 1660s, the king received two more, smaller yachts from the Dutch. The word *yacht* derived from the Dutch *jagt*. The king and his brother enjoyed yachting so much that by 1686 the Navy had acquired a total of twenty-six yachts of various sizes. The nobility and gentry copied the royal brothers and it became fashionable to own a small vessel. Thomas' *Duck* was typical. One of Charles' yachts, the *Katharine* was anchored in Calais harbour when the party arrived there on their outward voyage.

Thomas' kept his diary of the tour like a ship's log, detailing progress, winds and tides but added reports of the sightseeing the friends did: visiting churches, markets, the docks in Amsterdam, and even prisons and a *mad house*. With an attention to detail reminiscent of his early years in the East Indies, Thomas added notes about the currencies used and the prices in the markets.

The notable exception was any details of his business dealings but his accounts mention the goods he was carrying and payments he received. Sightseeing activities took most of their time in each town but Thomas and Long dined with a number of merchants during the trip and this was probably when much of the business was carried out.

From Calais, the *Duck* was sailed to Dunkirk and Ostend up to the start of the Bruges Canal. The yacht was left there in the care of her crew while the two friends took a side trip to Bruges on the *trekschiat,* a towed passenger barge. After returning to the *Duck,* the party sailed on to Flushing where they negotiated for the services of a pilot for the next stage of their voyage through what were, at that time before much of the land reclamation, the islands of Rhine-Meuse-Scheldt delta to Rotterdam. Leaving the yacht again, they set off for Gouda in a covered wagon before transferring to another *trekschiat* to Amsterdam, this time paying extra for use of a cabin. Disembarking about a quarter of a mile from their destination, they completed their journey on what Thomas described as a covered, horse-drawn sled while their goods followed on a barrow.

They spent some days in Amsterdam, one of the great cities of Europe at the time. Only a fifth of the population of London, its overseas trade was much greater. Following the example of many English tourists over the years, on the first day, they sought an English tavern. At other times, they dined with Dutch merchants. During his time in the East Indies, Thomas did business at a number of Dutch factories. Although, even at this time, English was widely understood in Holland it seems likely he was able to communicate the basics in the local language. Later in life, he possessed a Dutch-Malay dictionary and a New Testament in

Dutch. One day the pair dined on board a ship in the harbour. They were making the most of the opportunities to enjoy their meals. The facilities on the yacht can only have been limited and the food on board basic. In Dunkirk harbour, open flames such as fires and candles were prohibited on board ships. Whilst anchored here, meals had to be prepared in a special area provided on shore and were probably cold by the time they had been rowed back to the yacht.

After eight days, Thomas and Long ate at another English tavern before taking a waggon to Leyden followed by the *trekschiat* on to The Hague. They had now been travelling for three weeks and they needed some exercise. On the Sunday, they took a walk to Scheveningen, a small fishing town on the coast about a mile and a half away, before returning to The Hague and taking an evening walk along the promenade. From The Hague, they hired a waggon to take them to Delft. Here, Thomas was interested to see the earthenware made in imitation of the Chinese porcelain with which he was so familiar. They left Delft on the *trekschiat* back to Rotterdam and the *Duck*. The next afternoon, the yacht departed for Dordrecht and Flushing where they hired a pilot for a final side-trip to Antwerp staying there for a few days. Returning to the *Duck*, they took to the river passing through Termonde and Ghent. At Ghent, they dined with a merchant in the English trade. To pass through the city's canal, they hired three men to pull them. The next day, they hired a horse to tow them the rest of the way along the canal to Bruges and Ostend. The wind being against them, they were obliged to remain in the town for some days. Having made their way to Dunkirk, Thomas went ashore to carry out some business before they continued to Calais. On Saturday afternoon, the yacht set off to cross the

Channel but almost immediately a fog came down and lasted for the rest of the day but they made the Kent coast safely at Sandown Castle. Shortly after noon on Tuesday 12 July, Thomas and Long arrived safely back at Greenwich.

1699

We have seen how Thomas tried to profit from his knowledge gained whilst he worked in the East Indies. In February 1699, he had a further opportunity. The Court of Directors of the East India Company in London discussed the setting up of a settlement in the South Seas. Thomas Bowrey and a Captain Roffey, who both had personal experience of this region, were invited to present their proposals for such a settlement. At this time, the term South Seas to Thomas and the East India Company referred to the South Pacific Ocean generally rather than specifically the South American coast as it would come to mean in the future. Proposals about this would be developed by Thomas, and others, many years later. Where Thomas gained his knowledge of the region in the country trade, Roffey's experience was less conventional. Kerrill or Caryl Roffey or Rossey was a member of the crew of Charles Swan's *Cygnet* which departed on a voyage to South America in 1683. Swan turned pirate and the *Cygnet* moved onto the Philippines where his crew mutinied. They cast Swan ashore with a number of others, including Roffey. Swan probably died there but Roffey travelled onto Ternate in the Malacca Islands and then onto Batavia from where he took a ship home to England in January 1690 with a Thomas Gullock. Subsequently, Roffey became a Royal Naval officer.

Thomas' proposal still survives and, from this, it is clear he believed the East India Company should establish a trading settlement at Pattantecar, an island described as being off the west coast of Borneo, to give English traders the same advantages as the Dutch had at Batavia and the Portuguese at Malacca. The failure of the East India Company to secure a base comparable to Dutch Batavia has been seen as one of the reasons the English company never obtained the economic efficiency of their Dutch rivals. According to Thomas, Pattantecar was about six or seven miles long and close enough to the main island of Borneo to provide a suitable harbour. It was close to Sukadana, capital city of the North Kayong region, and was probably the island of Padang.

The Company had been interested in establishing a factory in Sukadana since they had been told of the opportunities there by Endimion Griffith thirteen years earlier. They had despatched two ships there from Fort St George but the missions ended in disaster. Nevertheless, their interest was sustained by an invitation to settle in his country from the sultan. This invitation was repeated in 1693 via Gullock. At that time, the Company's directors in London discouraged any new settlements. Although Thomas visited Borneo a number of times whist in the East Indies, no details of his voyages there survive. However, following his return to England, he had sought up-to-date information from Samuel Glover whom he had known at Fort St George. Glover had passed on the news he had received from Gullock and Thomas' later correspondent, Charles Sherer, that there was limited trade in pepper at Sukadana but presently no diamonds because they were at war with their neighbour, Landuk.

It was somewhat disingenuous of Thomas to recommend a settlement at a time when his informants indicated that trade there was so poor. Perhaps this was subsequently discovered by the Company because, although the court at first resolved to adopt the proposal, at the next meeting there was an objection. Following some debate, it was resolved to adjourn any further discussion of the proposals. At this point, the scheme for a settlement lapsed and was not discussed again.

During the summer, Thomas and his wife Mary spent four weeks in Bath with the Longs. There is some evidence that both Thomas and Mary suffered poor health and spent spells in both Bath and Tunbridge Wells in the hope of some healing. However, bathing in the sulfurous waters was also believed to be conducive for fertility. The couple never had any children and this may have been another reason for their visit. Although Bath is often associated with the Regency period, its restorative waters had been known, and taken advantage of, since pre-Roman times. Elizabeth I granted a royal charter to the town to care for the springs in 1591. Bath had become a fashionable destination from the 1670s. In 1687, James II's second wife Mary of Modena had stayed in the town, bathing every morning. Shortly afterward, she had conceived their son, James Francis Edward. By 1699, so many people were visiting the town that arrangements had to be made to accommodate the horses of the gentry on the town common. Taking the waters, drinking the mineral water at Bath, was a relatively new fashion compared to therapeutic bathing in the hot spring water. In 1668 Thomas Guidott, who had been a student of chemistry and medicine at Oxford, moved to Bath. Having studied the curative properties of the waters, in 1676 he published a book on his findings. Thomas, in his account book, recorded when he and Mary braved the noxious fumes to bathe. During their stay, they bathed eleven times each, Mary wearing a voluminous yellow canvas gown to maintain her modesty. She tipped the *cloth woman* for the loan of the garment. Other gratuities or fees were paid to the male and female guides, the sergeant, the chair-man and the pump woman. In total they paid two pounds and four shillings, about two hundred and eighty pounds today.

Thomas wrote a packing list of the items he sent from Bath in his trunk giving us an insight into what was considered to be essential for a holiday in the late seventeenth century. The list is long but included only two gowns and petticoats for Mary. Including her travelling apparel, three gowns do not seem to be much for four weeks but the two sent in the trunk – one in fine chintz and the other a silk and silver gown – were probably very expensive, fashionable and perhaps made from fabrics from the East Indies. Six aprons were taken to protect the expensive gowns. No bills have survived from Mary's dressmaker, unlike those from Thomas' tailors, and the list provides a rare glimpse of her clothing. The pair also took a limited amount of valuable jewellery: a pair of diamond earrings; a diamond buckle; a ring set *wound* (perhaps 'all round' like a modern full eternity ring) with diamonds and a gold ring. It is likely these items were made from some of the diamonds Thomas obtained from the East Indies.

The four ate well during their stay. Their bill for cooking their food included: boiling beans and bacon; frying beef steaks; roasting a rump of beef; boiling a chicken, bacon and sprouts; boiling peas; roasting a couple of ducks; dressing fish; roasting a breast of mutton; roasting a shoulder of mutton; boiling artichokes and peas; scalding and roasting a pig; and roasting a leg of veal. Other food purchased for just a few days, certainly less than a week, included: sole, crab and lobster; trout, shrimp and salmon; lemons, capers, anchovies, nutmeg and pepper; vinegar, onions and cucumbers; two loaves; cabbage and carrots; rolls (forms of both bread rolls and sausage rolls were known at the time); butter; strawberries; and tart, custard and cheesecake. This was all washed down with wine and a half-barrel of beer.

They had travelled in a coach from London to Bath via Gloucester. Before the invention of rubber tyres and suspension, coach travel was long and uncomfortable on the poor roads in the country at the time. Cramped into a tiny, airless carriage and jolted constantly as iron-rimmed wheels hit pot holes and ridges, the only relief passengers could anticipate was the stops at inns to change horses and take refreshments. On the outward journey, they had paid six pounds for the whole coach, presumably travelling with their friends, Nathaniel Long and his wife, plus two maids. The journey was about one hundred and sixty miles and cost about £800 for the six passengers in today's values. On the return journey, they paid three pounds for three places, travelling separately from the Long family.

After Thomas' return from Bath, he took another young man under his paternal wing. Within his papers there are receipts for clothing and rent for Thomas Loyd. Thomas Bowrey's connection to the young Loyd is not known although his father claimed his son was *bred to the sea*. The father, John Loyd, was from Ruthin, Wales. He owed Thomas Bowrey money but it is unclear if this was just for his expenditure on the young Loyd. Loyd senior wrote expressing his obligation to Thomas for all he had done for his son and mentions his brother, Edward. It is believed Edward Lloyd of Lloyd's Coffee House may have originated from Wales. Thomas was known to have been a customer of the coffee house and, although Lloyd is not an uncommon name in Wales, John

Loyd and Edward Lloyd of the coffee house may have been related.

In view of Thomas' difficulties with his crew on the *St George Galley*, it seems unlikely he had known Thomas Loyd from that time but perhaps he was planning to give him a place on a later ship because within a year, he was preparing for four new voyages. The *Gosfreight*, *Home Frigate*, *Tuscan Galley* and *Mansel* appear on a list Thomas drew up around the end of 1706 or the beginning of the following year. Other than this list and some invoices for compasses, nothing survives in Thomas' papers about these voyages. They carried cargos of over £45,000 in total, worth nearly £6 million today, but how much of this investment was Thomas' is not known. In these, and all his trading voyages from England, Thomas was only a part owner of the ships and their cargoes. As was standard at the time, the risk was spread across a number of investors, almost invariably including the ship's commander. All four ships eventually arrived home safely. Thomas' luck may have been improving.

CHAPTER 7

The Malay-English Dictionary (1700-1701)

It was an unlikely friendship, Thomas Bowrey the East Indies merchant born to the sea who had finished formal schooling by the age of nine and Thomas Hyde the Oxford academic, one-time librarian of the Bodleian Library, but they respected each other and gained mutual advantage from the relationship. Hyde had previously been disparaging about the linguistic skills of merchants but the pair worked together on a number of projects and continued to do so until Hyde's death in February 1703. After Thomas Bowrey returned home to England on the *Bengal Merchant* he concentrated on getting himself established and preparing for his marriage. The fiasco of the *St George Galley* could not be forgotten whilst the court case dragged on but he was at last in a position to complete the dictionary he had started on his voyage home. However, he could not give it his undivided attention because he had other, more immediate concerns. The first of these was his step-uncle.

HENRY SMITH

After Henry Smith incited the incident on the *Berkeley Castle* at

Bombay in June 1683, the East India Company officials at Surat immediately ruled him to be blameworthy. In addition, the Deputy Governor at Bombay, Charles Ward, complained Smith had earlier encouraged the unrest among the soldiers. Smith was suspended from the Council and all his other official duties at Bombay, he was ordered to hand over the account books to his deputy and summoned back to Surat to defend himself. At Surat, Smith made counterclaims against Ward who was later to complain Smith had maliciously entered items in the accounts detrimental to Ward. Although Ward convinced his superiors these were false entries, he was not fully exonerated. He was told he should have removed the books from Smith sooner. Smith's case was not helped when his wife sent her servant to Ward with a message in terms that were so indecent he was unable to repeat them.

On 2 October 1683, Smith was ordered to sail for Swally on the *Rainbow*. To the annoyance of the officials, his family accompanied him. When attempts were made to get Smith's wife to leave the ship, she refused *with a rude answer*. In the meantime, Ward convinced the officials at Surat of his belief that Smith was *an evil fellow* who had attempted to incite a mutiny. The officials resolved that Smith could not be permitted to remain in India and should be sent home on one of the ships about to leave from Swally. They concluded their judgement by declaring: *May God preserve your Honours from such servants!* This time, Smith was unable to talk himself out of trouble and was sent home on the *Coast Frigate* in 1684. The final verdict on Smith by the Company's officers was that he was *a most notorious, naughty, false, lying fellowe.* Smith's pregnant wife remained in Surat with a Mrs Bowcher. The pair were described as *a couple of fit companions.*

Nothing more is heard of Smith until 1700 when he wrote three letters to Thomas from Newgate gaol. It is clear from his signatures that this was the same Henry Smith who had been banished by the Company from first Bantam and then Bombay. On 3 June, Smith wrote that he and Captain Gullock's men had been given notice of their trial on 21 June. This is not the first Thomas had heard about Gullock. In 1693 Charles Sherer had written to Thomas about how, during the previous year, Sherer had worked for Gullock on a voyage to purchase diamonds in Borneo. Gullock had proved to be a *monster* and Sherer had left his service. Two years later, Captain Thomas Gullock was master of the ship *Adventure* bound for Borneo when the boatswain, Joseph Bradish, and some of the crew mutinied and seized the ship off the Spice Islands as a result of Gullock's behaviour towards them. At the end of March the following year, the *Adventure* arrived in America. The mutineers scuttled the ship off Rhode Island but were captured and imprisoned at Boston. Bradish escaped, joined up with the infamous pirate William Kidd and was subsequently recaptured with him. All were sent to England for trial. Bradish was tried at the Marshalsea and hanged on 12 July 1700. Kidd was executed the following year.

Smith shared his Newgate cell with the rest of Gullock's crew who were awaiting trial for piracy. He attempted to help them by recording their complaints about their brutal captain. It was to no avail and they were also condemned to be hanged. Smith was not part of the crew of the *Adventure* but had been charged in August 1698 with piracy and robbery of two Royal African Company ships, the *Hannibal* and the *Eagle*. The *Hannibal*, the larger, carried thirty-two guns and seventy men. The *Eagle* carried just ten guns and twenty-six men.

Over three days at the beginning of November 1697, officers of the court had taken ten remarkably similar statements from men who had been on board the *Hannibal* when it left Spithead for Cabo Corsa on the coast of Guinea two years earlier. The ten included the ship's surgeon, boatswain and mariners as well as Company soldiers and a clerk travelling as passengers at the start of their contract. They describe how, after they arrived on the African coast, seven on the crew refused the captain's order to hoist the long boat on board. There was no explanation why such a routine task should be refused but the captain had to be persuaded not to overreact and fire on the men by his chief mate. Tempers cooled and the captain entertained his officers to dinner that evening but there were further disagreements involving two of the men. The following morning, the mutineers seized the ship, her captain and his officers. Just three of the ten witnesses claimed that Henry Smith and two others, James Seaman and James Tatnell, were given the task of standing guard over the prisoners until they were put ashore in the longboat with sufficient provisions to sustain themselves for some time. Tatnell's evidence made no mention of Smith and Seaman had been unable to make a statement because he kept collapsing. There was no other mention of Smith's involvement. The mutineers on board the *Hannibal* next took the *Eagle* which was carrying a cargo including five hundred *elephants' teeth,* four hundred and eighty pewter spoons and four hundred and sixteen African slaves.

Six months after giving their initial evidence, two of the witnesses who had not originally mentioned Smith in their statements made supplementary depositions about his alleged involvement guarding the prisoners. One of them described Smith as a soldier, presumably one of those travelling as a passenger on board. In December 1699, the carpenter from the *Eagle* also made a statement confirming that his ship was taken by the *Hannibal*. According to him, one hundred of the slaves and two hundred of the ivory tusks were transferred to the other ship. The two ships then headed together across the Atlantic to Brazil. That the witnesses knew this implies that they had remained on board. Were their statements made in return for immunity from prosecution for piracy and were their statements so similar because they had been coached in what to say? No others from *Hannibal* were tried at the same time as Smith. In 1700 Edmund Halley, who five years later was to predict the return of the comet to be named after him, arrived at Pernambuco, present day Recife, in Brazil during the second of his three exploratory voyages. Here, he was detained for a short while by the English envoy sent there to recover the *Hannibal* and *Eagle* for the Royal African Company. The two ships had previously been detained by the local authorities.

In December 1699, Henry Smith was acquitted of the charge of piracy and robbery of the *Eagle* but he remained in custody in respect of a similar charge in respect of the *Hannibal*. He was to continue in Newgate for a further six months but was discharged the following June. No further details were recorded but, presumably, the jury was not convinced by the dubious witness statements. Smith still was not free. His final letter from Newgate dated 29 June said he would be released as soon as he had raised sufficient funds to pay his fees. It is possibly that Thomas helped him in this respect.

COMPILING THE DICTIONARY

It was not a good time for Thomas. Whilst helping Smith in Wapping, his relationship with his friend Nathaniel Long cooled. Thomas' initial letter on the matter does not survive but Long's angry response does. His anger is understandable. Just a few years after their joint trip to Holland, Thomas had tried to have Long arrested for debt. His friend was astounded Thomas could be so ungrateful, *base* and malicious especially after he had supported him so strongly in the affair of the *St George Galley*. Worse still, Thomas was claiming £1,000 when less than three hundred was due. Rather than apologising or relenting, Thomas responded that he did not agree and had his own grievances against Long. It is not known what these were because Thomas chose not to repeat them. He only wanted what was owed him. Nothing more survives of this dispute but there is only one more letter from Long in Thomas' surviving papers. This was from August 1704 when he wrote to Thomas in Tunbridge Wells with news of the rumours about the *Worcester*. The relationship had cooled and the letter is more formal than previously. Long is not mentioned in an early will Thomas drafted two years later but by the time of Thomas' death, things had improved. In his final will, Thomas names Long as his good friend.

The result of this disagreement was that were no more combined trips to Bath for the two families. For four weeks in the summer of 1700, and for the next five summers, Thomas and Mary travelled on their own to another spa town, Tunbridge Wells. Perhaps Bath held too many memories.

Tunbridge Wells came into being early in the seventeenth century when a courtier to James I became convinced that the spring waters there had healing properties. A visit by Queen Henrietta Maria in 1630 ensured the town's popularity as a spa retreat. Fifty years later the Walks, the tree-shaded paved and colonnaded promenade now known as the Pantiles, were built leading to the springs and it became one of the most fashionable destinations for fashionable society. Lodging houses were built around the Wells but visitors purchased their own provisions from the local market. Thomas again kept account books for his holiday detailing their food from this market. Their diet was much the same as at Bath with the additions of local Kentish cherries daily. Unfortunately, little more than food was included so it is not known if the couple enjoyed shopping in the shops provided for tourists or gambled on the lottery or hazard board. They paid for three places in a coach for the journey there and back. The total cost of the trip was ten pounds eight shillings, the equivalent of over £1,400 today.

Not all of Thomas' relationships at this time were as taxing as those with Smith and Long. He had been keeping a paternal eye on Robin Lesly and his siblings, the nephews and niece of Robert Masfen. The children had left England to return to their mother in India and Robin wrote expressing his gratitude and excitement about his apprenticeship there. No doubt Thomas' sadness at the children leaving was balanced by the satisfaction at seeing Robin following in his footsteps.

Thomas' business affairs were picking up pace and he recorded his involvement with five ships in 1700 and the early months of 1701: the *Mansell*, *Ekins Frigate*, *John Galley*, *Scipio* and *Anne Frigate*. This time the results were not as favourable. Of the four, only the *Scipio* under the experienced Captain George Luke Burrish returned safely to England. Thomas and

John Spencer had purchased an East India Company licence for the *Scipio*'s voyage from an unknown third party and obtained permission from the king to export four hundred and forty iron guns to India. Thomas' investment in the outward cargo of glass and guns amounted to almost £1,000 but he more than doubled his money on the textiles brought home in return. Compared to many trading voyages, this was not a huge investment for Thomas but it was a success.

Of the other ships, the *Ekins Frigate* was sold to the East India Company in India. Nothing survives in his accounts but presumably Thomas did not lose on the deal. The *Anne Frigate* was originally a French ship which had been taken as a prize. Renamed, she sailed for the East Indies with a cargo worth a total of £6,800 and Thomas Gullock, whose crew Henry Smith had helped defend, on board as supercargo. She traded in Bencoolen and Batavia but was blown up near the Isle of Wight during her return voyage destroying any return cargo and profits. History does not record how this happened.

The fourth ship, the *John Galley*, was plundered by pirates. An early Lloyd's list in Thomas' papers names the galley but not her intended destination. Another document, an invoice, throws some light of where she was heading and what may have happened. The *John Galley*'s cargo included brass collars and *manilloes*, bracelets used for trade, often to purchase salves, in parts of Africa. The collars were almost certainly intended for the restraint of slaves. The most likely first destination of the galley was East Africa, probably the island of Madagascar, well known to mariners as a place to restock with water, limes and other provisions, but she never arrived. After departing from London in December 1700, the ship was forced to return home after being attacked and plundered by Barbary pirates. Having incurred a loss from the first voyage, Thomas did not risk investing in her for the second but she set out again the following season with the same outcome.

Corsairs operated from the North African coast between modern-day Libya and present-day Morocco. These state-sanctioned Barbary pirates preyed on Christian shipping, enslaving those they captured. Many used a type of galley called a *xebeck*, rowed by slaves. The speed and manoeuvrability of these vessels was terrifying especially for the crew of a becalmed ship. Although vessels to and from the East Indies were at risk from the Corsairs for a relatively short part of their voyage, they were greatly feared by European sailors who faced enslavement for life unless their friends and family were prosperous enough to pay their ransom. In contrast, capture by European pirates although it may have resulted in death did not always have such dire consequences. It may have involved little more than giving up supplies, arms, other equipment and cargos, especially silver and gold, before being allowed to continue on their voyage. If the pirates were short-handed, the crew of a captured ship may have been forced to join the pirate crew but this was not considered as dreadful as being enslaved by Africans. Often, sailors of an adventurous nature or unhappy with their current captain would be only too happy to *turn pirate*.

As Thomas' thoughts returned to the East Indies he took up work again on the only book he published in his lifetime, his dictionary. As he explained in the Preface, his reason for doing this was primarily *for the Promotion of Trade* where Malay was spoken. Even as early as the end of the seventeenth century, Malay had been widely used for several hundred years in

Southeast Asia. More than that, it was a contact language widely used as a lingua franca by speakers of other first languages. It had been an international language of diplomacy, as well as trade, alongside Arabic and Persian before Europeans had arrived in the East. The advantage of Malay over many other languages is that it has a straightforward sound system and an easily learned grammar. It has only two basic sentence structures; it is not tonal and words are not heavily stressed; and it has no verbal tenses, no morphological plural forms (the plural form is often indicated by repeating the noun), and no definite or indefinite articles.

When European traders arrived in the East Indies, they had issues with communication. The only Europeans proficient in Asian languages were the Jesuits and other Catholic missionaries who had been in the region for much longer. The Portuguese arrived in the area in advance of the English so the East India Company initially used a little Portuguese but also sent letters to Asian rulers in English or Latin. Their linguistic difficulties severely impacted on their communications and they were concerned that they were at the mercy of untrustworthy interpreters. I have been unable to find any examples of such duplicity and the fears may have been unfounded because interpreters were well paid and were unlikely to risk a trust that was not easily won. Around one percent of a transaction's cost was allocated to pay local interpreters and clerks. Thomas was known to have used an interpreter in his early years in the East Indies but quickly became proficient in Malay and other local languages.

It is believed Europeans in India learned local languages from each other rather than from native speakers. This, and the ease of learning Malay, resulted in the Europeans following the lead of the Chinese and adopting it as their lingua franca. It became known as the *Latin of Asia*. It was not until an English settlement was established on Penang in 1786 that the English language gained a foothold in the region. Despite this reliance by the English on Malay, by the time Thomas departed from India, there was no Malay-English dictionary available to them. Some earlier works existed. By 1525, Antonio Pigafetta, who had accompanied Magellan on his circumnavigation of the world, had published Malay-Italian, Malay-French and Malay-Latin word lists. Yang Lin had compiled a Chinese-Malay vocabulary in 1560. The East India Company's first published pamphlet, printed in 1603, had included a list of fifty-two Malay words and phrases. Other than this list and a 1614 translation by Company merchant Augustine Spalding of a Dutch book there was nothing available to help the English-speaking merchant and factor.

Thomas dedicated his dictionary to the governors, directors and committees of both East India Companies who had encouraged its publication in 1701. It was the only such work available to the English in the Malay-speaking world until *A Short Vocabulary, English and Malayo* was published in Calcutta in 1798 and James Howison produced a Malay dictionary in 1801. It is believed both of these were based on Thomas' work. William Marsden subsequently produced his own Malay dictionary in 1812. In it he commented on that by Thomas. Marsden acknowledged that, although the work of someone unable to read or write the Malay Arabic-based script, the dictionary was of considerable merit. Marsden believed Thomas' claim that his dictionary was based on the knowledge of the language he had picked-up as a trader in the region and compiled from his memory.

As the dictionary contains 594 pages, it would have been a huge achievement from memory. How was this done? Thomas' surviving papers contain a manuscript notebook that is probably the early draft of the dictionary he produced on his homeward journey. This list contains only in the region of four hundred and eighty words. Obviously, he continued to work on the dictionary once in England but he also had some additional assistance. In his Preface, Thomas ungratefully wrote:

> I do acknowledge my self obliged to some helps I have
> attained for several Malayo words in the following work;
> for the truth of which I will not be answerable.

Following the English to Malay and Malay to English sections, the dictionary also contains a section on Malay grammar, rules for pronunciation, dialogues, tables of times and dates, and a map of the area in which Malay was spoken. Where did Thomas obtain his help?

THOMAS BOWREY AND THE ORIENTALIST

It is not known when Thomas Hyde and Thomas Bowrey first met. Nothing of their correspondence survives before April 1700 and, from then, only the letters from Hyde. On two occasions Hyde asks after John Russell who was the rector of St John Wapping and a friend of Thomas. Russell had studied at Balliol College, matriculating in 1679 at the age of eighteen. He arrived at Wapping in 1689, the same year Thomas returned from the East Indies. Hyde was librarian at the Bodleian, Oxford, between 1665 and 1701 so it is possible Hyde and Russell knew each other from that time. Earlier, Hyde had used the East India Company to obtain information for his publications. If he and Thomas were not introduced by Russell, they may have known each other through the Company. Hyde's letters make it clear the Hydes and Bowreys already knew each other well by 1700.

Hyde was an expert in oriental languages and their scripts. He acted as an official interpreter for Charles II, James II and William III. Despite earlier disparaging comments about merchants, Hyde appeared happy to collaborate with Thomas, trading his experience for information, especially about the plants that grew in the Malay Peninsula. Hyde was also keen to use Thomas' contacts, at one point asking him to obtain further details about a merman discovered and killed off the coast of Denmark. Thomas collected items for Hyde from his contacts. In 1700 and 1701, Silvanus Landon wrote to Thomas twice from Banjar on Borneo. In addition to some *Malabar characters*, the first letter confirmed that he had sent a *sumpitan*, or blowgun, with arrows and a number of birds' nests. These items were probably for Hyde.

Landon's letters also hint at plans Thomas may have had for returning to the East. He suggested that Thomas would be the best person to become the head of the factory at a new settlement there. There is no evidence that Thomas seriously considered this proposition but, perhaps, it is what he had intended if the East India Company had accepted his proposals a few years earlier. Landon, in a postscript to his later letter, requested Thomas pass on his regards to Madam Etherington. Thomas had invested in Richard Etherington's voyage on the *Resolution* a few years earlier.

In return for the information from his contacts, Hyde supplied Thomas with a translation service for his letters to India, word lists, advice about pronunciation and assistance with having copper plates engraved. It was Hyde's suggestion that Thomas commented in his Preface to the dictionary that the Malays had adopted a number of Arabic words. He believed this was something not previously understood in the West.

Eventually, on 25 November 1700, Hyde wrote that Thomas' work was done. The dictionary was published the following year, printed by Samuel Bridge. Although primarily intended for use by East India Company servants, it was also sold by three London booksellers. Thomas tried to have his book sold in Oxford but Hyde advised him that the booksellers he approached considered it too expensive. Unfortunately, without Thomas' side of the correspondence, the price he was expecting is unknown but, if the Company expected a discount for sponsoring the work, he may have been trying to recoup his losses.

Hyde may not have been the only person who helped Thomas in the production of the dictionary.

HENRY SMITH AND THE DICTIONARY

The library of the School of Oriental and African Studies, University of London, holds a copy of Thomas Bowrey's dictionary once owned by William Marsden who published his own in 1812. This copy contains many annotations, clearly disputing some of the entries and, at the end of the English-Malayo section, in the same hand:

<u>Soe far Corrected by Henry Smith</u>
My Dictionary w^(ch) ye foregoeing should have bin only the
Coppy off is Soe Strangely Perverted thro (~~thro Ambition~~

&) Ignorance of ye Genuin Elegancy & meaning of ye words in this Language, that it would have Puzled a Learned Native Malayer, to have pickt out ye meaning of the Short Sentences, for they are very Concise in there discourse useing noe Circumlocutions or tautologie.

The signature matches that of Henry Smith in Bombay and Newgate gaol. If what Thomas' step-uncle claims was true, why would he give his dictionary away and allow Thomas to publish it as his own? One recent author has suggested it may have been in repayment for help Thomas had given him when imprisoned in Newgate. In view of his history with the East India Company, it is unlikely they would have wished to be associated with anything connected to Smith. However, as Hyde appears to have reviewed a final draft of the dictionary in November 1700 and Smith cannot have been released before July, Thomas would have had less than five months to combine the two bodies of work. Surely this was impossible especially if Smith, as claimed, had provided the bulk of the material. It is possible that Smith, reluctantly, passed his work to Thomas before embarking on the *Hannibal* in 1695 because of opposition from the Company. Would this devalue Thomas' contribution? To evaluate this, it is necessary to understand a little more about the Malay language.

WRITTEN AND LITERARY MALAY

Written Malay is as least as old as written English. The earliest inscriptions, although rare, used Indic-based scripts and are to be found across the whole of the Malay Archipelago. By the fifteenth-century, Malay spread as a language of trade and diplomacy and also as a result of the spread of Islam. Not only did Malay absorb a large Arabic vocabulary but also adopted an Arabic-based script known as *Jawi*. The Malay Roman script, known as *Rumi,* was not adopted until the period of British administration, long after Thomas' time. Because of this, Thomas had to develop his own method of Romanising Malay for English speakers. The Dutch had already done this using their own spelling and phonetics but Thomas is believed to have been the first to have done so for English speakers. When Malaysia and Indonesia agreed on a standard Romanised spelling system to replace *Jawi* in 1972, it was based on the existing Dutch and English systems and the culmination of the evolution of a written system in part started by Thomas.

While there may be doubt about how much of the dictionary was Thomas' own work and even the quality of the Malay it presented, the development of a Romanised form of written Malay is generally accepted as a major achievement. Hyde assisted him with pronunciation but the rules Thomas developed to depict the pronunciation of the language were his own and considered by modern linguists to have been extremely accurate.

The adoption of a written script enabled the rich Malay oral tradition to be recorded and the development of a new literature. From that time, there have been three types of Malay in use: colloquial, formal and bazaar. Colloquial Malay is a verbal form used among native speakers and by immigrants to the region. Formal, or standard, Malay is a highly developed and complex form of the language used for literature, education and administration, in both the written and spoken form. The third type is bazaar, *pasar,* or low Malay used as a trade language. It is this third type of Malay that was used as the *lingua franca* for trade in the Malay Archipelago and is a reduced form; grammatically simpler with a smaller vocabulary.

That Smith was a senior clerk and accountant with the East India Company may explain his criticism of the work. He is more likely to have used formal Malay than the bazaar version used by merchants. Thomas is clear in his Preface that the Malay to which he had been exposed was that used in the trading ports as a commercial language and that he intended his dictionary to be used by merchants. It is likely he would have ignored much of Smith's feedback.

THE IMPORTANCE OF THE DICTIONARY TODAY

Thomas included a map showing the distribution of the Malay language indicating that it remains virtually unchanged today and Malay is still an important world language. It is one of the official languages of Malaysia and Singapore and, in a slightly different form, of Indonesia. Even today, it remains an important contact language easily learned by native speakers of other languages and is the most important in the region being easier to learn than European languages. Malay is spoken by over two-hundred million people in Southeast Asia. It is now the sixth most widely spoken world language. Because of the importance of Malay, Thomas' dictionary still has relevance today. The National Library Board of Singapore makes it freely available online. It has been claimed that anyone following Thomas' vocabulary and rules for pronunciation would learn to speak Malay as well as it is often heard.

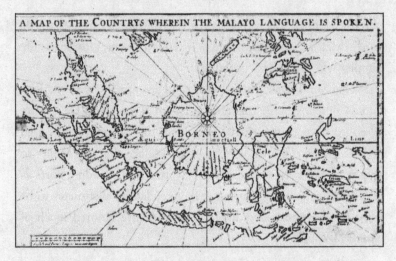

A MAP OF THE COUNTRYS WHEREIN THE MALAYO LANGUAGE IS SPOKEN.

Map of the Countrys Wherein the Malayo Language is Spoken.
[From Thomas Bowrey's 1701 *A Dictionary: English and Malayo,
Malayo and English.*]

The first known academic use of the dictionary is believed to
have been that by James Howison in 1801 and it has continued
to be of interest academically ever since. Stamford Raffles,
who established the British trading post of Singapore in 1819,
is thought to have studied the dictionary on his 1805 voyage
from England to Prince of Wales Island, now Penang Island in
Malaysia. John Leyden, a scholar of the Malay language and
great friend of Raffles and his first wife Olivia, said Thomas'
grasp of working Malay was something to be envied. The most
recent study, included in her *Hybrid Knowledge in the Early East
India Company World* by Anna Winterbottom, was published in
2016 and at least one further study is currently underway.

LATER LANGUAGE PROJECTS

It is clear from Thomas' correspondence with Hyde and the East
India Company that he intended to publish a further book on
the languages and alphabets of the East Indies to aid mariners,
merchants and factors in the region. Hyde had copper plates of
the *Syam* (Thai) and *Singala* (Sri Lankan) alphabets engraved
on Thomas' behalf and advised him on the languages. It is not
clear, however, if Thomas was proficient in these other languages
because Hyde refers to the works of others, such as Robert Knox,
from which Thomas appears to have been working. It is likely
these later project came to a sudden halt when Hyde died in 1703.

In 1677, Hyde had published the four gospels and the *Acts of
the Apostles* in Malay. Although this work was intended for use
in the Malay Peninsula, it uses Roman characters. It had a preface
by Dr Thomas Marshall, Rector of Lincoln College Oxford, who
some sources claim assisted Thomas with his dictionary although
this is unlikely as he died in 1685, before Thomas returned from
the East Indies. A second edition of this work was published in
1704 at the expense of the East India Company. According to the
Dictionary of Printers and Printing published in 1839 this edition
was superintended by Thomas and he added Hyde's specimen
of the Malay characters together with a map of the Malay
Peninsula. Although it may have been this edition that Thomas
had in his book collection in 1711, only one copy is known to
have survived in the World today and that is in the Stuttgart State
Library. Thomas' involvement cannot be verified because that
copy contains no mention of him, nor does it contain the map or
Malay characters.

THOMAS BOWREY AND THE HOAXER

Another letter in Thomas' papers, unfortunately undated, opens up the possibility that Thomas was taken in by a notorious hoaxer. The letter concerned the pronunciation of the language of Formosa, present-day Taiwan, when written in Roman characters and included a set of ten rules for that pronunciation. The letter was signed G. *Psalmanaa Zaar* and would appear to have been from George Psalmanazar, a Frenchman who claimed to be from Formosa. As such, he would probably have been the first native of that island to visit Europe. Having initially claimed to have been from Ireland in order to travel in France incognito, he later changed his claim when he realised Irish pilgrims were not uncommon there and he was liable to be exposed as a fraud. In this latter guise Psalmananzar travelled through Europe between 1700 and 1702 before moving onto England in 1703 and achieving celebrity there.

In 1704 Psalmananzar published *An Historical and Geographical Description of Formosa* in which he described the *Formosan language*. Following his death in 1763, his *Memoirs of ** **, Commonly Known by the Name of George Psalmanazar; a Reputed Native of Formosa* was published admitting he was an imposter. It would appear Thomas was taken in by Psalmanazar and, unknowingly, contacted him for assistance having read his book. Whether or not Thomas eventually recognised the deception will never be known.

CHAPTER 8

The Voyages of
the *Prosperous* & the *Worcester*
(1701–1703)

In the spring of 1707 Captain Thomas Bowrey, owner of the *Prosperous,* stood up before a House of Commons committee and related the story of the ship being taken by pirates at Madagascar several years earlier. Previously, John Webber, who had been on board the vessel, gave his evidence. Both men stressed that the majority of the pirates were Englishmen. A number of other mariners also told their tales of piracy and, on 8 April, the committee's report was presented to the House.

It is likely that the failure of Thomas' planned voyage on the *St George Galley* played heavily on his mind. However much he may have denied it, he had lost his nerve. Just one of many reasons for this may have been the dubious legality of the venture. He had spent much effort chivvying Nathaniel Long to obtain the licences necessary to make the voyage legal but they were not easily obtained. When the act of Parliament establishing the New, or English, East India Company was passed in 1698, he recognised a lifeline. One provision of the act was that subscribers might trade individually as well as under the New Company. Thomas' name appeared in the list of subscribers.

The East India Company's charter granted it the monopoly of all trade between the East Indies and England but the perceived lucrative nature of the business attracted many other merchants such as Thomas who wanted their share of it. Although the Company jealously guarded its monopoly, it occasionally gave into pressure and granted licences to independent, or *permission* ships. These licences strictly controlled the ports to be visited and the goods allowed to be traded. Too few licences were granted to satisfy demand but, without the expenses of permanent bases, the potential for good profit resulted in many private merchants being willing to risk forfeiture of both their ship and cargoes to undertake voyages as interlopers. Their crews were subject to severe penalties if caught but they were well paid and it was not usually difficult to attract good men. It is not known if Thomas was able to obtain licences for all his trading voyages but the risk of forfeit was likely to be one he wished to avoid if at all possible.

Thomas was aware of the fate of his *John Galley*'s first brush with the Barbary pirates in 1701 as he started the preparations for more new voyages. The incident would add to his concerns about the risks they would face. Five of his ships destined for the East Indies departed during the autumn and winter of 1701-1702. Two of these, both commanded by experienced captains, the *Frederick* and *London*, were to return safely. The *Constant Friend* was not so lucky. Departing London in November 1701 under the command of John Lackie she sailed, in the first instance, for Madagascar where they took on slaves destined for Achin. Although the West African slave trade to the Americas is more widely recognised, there was also a trade in slaves from East Africa to the East Indies. This was encouraged by the East India Company during Thomas' lifetime because they found most

Englishmen were unable to carry out essential manual tasks such as blacksmithing in the climate.

Pirates from the Caribbean had migrated to the island of Madagascar a decade earlier. The *Constant Friend* was attacked by them at St Lawrence, narrowly escaping being taken. After selling the slaves at Achin, they sailed for Surat via Malacca, arriving in February with a cargo valued at £4,000. Here Lackie presented his licence to the East India Company president proving his was a *permission ship*. Lackie's luck did not last. He died whilst still at Surat and was buried *as a captain* by his friends. The ship's chief mate, John Spivey, was appointed commander by the Surat consul. No more is known of the *Constant Friend* other than it was lost somewhere in the East Indies and never returned home. A great deal more is known about two the final two of the season's ships: the *Prosperous* and the *Worcester*. These were to play a major part in Thomas' life for many years to come.

THE STORY OF THE *PROSPEROUS*

The story of the *Prosperous* had begun in September 1701, six years before Thomas Bowrey's appearance before the committee of the House of Commons, when the two hundred and thirty ton ship armed with twenty-four guns had departed from London under the commanded of Captain John Hilliard who also acted as supercargo. On board was Thomas' cousin, Thomas Studds, one of the full complement of forty-four men. Hilliard had a salary of ten pounds per month, the equivalent of over £1,500 today; whist Studds received the lowest wage, one pound five shillings a month.

One of the crew, Edward Long, the assistant supercargo, was the son of Thomas' friend, Nathanial. Both were included in the six investors in the voyage. Despite being described as the owner when he appeared before the committee, Thomas was only one of six owners. He had taken only five of fifty-six shares in the ship. Long senior held four. Edward Hilliard had invested on behalf of the commander, taking thirty-six of the shares. The freighters had purchased a licence for an outward cargo of £2,000 to the East Indies. John Hilliard again owned the largest share, eight of the total twenty-eight. Thomas again held five shares. It was a mixed cargo of sixty secondhand iron guns supplied by Thomas plus new iron guns, iron shot, anchors, iron and lead, glassware, sword blades, cutlery, cheese, spirits, hats, silk stockings and woollen cloth. Thomas had traded in old iron guns and anchors for most of his time at Wapping. It was a good trade. Ships carried a number of anchors, up to nine on the largest ships. Different conditions required different types of anchors and they were often lost or, even, sacrificed in times of danger. The *Prosperous* also carried two hundred small arms with ten barrels of powder, four thousand flints and eight thousand bullets which cannot all have been for their own protection. Thomas' total investment in the ship, cargo and wages was a little over £1,000, the equivalent of almost £155,000 today.

From the start, the *Prosperous* was an unlucky ship. The voyage to the west coast of Madagascar was difficult but they eventually arrived during the following May at the end of the rainy season. Hilliard immediately commenced negotiations with the local king who promised to supply two hundred slaves within two months. This had always been the intention. The *Prosperous* included medicines for the slaves in her cargo. With good harbours, coves and beaches as well as plentiful provisions it seemed that life was improving for the crew. Glad to be on dry land again after their tedious voyage, the carpenter erected a tent on the shore within which to build the sloop, or service boat, they had brought in parts from England. A second tent was erected for storing trade goods to reduce the number of trips between ship and shore. However, the ship's long boat continued to make such journeys to restock with water.

The presence of crew members of the *Prosperous* ashore had been noted by a group of pirates led by Thomas Howard visiting from other parts of the island. The pirates set about convincing a number of the crew to join them. They included the boatswain's mate, Richard Ranton. At midnight twelve days after they had first anchored, as the turned members of the crew lay in wait on board, a group of pirates, together with Ranton, approached the ship in a boat. When the young midshipman on watch, John Orp, challenged them, Ranton answered it was the *Prosperous*' longboat returning from shore with water. Orp passed them a rope and returned to what he was doing. The first pirate to board fired at Orp who, although not hit, played dead to save his life.

In a brutal attack, the pirates shot Daniel Perkins, the first mate, in the mouth at point blank range when he refused to surrender. The shot went through the middle of his chin and emerged from the side of his neck between the jawbone and his jugular vein, shattering his lower jaw. Simultaneously, the other pirates with the help of the turned crew seized the steerage where some of the crew were sleeping, firing indiscriminately as they did so. Ranton fired several shots at the second mate, Daniel Saunders, as he lay asleep in his hammock. Although injured, Saunders managed to escape to a boat tied to the stern of the ship.

The pirates fired frequently at the door to the great cabin hoping to kill the captain as he emerged to see what was happening. Hilliard, however, managed to reach the quarterdeck by another route and without harm only to be shot twice in the right arm, breaking it in a number of places, and once in the left. Another crew member was shot and injured in his throat as he attempted to assist the captain and first mate.

Having demonstrated their brutality, the pirates offered the crew the opportunity to escape in the boats. The only alternative was a violent death. The crew chose to abandon the *Prosperous*, taking the wounded with them. Having gained control of the ship, the pirates finally showed a little compassion and sent ashore the supplies required for the carpenter to complete building the sloop, they had named *Linnet*, and it was on this twenty-eight of them departed from Madagascar on 3 August. Their number included the second mate Saunders, who had fully recovered from his wounds and Perkins who was still very sick. Hilliard and another man had already died of their injuries.

The *Linnet* stopped first at Johanna, probably Anjouan in the Comoros Islands, for fresh water. By this stage, five of the crew had had enough and decided to remain behind as the *Linnet* continued on to Surat on the north-west coast of India where they arrived six and a half weeks after leaving Madagascar. It was their misfortune to arrive at the port at a time when there was great concern about piracy in the region. The local governor was even concerned the East India Company ship sent to drive them out may have been an English pirate. Both the local and East India Company officials were initially suspicious of the story they were told by the *Prosperous'* crew. Surely the *Linnet* was too well built and in too good a condition. They had no paperwork to confirm what they said. Although the Company officials quickly came to believe their story, the local governor seized the sloop and imprisoned her crew. Despite the men's later complaints to the contrary, the Company provided food for them daily, their doctor tended the wounded and they prevailed upon the English consul to call for their release.

The men were finally released in February or March 1703 after the intervention of the Mughal. By this time, they had fallen out among themselves and were in dispute about the sale of the *Linnet* in order to enable them to repay the debts they had built up with the East India Company for their food and care. They were now destitute and desperate for a ship on which to return home. At this point the records run out and the fate of the men is unknown. Probably they were able to work their passage home on another permission ship and may have been the first to break the news to Thomas. He certainly knew some time before a friend and fellow London merchant, Walter Combes, departed for the East Indies during the winter of 1703/04. Combes wrote to Thomas from Mauritius the following April advising him the *Linnet* had been sold by the East India Company in Surat and promised to attempt to recover the proceeds on Thomas' behalf. He also had news of the *Prosperous*.

Back in Madagascar, the pirate Thomas Howard had taken over the command of the *Prosperous* and the next stage of her story is entwined with that of two others: the *Speedy Return* and another of Thomas' ventures, the *Worcester*. To understand this complex story it is necessary to take a detour into Scottish history.

By the beginning of the eighteenth century, Scotland had been through a decade of particularly difficult times and, despite their joint sovereignty since 1603, its relationship with its southern neighbour England could not be much worse. The question of the Union of the two countries hung in the air but would not be resolved until 1707. Scotland had endured seven years of famine caused by bad weather and obsolete agricultural techniques. The merchants of England believed they had a monopoly of overseas commerce and were active in trying to exclude Scotland from this trade.

The relationship hit an all-time low with the failure of the Scots Company's Darien scheme. The Company of Scotland Trading to Africa and the Indies or Scots Company was the Scottish rival to the East India Company. Although also set up by a royal charter, it was not recognised by the English company. The Darien Isthmus, the narrow strip of land joining North and South America, separating the Caribbean Sea and the Pacific Ocean now known as Panama, was chosen as the location of a trading colony. As the future Panama Canal was to prove, this area was seen as an alternative route for the East Indies trade. Up to half the available wealth of Scotland was invested in this venture, much of this from ordinary people who saw it as a patriotic act as well as an investment. There was a strong feeling among the Scots that both nature and the English had treated them badly but their country deserved to be as great a mercantile power as their southern neighbour.

Unfortunately, the project was doomed to failure: the climate was unsuited to Europeans and the native population was hostile. The colony lasted barely eight months and the colonists fled in July 1699 leaving behind those too sick to move. The escapees were also in poor health and many died on board ship. William III of England, William I of Scotland, had always been lukewarm about the scheme. At the time, England was at war with France and he had no desire to antagonise Spain. The Isthmus was part of the territory claimed by Spain as New Granada. Consequently, William ordered the English navy and the English colonists in North America not to assist those escaping from Darien. Not only were the participants of the expedition decimated and the few survivors humiliated but the Scots Company was almost bankrupted.

Newspapers had not been regularly published in Scotland until 1699. The fledgling press ensured that for the first time the public were fully aware of all these issues. Negative public opinion was stirred up in Scotland and there had been riots. When, in 1700, the belated news reached Scotland of a skirmish won by the Darien colonists over the Spanish, one newspaper called *for all true Caledonians* to put candles in their windows. Some individuals threw stones at any dark windows.

THE *SPEEDY RETURN*

The Scots Company's response to its losses was to despatch two ships to the East Indies in an attempt the trade itself out of its financial difficulties. On 26 May 1701, the *Speedy Return*, a three-masted ship, and her smaller companion the *Content*, a two-masted brigantine, departed from Newport, Glasgow, with Captain Robert Drummond in command. Both the ships and Drummond were veterans of the Darien affair. His brother, Thomas, also a veteran of the Darien expedition, accompanied him as supercargo. However, despite the acknowledged purpose of the voyage, an examination of the ships' manifest shows they were carrying goods such as hats, shoes and stockings. There was no market in the East Indies for such goods manufactured in Scotland. Silver was necessary to trade for spices but silver was what the Scots Company did not have. The implication is that their intention was to trade with the pirates at Madagascar. Pirates did have silver. As will be seen, this is exactly what they did and it was to have disastrous consequences for all concerned.

The Scots Company vessels, the *Speedy Return* and the *Content*, arrived in Madagascar having stopped at Madeira to trade in wine on the way. They anchored off St Mary's Isle, present day Nosy Boraha, a Madagascan pirate settlement confirming the intention to trade with pirates. Here they sold strong liquor to the residents and agreed to transport a consignment of slaves to Isle Bourbon, present-day Réunion to the east of Madagascar. In July 1702, after returning to Madagascar, the ships headed south along the east coast of the island to Maritan, in search of new customers. Maritan was where the pirate John Bowen had raised a new settlement.

Captain Drummond, his surgeon and the officers of the *Content* including the captain's brother, Thomas, went ashore. Nine hours later, Bowen boarded the *Speedy Return* on the pretence of trading but, instead, took it over and, later, also captured the *Content*. Some days later, Bowen took the two ships to Isle Bourbon and then the short distance to Mauritius in an unsuccessful search for prey before returning to Madagascar. Robert Drummond, his chief mate Charles Broudly, the carpenter James Davis and a foremastman John MacClachee had been left stranded at Maritan. The rest of the crews of the two captured ships had been forced to join Bowen's pirates.

On their return to Madagascar, the *Content*, which was damaged by hitting a rock during the voyage, was driven ashore and burnt, the crew having first been transferred to the *Speedy Return*. At this point, Bowen decided to seek out another pirate group headed by Captain Thomas Howard, the pirate captain of the *Prosperous,* with the objective of joining forces with them. The two ships continued attacking shipping, together and separately, until they came together again at Surat on the west coast of India where they captured two larger and better armed ships in September 1703. Having obtained more powerful vessels, the pirates no longer had use for either the *Speedy Return* or the *Prosperous* and they were burnt at Rajapore on the Malabar Coast.

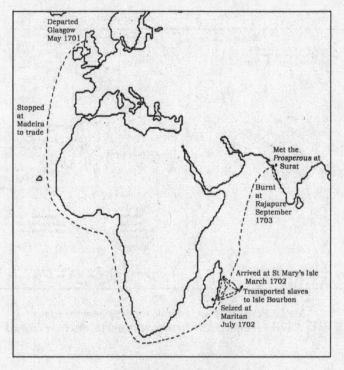

Voyage of the *Speedy Return*.

Having renamed his latest prize ship *Defiance,* Bowen set off on a cruise down the Malabar Coast together with Howard before Bowen sailed back to Mauritius. Here he disbanded his company. With forty of his men, he went into retirement but died of an intestinal complaint six months later. The *Defiance* and her remaining crew were taken into Howard's group. During this stay in Mauritius, two of the forced men from Drummond's crew, Israel Phipenny and Peter Freeland, escaped and secured a berth on the *Rapier Galley*, a London-based East Indiaman bound for England where they would arrive just in time to provide vital evidence about what had happened to their ship in the case of the *Worcester.*

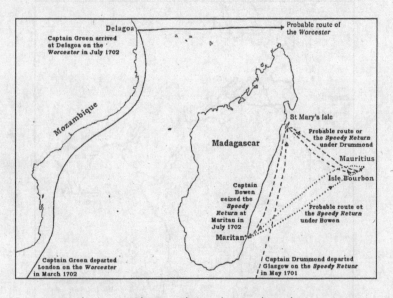

Madagascar and Mozambique showing how the routes
of the *Worcester* and *Speedy Return* were unlikely to have crossed.

THE VOYAGE OF THE *WORCESTER*

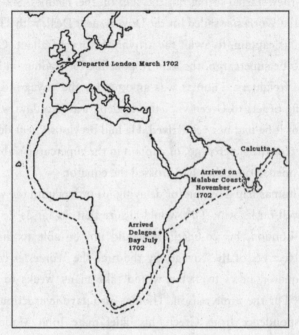

Outward voyage of the *Worcester*.

Late in 1701, Thomas Bowrey and a group of friends and associates chartered the privately owned *Worcester* as an independent, or separate stock, ship for their own sixteen-month trading voyage to the East Indies. Little did anyone realise at that time how disastrous both the situation in Scotland and the voyage of the *Speedy Return* would be to those connected with the *Worcester* and the impact it all would have on Britain for centuries to come.

The charter party, or contract, for the voyage was signed on 16 December 1701. This document set out all the terms for the voyage from the size of the crew and arms to be carried to the route to be followed and the goods to be traded. The following week they started fitting out the ship on the Thames. Six weeks later, the *Worcester* sailed for the Downs, near Deal, with Thomas Green as captain, to await the arrival of Robert Callant. Callant was to be supercargo, the man responsible for trading on behalf of the freighters. Thomas was anxious for the voyage to start, sending orders to Green via letter to depart in two days without Callant if he had not yet arrived. He had previously sent detailed orders for the supercargo, or captain in the supercargo's absence, to be opened once they had crossed the equator.

Thomas had a reason for delaying his orders until the voyage was well on its way. This would ensure that, as far as he could from London, his competitors would not be able to discover the objectives of the voyage. By the time the *Worcester* crossed the equator, news from her would take many weeks to reach home. For the same reason, Thomas also gave instructions that correspondence from Green, his chief mate John Madder or Callant should be written in a rudimentary cypher. Later, despite this instruction being ignored, this requirement for secrecy was to backfire.

Callant arrived in Deal ahead of the *Worcester* but, still, things were not to go according to Thomas' plans. The ship's main top mast had been damaged. A new one had to be purchased and fitted by the carpenter. On 3 February, Thomas lay awake at night at home in Wapping listening to a storm raging outside and worrying about his ship. In the morning, he dashed off a letter to his supercargo asking for reassurance. Callant, not yet on board but clearly understanding his employer's concerns, had already written to say that although several ships were missing, the *Worcester* was safe. Green had not thought to do so and Madder did not write until the following day.

Whilst waiting in the Downs, there was an almost daily exchange of letters between Thomas and the ship. From these, it is clear that Green was a reluctant correspondent. Thomas clearly did not fully trust his captain and would ask for the same information from both him and, in secret, from Madder. This was not the only evidence of lack of harmony among those on board stirred up by Thomas' attempts at total control of the activities of the ship and crew. Callant reported Green as carrying private cargo on behalf of one of the freighters in contravention of the Charter Party. Thomas' response was to ask Callant to forbid any further contraventions saying that he would ask Green to account for his actions on his return.

The bad weather continued, delaying the *Worcester*'s departure further. Later in the month, Callant reported that the *Worcester*'s oars were damaged and had to be replaced. Next Thomas received news which confirmed that his concerns were justified. Another ship, whose captain was drunk, fouled the *Worcester* and carried away her bowsprit. This was particularly galling because the wind was finally blowing favourably enough for them to leave the Downs. Once the *Worcester* was able to make a fresh attempt to sail at the beginning of March, she was again driven back by the weather.

Luckily for the officers on board the *Worcester*, Thomas became distracted from worrying them by another project – whaling. For a few days, his letters to the ship concerned the necessary preparations for this venture rather than the ship's delayed departure. Ever aware of new business opportunities, he saw that the failure of the Greenland Company had reopened the market to any merchant-adventurers looking for a new venture. The Company had a long-term monopoly of the London whaling trade. Whales were to be found at Delagoa Bay on the *Worcester*'s proposed route and their baleen, whalebone or whale's fin, for corsets and oil, for lighting and lubricants, had great commercial value. He enthusiastically researched the trade and sent instructions in his letters to Madder.

Two professional harpooners were recruited, accommodation was built for them on board and Thomas was excited about the additional possibilities these would add to the voyage. As cabin space was reserved for officers and important passengers, providing separate accommodation was an indication of their perceived value. A whaling venture was not included in the contract but Thomas clearly believed that he was free to deviate from this. It is easy to sympathise with Green who was criticised for accepting cargo for another of the freighters.

This reprieve from harassment by Thomas of those on board the *Worcester* did not last long because he worried that the delayed start to the voyage would affect the opportunities for whaling. He bombarded them with often contradictory instructions about this new venture and, possibly as a result of this, no whaling was ever carried out. The harpooners effectively became dead-weight passengers.

Finally on 8 March, the *Worcester* was able to set sail. One can only imagined the conflicting emotions Thomas felt: glad that the voyage had at last started but concerned that he would now have little control over what happened on the voyage. In contrast, the officers on board were probably relieved. Thomas had continued to send his orders until the last opportunity. In fact his last letter was undated but clearly written on or after the departure date because it contained the news that King William had died. This letter never reached the ship. Whilst those on board remained eager to please their anxious employer, there were clear signs in the correspondence that has survived that they believed many of his orders to be unreasonable. On 2 March, Callant wrote that he had noted what was written and would follow all orders and instructions but protested about the imposition of an assistant to watch him when he was already employing his own from his own pocket.

Thomas did, of course, expect to receive occasional news from the ship whenever they were able to find a vessel returning to England willing to act as postman. The first report from Callant dated 27 March, and despatched on 11 April, reported that the ship was not sailing well, being heavy in the water, but they were pushing her hard to make good time. Was Thomas reassured by this news of the ship's progress or did he worry, correctly as it turned out, that they were pushing the ship too hard and she would be damaged? Whatever his reaction, this was all the news he was to receive until the *Worcester* arrived on the Malabar Coast of India eight months later.

Meanwhile, the ship arrived at Delagoa Bay in present day southern Mozambique on the east coast of Africa around 10 July. Here the crew assembled the dismantled sloop they had carried in her hull. This small, single-decked vessel would be used as an inshore coastal trader and they christened it *Delagoa* after the bay. There is no evidence of any whaling activity having taken place as planned by Thomas. It is unlikely to be because his orders were completely ignored. After all, the harpooners were on board as a constant reminder. Perhaps no whales were found or the harpooners were already sick after the long voyage.

It was while here that several of the crew reported seeing a mermaid, perhaps whilst searching for whales. The reports of the sighting were recorded later by Thomas in his *Notes on Delagoa*. The creature appeared to a number of the crew three times close to the mouth of the Delagoa river. It was only about ten yards from their boat, looked the men in their face before diving under the water. It was the size of a large woman, had a tawny complexion, large pendulous breasts and long dark hair. They had probably seen a dugong, similar to a manatee or sea cow, often believed to be the origin of mermaid myths. Although in some parts of the world mermaids were considered lucky by seamen, in British folklore they were usually seen as unlucky omens. How many of the crew had a premonition of what was to come because of this sighting?

They left Delagoa on 26 August. If Green followed his instruction, he sailed between the east African coast and the island of Madagascar thus avoiding the known pirate colonies on St Mary's Isle and at Maritan. The *Worcester*, *sailing very heavy*, took another two and a half months to arrive at Anjengo on the coast of Malabar on 14 November 1702. She then spent the next few months trading along the coast. At Anjengo, they traded silver dollars, anchors and sword blades brought from England as well as elephant ivory from Delagoa for pepper and *spoiling trade* or perishable goods, probably provisions for the crew. It was reported locally by hostile East India Company officials that they sold their European goods too cheaply. We can only wonder if Thomas would also have been annoyed at this news. At Cochin they traded guns for more pepper. Pepper was an extremely valuable East Indies product used, in England, both to spice up food and for medicine and was the cargo with which Thomas most wished to see the *Worcester* return.

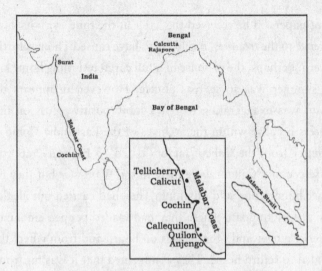

East Indies showing the Malabar coast.

For some time during December, it appears that Callant, his assistant and three or four of the crew were detained ashore for some time at Quilon by the Indian locals in a dispute over the price agreed for pepper. Whilst on the coast, a passing Dutch ship had informed them that Captain Drummond had *turned pirate* and the *Delagoa* had been made ready in case of attack.

By January 1703, the *Worcester* was leaking badly and in need of a refit but the Governor of Cochin would not allow the ship to be refitted there. On 31 January, Callant wrote from Calicut that their problems had hindered them carrying out Thomas' instructions but nevertheless he hoped to be home by the following August with a full and profitable ship. They already had one hundred tons of pepper and twenty tons of cinnamon sticks plus asafoetida and other drugs. This letter, sent via the *London*, is included in Temple's *New Light on the Mysterious Tragedy of the Worcester* but I have been unable to find it within Thomas' extant papers. If he received the letter at the time, with its vague reference to the *troubles*, it is likely to have caused Thomas further concern. Perhaps, the promise of a full cargo returning home later that summer was some reassurance. However, it appears that Callant was exaggerating to put a more positive gloss on their progress because within the archives of the East India Company is a letter from the Calicut factory dated 13 February reporting that Green and Callant were there in the *Worcester* but they had neither bought nor sold anything. They had carried out all their trade at Calliquiloan, where they had loaded pepper, cinnamon, turmeric, ginger and other goods on board and from where they intended to return home. They commented that it was far from a full cargo.

Around the same time at Calicut, according to the memoir of Alexander Hamilton, Green and several of his crew boarded Hamilton's ship at sunset very drunk and attempted to sell him guns, powder, shot and glassware *at a very reasonable rate*. At another time he reports Callant again as drunk. He also claimed that the *Worcester*'s surgeon, Charles May, asked him for a job as *his life was uneasy on board of his ship*. Despite his poor opinion of his visitors, Hamilton purchased the glassware and five barrels of red lead. The overall impression from the records is of a trading voyage that was far from being as successful as Thomas had hoped.

Despite the leak, for the next three months the *Worcester* continued trading on the coast between Tellicherry and Anjango. The armed *Delagoa* was sent to trade separately but ran aground leaving Quilon and was lost with her cargo. Leaking and without the sloop, further trading opportunities for the *Worcester* were severely restricted.

During April, the *Aurengzeb* commanded by Captain Blewett arrived on the Malabar Coast near to Anjengo. It was here a few days later that a storm blew the *Worcester* close to Blewett's ship. Green was concerned and desperate enough to empty the water casks and throw some of the cargo overboard to lighten the ship. The *Worcester* signalled to Blewett that she was in distress and he went, with his chief mate, to check on her condition. They saw that the ship was *very leaky* and that a cable had parted. Blewett confirmed to Callant that the ship could not return to England without repairs. The two ships were brought together again by more bad weather a few days later. The *Worcester* saluted the *Aurengzeb* with five guns as was the practice at the time. When the *Worcester* arrived at Cochin on 23 January, they saluted the factory with seven guns. May, the ship's surgeon was ashore at the time and heard the guns. He was to recall the incident months later.

The two ships stayed together for three days during which time the captains, supercargoes and others of the crews often went aboard each other's ships. Having replenished their supplies from the shore, the *Worcester* supplied the *Aurengzeb* with fresh water. The chief and second mates of the *Aurengzeb* went ashore and reported that the *Worcester* had sprung a leak to the governor of the English fort at Anjengo. They were concerned about her getting safely to Bengal. On 4 May, Callant and Green went ashore at Anjengo to ask the governor where they could take the ship for a refit. He advised them in writing to go to Bengal. The next day, the *Worcester* departed for Bengal, many of the ship's crew being sick with fevers and fluxes. A number of the crew had died including the two harpooners. Callant probably fell ill at this stage because he disappears from the records. There is no record of the voyage through the Bay of Bengal but, if they were in danger of sinking, the ship's carpenters could have carried out the risky procedure of going overboard to find and stop the leaks with tar or pitch whilst the ship was heeled over first to one side and then the other.

One reason for heading to Bengal was to avoid the annual monsoon on the west coast of India. However, the local officials of the East India Company there had not been welcoming and it was possible that Green believed that he was likely to receive more favourable treatment in the Bay of Bengal where Thomas had spent many years and had many contacts. The *Worcester* arrived at Calcutta, at that time a new and small factory, on 11 June 1703. Here their reception was, indeed, more favourable and they traded saltpetre and red wood in addition to having the ship repaired whilst laid on shore. Sound, at least for now, they departed for England on 17 November carrying a letter from Fort William, the Calcutta, factory to the East India Company in London.

Meanwhile, Thomas had received worrying news from the East. In similar terms to all his correspondence since he returned home, his young prodigy Robin Lesly had written from what is today Iran that business was calamitous and that merchants were afraid. He was hoping to return to England. His step-father, Charles Sherer, had to take work with the New East India Company at Hugli. Whilst the *Prosperous* and *Worcester* took up most of Thomas' attention at this time, he prudently also continued to spread his risks. He invested in seven other ships destined for the East Indies that departed during the autumn and winter of 1702-1703. Thomas took out a bottomry agreement on the *Resolution* and exported a range of domestic items from frying pans to bird cages on her. In return, textiles were purchased on his behalf and these sold by his agent in Amsterdam following her safe return at the end of 1704. Whilst they were away, Thomas sent a letter to two of the crew, Morregh and Wilkinson, requesting that they write to him from each of their ports with information on the prices of various goods. Four others, the *Alexander Galley*, *Rapier Galley*, *Trumball Galley* and *Marlborough*, also returned safely but the *Black Boy* was cast away at Batavia. There is no information on the outcome of the voyage of the seventh, the *Marianna*, in Thomas' papers or elsewhere.

CHAPTER 9

The Fate of the *Worcester* (1704-1705)

The country had experienced a fortnight of strong winds. The whole of England talked of the awful weather, chimney stacks were blown down, tiles fell from roofs and several ships were lost. It did not die down. The ferocity of the wind continued to increase. Thomas, aware of the danger, became increasingly concerned for his ships. During the late afternoon of Wednesday 24 November 1703, it blew even harder and the fair weather turned to rain. There were furious and frightening gusts of wind. It had become dangerous to be outside as the walls of houses fell and roof tiles showered down. The violent weather continued through the next day, the following night and the Friday morning. It was already a storm that everyone would remember for a long time. As night approached and Thomas checked his barometer, the mercury had sunk lower than he had ever seen before and he knew that it would be a terrible night.

As the night progressed, there was little sleep as people throughout England were afraid that their houses would fall down around them but they dare not leave them for fear of greater danger outside. In some areas, lightening or hail added to their distress. The storm did not start to abate until seven on the Saturday morning. As it did, the mercury rose. There had been many bad storms over the preceding few years but this had been by far the worst. When people finally ventured outside, they saw that their roof tiles had been blown with such force that they landed up to forty yards from their house yet were still buried deep into the hard soil. Timber, iron and lead from the tallest buildings were blown even further. It would be a few days before Thomas learned that the newly erected Eddystone Lighthouse had been destroyed. His home and household safe, his immediate concern was for his ships.

THE *RISING SUN*

As the *Worcester* departed Bengal, Thomas Bowrey was investing in five more voyages. His involvement in the *Rochester*, *Anne Galley*, *Horsham Frigate* and *Arrabella* were minimal and little is known about them other than the first two returned safely and the *Arrabella* was *cast away* in unknown circumstances. More is known about the fifth, the one hundred and forty ton *Rising Sun* with an outward cargo valued at almost £1,000.

Thomas purchased the *Rising Sun*, recently returned from an East India Company charter, in 1703. It was not the ship of the same name that took part in the second Scots Company expedition to Darien four years earlier. That ship was lost with all hands in a hurricane off Charleston. In November, the *Rising Sun* was one of about 700 ships in the Pool of London at the time but it had been luckier than most. When the storm hit she was on the Thames being fitted out for her voyage and her outward cargo loaded. She was damaged but survived although her masts, cables and anchors as well as the ship's longboat were lost. Her captain, Thomas Wybergh, believed that the mast ended up on the coast of Holland but the anchors could not be located, especially as he could remember no details by which to identify them. It was impossible for the London shipyards to effect all the repairs required and priority was given to the ships of the Royal Navy and the East India Company. An independently owned ship had a low priority. If her voyage was not to be delayed for longer than necessary, Thomas had to look further afield and the *Rising Sun* was taken to Flushing for repair. It is clear from Thomas' papers that the ship was almost ready to sail when the storm hit. The delay and cost of repairs were of great concern but were not the only ones for Wybergh.

Once in Flushing, the ship's crew's troubles were not over. In a letter, Peter Tom, one of the owners, informed Thomas of his concerns about the supercargo, Captain Samuel Rowley. In Tom's opinion, Rowley fell far short of the prudence and sobriety needed to provide good management for the voyage. He suggested that Thomas would have been better taking a man out of the Bethlehem Hospital, an institution for the insane. Tom apologized for being so frank but Rowley had been responsible for the loss of a boat with two men and a boy on board. He finished his letter by stressing his own good character and suitability for Rowley's job. It is questionable whether Rowley was as bad as he had painted or if Tom was simply taking the opportunity of his captain's absence to engineer an opportunity for his own advantage.

On another occasion, three copies of the same letter were sent to Thomas from Flushing. Jointly from Wybergh and Tom they said it was impossible to control their crew in a place where the demand for men to crew privateers was so great. They believed that local law did not support them in controlling their men. A postscript added that the crew was their greatest concern. The men were the masters and Wybergh and Tom forced to comply with what they wanted. They had never before had so many problems. Seven men were lost at Flushing. Six deserted and another was discharge. Mutiny was a frequent hazard for all sea captains especially when a voyage was not going to plan. If the crew believed that they would not receive the rewards they expected and they could see greater advantages elsewhere, mutiny was an attractive option. The sea was a dangerous place and the risk of execution not such a deterrent in these circumstances.

On 13 February 1704 Tom wrote again to Thomas. The letter contained the news he had been awaiting for so long. Finally, there was a favourable wind. The previous morning, a fresh gale blew up and at eight in the evening they set sail on the flood tide in convoy with a number of other ships for the East Indies. Despite the trouble with the crew, they had managed to get the full complement of thirty men on board before they departed. Tom was relaxed. He expressed the opinion that the captain was an honest and good-humoured gentleman and passed on the regards of the boatswain and carpenter to Thomas and his family. But it was a case of speaking too soon.

A postscript to the letter said that the wind had dropped; the *Rising Sun* had anchored and, next morning, returned to Flushing. What had actually happened was that ship had touched a sandbank. Although not stuck, they were forced back into the harbour to check for damage. The rest of the convoy had continued on its way and there was now no other ships to travel with. They finally left two weeks later under a fine easterly wind. Their eventual departure was reported to Thomas by his agent in Flushing, Leenert Sonsbeeck, who also thought it necessary to pass comment on the captain. In his opinion, Wybergh was an honest man but *no seaman* and because of this he had experienced a great deal of trouble with his crew. Sonsbeeck offered the opinion that the War of Spanish Succession was causing restlessness among mariners.

Sonsbeeck wrote to Thomas again a month later with a story he knew would be of concern. One of Sonsbeeck's own ships, homeward bound from Guinea, was attacked by a French privateer with seventeen guns and many men. The fight lasted six or seven hours but the ship eventually forced the privateer away. By this time, they were close to Plymouth but were not safe because they encountered a second French privateer, this time with thirty-four guns. This one did a great deal of damage to Sonsbeeck's ship's masts and sails. By then, it was evening and the damaged ship anchored overnight, putting into port the next morning. As the ship was laid on a bank for repairs to be undertaken they were approached by an English man-of-war, the *Woolwich*, commanded by Captain Thomas Eckings. He seized the stricken ship and her boats, and took the ship's crew and papers to London. Eckings claimed that the ship's commission was invalid. Sonsbeeck requested Thomas to speak to his friends and try to have the ship and cargo released.

This news cannot have been welcome by Thomas, reminding him of the risks to his own shipping but by May the *Rising Sun* had arrived safely at the Cape of Good Hope where they rested to restock with fresh water and to prevent scurvy among the crew. Although they had lost the convoy, they had travelled with a Dutch ship after the Isle of Wight. Peter Tom took the opportunity to send a letter home by one of the ships returning to England. Everyone on board was in good heart but they would be arriving late in the season for the East Indies trade. It was not all bad news. The returning ships had advised that good prices were being paid.

All Thomas could do at such a distance was to wait, hope that the voyage went well and try to find warehousing for his returning cargos. Meanwhile there were family problems to deal with. On 15 August 1704 while Thomas and Mary were staying at Tunbridge Wells, Mary's father Philip Gardiner died aged sixty-eight. He had made his last will and testament four years earlier expressing the wish to be buried at Great Clacton if he died in Essex or at Wapping if he died in London. He was buried in the sacrarium of the parish church at Clacton twelve days following his death. Gardiner left his elder daughter, Elizabeth, a property at Jaywick and made her the executrix of his will appointing Thomas to supervise. As the will was proved the day after the funeral, Thomas had a busy few weeks to distract him from his shipping concerns.

By December, the *Rising Sun* was at Fort William where Wybergh was reprimanded for flying French colours opposite the East India Company fort. Both merchantmen and the ships of national navies at the time carried flags of many nations in addition to their own. They would use the flags of another country to intentionally deceive: either for safety reasons or to trick enemy shipping before attacking. For this reason, crews, especially those of the Royal Navy, would learn to recognise individual ships by sight. At this time, England was at war with France. Perhaps the *Rising Sun* had only recently arrived having passed French ships. Whatever the reason they were flying the wrong colours, the officials at the fort were not happy because it could well cause them difficulties if the local authorities were to notice. On hearing this, Wybergh replaced the French flags with English.

Whilst at Fort William, the *Rising Sun* met up with two other ships in which Thomas had an interest: the *Mary Galley* and the *Macclesfield*. The three crews took the opportunity to swap correspondence. At the same time, back in London, Thomas had received a letter from Solloman Middleton, a crew member shipped at Flushing. Middleton had jumped ship at Fort William, returning home on another and had written complaining about Wybergh. Thomas believing Wybergh had failed to follow his orders, appeared before a public notary and swore his affidavit authorising Charles Newman, captain of the *Tankerville* to take possession of the *Rising Sun* and her cargo, and then return the ship immediately home. Newman never met the *Rising Sun* which arrived back at Amsterdam on 27 July 1706 and at Gravesend the following 18 August. Four days later, Wybergh paid the customs duties due on his cargo. The following December, Thomas sold a range of textiles brought home by the ship at the Marine Coffee House in Birchin Lane, London. The sale was by candle. Through his many contacts, Thomas constantly checked prices achieved in the east and back home. He sold his stock in the place, and by the method, where he was likely to obtain the best price.

The sale was not the end of the story of the *Rising Sun*. Despite a relatively uneventful voyage after leaving Flushing, the animosity between the senior officers on board and Thomas' suspicions of them continued. Rather than being grateful for his ship's safe arrival, Thomas proceeded to accuse Wybergh of failing to make sufficient profit from the voyage. He started a court case against him. The Court of the Queen's Bench appointed Captain Samuel Jones, a London merchant, to arbitrate between them. Thomas' complaint was that Wybergh had failed to follow his orders to call at Mozambique, Ceylon and three ports in India.

Failure to do so cost Thomas 7,000 rupees. In addition, Wybergh
had not given an adequate account of the losses and damage to
cargo for which Thomas was claiming a further 3,775 rupees.
Wybergh's failure to follow orders to purchase specific items in
India added a further £600 to the claim for damages. Exaggerating
his case, Thomas further alleged that the malicious and ungrateful
Wybergh would ruin him if Jones' judgment went against him.
The equivalent value of Thomas' claim today is over £290,000.
This is a large sum but, at this this time, Thomas continued to
invest in other ventures. He was far from destitute and Jones
was not swayed. He awarded Wybergh £771, equivalent to over
£120,000 today, against Thomas.

THE ARRIVAL OF THE *WORCESTER* IN SCOTLAND

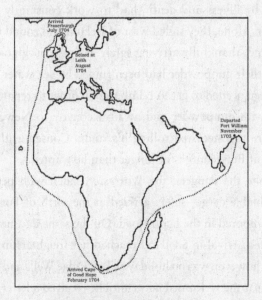

Return voyage of the *Worcester*.

The *Worcester* and the *Rising Sun* passed each other off the west coast of Africa but the two ships did not meet. The *Worcester* had arrived at the Cape of Good Hope from Bengal on 21 February 1704. Here, Robert Callant died and Thomas Linseed took over as supercargo. Thomas Bowrey had warned Callant by letter to be careful of hostile French privateers. He was to avoid the English Channel on the return voyage by sailing round Ireland in a convoy with an armed escort. The ship left the Cape with a Dutch convoy including two other English ships in which Thomas had an interest, the *London* and the *Resolution*, on 26 March.

The only surviving report of the final leg of the *Worcester*'s journey home was written by Green. In May, the ill-fated ship again sprung a leak and was no longer able to keep up with the convoy. A leaky ship sailed low in the water, was in constant danger of sinking and was at risk from hostile shipping. The crew, already depleted by illness and death, had to work constantly pumping out water. Alone, they sailed west of Ireland and round the north of Scotland, thankfully arriving safely at Fraserburgh on 19 July. Most of their gunpowder had been ruined by sea water from the leak. Green needed to get to Edinburgh in order to repair his ship, restock with gunpowder and await a convoy to Newcastle but there were privateers patrolling his route. Consequently he was detained at Fraserburgh for longer than he wanted.

Despite the dangers, the *Worcester*, laden with pepper and other valuable cargo, safely arrived at the Firth of Forth on 28 July and moored in the Leith Road. On the same day, news of the *Worcester*'s arrival in Scotland reached her freighters in London. Thomas, however, was on holiday at Tunbridge Wells and probably did not hear the welcomed news until he received a letter dated 31 July from Thomas Hammond, another of the freighters.

THE *ANNANDALE* INCIDENT

Whilst the *Worcester* was still undergoing repairs in Fort William, Calcutta, back in Scotland the increasingly desperate Scots Company decided on an attempt to recover a cargo lost in the Malacca Strait on an earlier disastrous trading voyage by the *Speedwell*. Having lost the *Speedy Return* and all their other vessels, in October 1703 they purchased a majority share in an armed London merchantman. It is interesting to note that there was correspondence dated between 17 July and 21 September 1703 in Thomas' papers that appears to indicate that Thomas had been negotiating with Roderick MacKenzie, Secretary of the Scots Company, to purchase shares in the company. In this correspondence, MacKenzie denied that they were interested in purchasing the ship.

At the time of purchase by the Scots Company, the ship was being fitted out on the Thames but her previous, English, owners had yet to purchase a trading licence from the East India Company. The new owners renamed the ship the *Annandale*. On 1 February 1704, English customs officers accompanied by an armed naval party boarded the *Annandale* on the pretence of searching for stolen money. The naval lieutenant promptly pressed twenty-one of the *Scots Dogs* and the remaining Scots seamen were subject to abuse. When the *Annandale*'s officers protested, they were told that their letter of marque issued by the Queen's Commissioner for Scotland, which should have guaranteed them free passage, was not recognised. The *Annandale* was moved to Dover to await the results of legal proceedings.

The case was heard before the bar of the Court of Exchequer on 28 June. The verdict given six days later was in favour of the

East India Company's claim that the ship was not licenced for her intended voyage. The Scots Company appealed but the appeal was delayed until the autumn. Before the ship could be refitted to sail from Dover, an additional claim for £3,000 damages for losses he claimed to have suffered was served on her by John Ap-Rice. He was her original owner and retained a minority share in the ship. The *Annandale* was taken to Deptford on the Thames to await the results of the appeal and additional legal actions. On 11 August, the directors of the Scots Company presented a petition to the Queen's High Commissioner to the Scottish Parliament claiming that the blatant, state-approved, English aggression against the *Annandale* and her crew demanding retaliation in kind.

THE FATE OF THE *WORCESTER*

That retaliation was not long coming. On the day the petition was presented to the queen and whilst Green, his senior officers and many of his crew were ashore in Leith and Edinburgh, MacKenzie gathered together a group of his friends and acquaintances on the pretence of offering them dinner, a meal taken in the middle of the day at the time. After arriving at Leith, he revealed his true purpose to them. Armed with pocket pistols, swords and bayonets, MacKenzie, three of the gentlemen and a servant rowed out to the *Worcester* with some wine, brandy, sugar and lime juice, requesting a tour of the ship. After boarding the ship, another four of the party joined them whilst the remaining officers on board were distracted by the first arrivals *tongue-padding* and entertaining them. The remaining men from the dinner party made pretence of visiting a man-of-war before also approaching the *Worcester* and surreptitiously boarding her. The three separate groups pretended not to know each other but wandered around the ship, stationing themselves to guard the gun-room and other strategic points. From this position of strength, the *Worcester* was seized by MacKenzie on behalf of the Scots Company. He started an action in the Scottish High Court of Admiralty to take the ship and her cargo in compensation for the seizure of the *Annandale*. He did this despite knowing, from his correspondence with Thomas, that the *Worcester* was not an East India Company ship. The officers and most of the crew were put ashore to await the release of the ship.

There had been premature reports in London of the *Worcester* having been seized from 1 August, obviously causing concern to Thomas but it is clear from a passage scored out in a draft letter he wrote to Charles Sherer on 13 September 1704 that he was unhappy less about the seizure of the *Worcester* than other matters. He wrote that he did not believe that Callant, the supercargo, had followed instructions. Consequently, the voyage would not be as profitable as it could have been.

Thomas had clearly heard reports about some of the misfortunes that befell the *Worcester* and her cargo on the Malabar Coast. He appears not to have been too disturbed by the rumours because he did not return home from Tunbridge Wells immediately despite correspondence sent by his concerned friends. However, as soon as the news of the actual seizure of the ship reached Thomas he did return and, together with the other freighters of the *Worcester*, started the fight to have her released and they were initially winning the argument that she was not an East India Company ship. However, MacKenzie soon suspected that Green was guilty of dubious practices. Thomas' paranoid orders to use a cypher in their letters to him intended to stop competitors discovering the plans for the voyage were mistakenly seen as highly suspicious proof of intended wrong doing. Some of the *Worcester*'s crew had been overheard saying incriminating things about what had taken place whilst in the East Indies. These suspicions grew and, on 7 December, Andrew Robison, one of the ship's gunners, was arrested at Bruntisland for piracy, robbery and murder. The next day Green and seventeen more of his crew were also apprehended on the same charge. The Scottish newspapers, reporting both fact and rumour, declared the prisoners guilty, linking the circumstances of the trial to the ongoing constitutional conflict between Scotland and England. The incident provided a focus for the Scots' seething resentment against the English. An acute crisis was threatening the British composite monarchy. Despite neither the *Speedy Return* nor Captain Drummond being named in the charges, it was generally but erroneously believed that their loss was due to Green and his crew.

The trial for piracy, robbery and murder against Green and his crew started on 5 March 1705. In the intervening period, MacKenzie had worked on the crew, attempting to obtain confessions from them in return for pardons. The turned crew members included the surgeon, May, who claimed that he had witnessed the attack on the *Speedy Return* by the *Worcester* and *Delagoa* whilst he was ashore at Callequilon. It is clear from his testimony, and that of the other witnesses, that there was a great deal of ill feeling between them and John Madder and it is possible that this may have provided further incentive for some of the crew to witness against him and Green. However, evidence came to light later that May had been induced to turn against the others by the young daughter of the Governor of Edinburgh

Castle where he was held prisoner. On 14 March, all the accused, with the exception of John Reynolds, were found guilty. Reynolds had been fortunate enough to have been ashore at the time of the incident. The court met again a week later to pass sentence. Green, Madder and two other defendants would be hanged on 4 April and the remaining nine would be executed over the following fortnight. As the result of an intervention by Queen Anne, the first hangings were postponed by a week. Following sentence, some of the convicted confessed to MacKenzie on the promise of a reprieve. The sentences did nothing to cool public opinion in Scotland and, over the next week, the pressure to carry out the executions reached fever pitch.

At the end of March, the *Rapier Galley* landed at Portsmouth with two of the crew of the *Speedy Return*. John Green, Thomas' brother, obtained affidavits from Peter Freeland and Israel Phipenny on the fate of their ship. The affidavits were rushed to London from where copies, together with the queen's plea for clemency, were sent on via messenger to Edinburgh. He arrived in the city three hours before the scheduled execution of Green, Madder and John Simpson, gunner. The crowd had started to build in Edinburgh the day before.

By first light, an angry crowd of tens of thousands of people had lined the route from Edinburgh Castle to the execution site on Leith Sands, chanting and determined not to be robbed of their vengeance for all the English treachery of the previous decade. It was a very ugly crowd. Only a handful of Scottish privy councillors were brave enough to appear at Old Parliament House to consider the new evidence arrived from London and those who had had arrived early before the crowds had built up. Feeling intimidated by the crowds, who could be heard inside the chamber, they dismissed the affidavits. Despite this, as the councillors tried to leave, a section of the crowd rushed the chancellor in his coach believing the prisoners had been reprieved and he was lucky to escape with his life.

The crowd continued to grow. By the time of the executions, it was estimated to be 80,000 strong and no one was likely to be brave enough to deny them what they demanded. But, as he waited at the gallows and Green saw the *Worcester* across the Firth, he continued to hope until the end that a messenger would bring a reprieve. None came. He was the first to hang followed closely by Simpson and then Madder. Breaking with the tradition for pirates, the bodies were not hung in chains to be washed by three tides but taken to their lodgings to be prepared for burial. Had this not happened, the crowd was likely to have torn the three apart. The three were given a Christian burial. The record of the burials at South Leith Church reads

Capt. Tho. Greens, Commander, Capt. John Maither, Mate, James Simpson, Gunner, of the English East India Ship called the Worcester *of London, being sentenced to death for Pyrracy & Robbery, were hanged (the First in the Thirtieth & third year of his Age, the second in the Fortieth and Fourth year of his Age, the Third in ye Thirtieth and nynth year of his Age) within the Seamark near to the Saw-Miln, on the Eleventh day, and were buryed on the said day.*

By 1705, Thomas Bowrey had experienced two public and devastating losses in the *Worcester* and the *Prosperous*. Investing in two of Sir George Matthews' voyages, those of the *London* and the *Little London*, reduced both his work and risk involved. Matthews and his ships had been hired many times by the East India Company and previously by Thomas. He was a safe and experienced commander who, in 1712, was to be elected Member of Parliament for Southwark. Although there is no record of the size of Thomas' investment in these ventures, the combined value of the outward cargos was £7,000. For another of Thomas' interests at this time, the 400-ton *Windsor Frigate*, the total investment was £7,400 but again there is no record of Thomas' investment in this voyage. He limited his involvement in fitting out the ships, affording him a well-earned rest following the departure of his *Mary Galley*.

THE *MARY GALLEY*

In early August 1704, Thomas was recuperating at Tunbridge Wells with his wife. Letters from the time provide a small window into their private life of which, in the main, almost nothing survives. Earlier in the year he had been unable to join his *Molly* during her stay in Bath due to the demands of supervising the construction of his ship. Mary had pleaded with her *Tommy* for him to join her but he did not think it was possible for him stay away from London for so long. He tried to encourage her to join him at Nathaniel and Sarah Long's house in Richmond to sample the first beans and peas of the season instead. By August, Thomas was exhausted and Mary ill. As soon as they could get away together, they spent over three weeks recuperating at Tunbridge. Whether Mary was well enough to re-join Thomas in time for the launch of the ship named after her is unknown.

Thomas' release from his ties to the capital came as he celebrated the launch with a dinner on board on 22 July. No guest list survives but it was no doubt attended by his fellow owners of the ship. Thomas owned half while her captain Joseph Tolson had a sixth share; Thomas Hammond and Elias Dupuy each had one twelfth; and the purser Elias Grist and Richard Tolson a twenty-fourth share each. Hammond and Dupuy had also been part owners of the *Worcester*. Judging by the quantity of food served by Samuel Pepys when he hosted dinner parties, it is likely there was at least another six guests, one of whom was likely to have been Richard Wells, the ship's builder. Thomas probably took this opportunity to present Wells with a gift of a piece of silver that cost thirty pounds, worth the equivalent of more than £4,500 today. It was a handsome gift indicating just how pleased Thomas was with the result. Thomas Warham was employed to cook the meal, comprising a sirloin of beef, a boiled ham, four lobsters, eight fowl, six chickens, four tongues, two tarts and custard, an almond cheesecake, a dish of fruit, bread and pickles. It is likely this food was served as two courses, savoury dishes mixed with sweet as was the custom of the time. It was all washed down with a gallon of brandy, a gallon of Rhenish wine, fifteen flasks of Italian red wine and twenty-four bottles of ale. Warham supplied the table linen, pewter plates, knives and forks.

Thomas Studds, the son of Thomas' Middleton cousin Hannah, was to be one of the crew of the *Mary Galley*. That Studds' father had died many years earlier may explain why Thomas had taken on the responsibility of equipping him for the voyage. He had paid for Studds to have lessons in navigation and arithmetic, as well as providing the clothes and other items he would require, ranging from four pairs of drawers to a pewter chamber pot.

In total there were just twenty-six officers and crew on board when the *Mary Galley* departed from the Thames. She carried an exotic cargo including hubblebubbles or glass hookah pipes, *paun* boxes for keeping betel-leaves and spire drinking glasses with air-twist stems. Two of these items were notable in not being the usual trade goods taken to the East Indies. It appears Thomas was using the knowledge he gained whilst in the East Indies to improve his chances in a difficult market.

The ship was granted a licence by the East India Company on 3 October 1704 and departed from Gravesend two weeks later. At about five in the evening of the 26th of the month, Tolson sailed out of the Downs. As the day broke the next morning, they had just drawn level with Brighton when two sails were spotted in the distance, one to the north between them and the shore and the other in the direction they were travelling. Tolson was suspicious especially when the one ahead of them added more sail as if to intercept them. He changed tack. The other ship followed suit. It caught up with the *Mary Galley* and fired three shots at her. Tolson ran. The two ships gave chase. They were flying Dutch colours but Tolson recognised them as being French built and judged them to be privateers. The first was armed with thirty guns. His suspicions were justified. Tolson fired back and hit his target. He easily out sailed them. This was the first time his new vessel had been tested and he was well pleased with her performance but the danger was not yet over. Three hours later, three sails were spotted. This time he could see no way of avoiding converging with them other than by out running them. He headed for Spithead as fast as the ship was able. One of the ships rowed into Portsmouth harbour with him, planning to cut him off before the *Mary Galley* reached safety. Fortunately, Tolson discovered the galley could be rowed at two knots, again outpacing the enemy. By the time he wrote to Thomas with the news of the attacks, Tolson had arranged to proceed in convoy with HMS *Litchfield* as far as the Cape Verde Islands about 1,500 miles west of the coast of Senegal.

After all the previous unfortunate incidents to his ships, Thomas may not have been so sanguine. He had previously given orders the *Mary Galley* should not join any convoy that may try to discover their trading objectives or interfere with the ship. He responded by sending instructions on how to sail the ship and to keep details of their trading objective from everyone except Dupuy, the assistant supercargo, and Griffin, the first mate. Grist was especially to be kept in the dark despite being a co-owner. Even before departing, Grist had shown himself to be unreliable, almost failing to join the ship at Gravesend and causing Thomas to doubt his sincerity. Yet again Thomas was showing a lack of trust in his captain and senior officers.

Even after the *Mary Galley* left English waters, Thomas continued to send Tolson instructions to be guarded in his business dealings. There were obvious difficulties in attempting to manage the details of a voyage from such a distance as demonstrated by a letter instructing Tolson to go first to Bengal and then the Maldives. It was not received until the ship arrived at Calcutta in West Bengal having sailed first for Batavia. Thomas expected these instructions to supersede those delivered in England. Even the sailing direction for the Malay Archipelago based on Thomas' extensive experience in the region arrived far too late. The only constant was the exhortation to be frugal. Tolson's failure to follow orders he did not receive until too late was to form the basis of a complaint against him by Thomas after his return.

The *Litchfield*'s captain turned out to be an inconsiderate convoy leader and out-sailed the *Mary Galley*. Separated from her protector by about four miles of ocean, she had a further encounter with French privateers. Tolson scared one off by firing at it and the other was taken as a prize by the *Litchfield* and despatched to England. The small convoy continued on its way with Tolson struggling to keep up with his escort. It was an eventful voyage. Before arriving at the Cape Verde island, they had spotted yet another French ship and ridden out a storm. The *Mary Galley* continued alone towards the Cape of Good Hope as misfortune continued to follow them. They lost part of their foremast and were pushed further west than intended as they crossed the equator. At Tristan da Cunha, about 1,500 miles west of modern South Africa, they met with contrary winds but they finally arrived safely at the Cape of Good Hope in January 1705. Here they took the opportunity of cleaning some of the ship's hull and heard the disturbing tale of mutinies on board the *Abingdon* and *Josiah,* two East India Company ships on their way to the Malabar Coast of India.

From the Cape, Tolson's route took them to Batavia via Bencoolen on the west coast of Sumatra and other ports on the same coast. They made slow progress due to the lack of wind. A month out from the Cape, the ship lost part of her main mast. They stayed at Batavia from 23 April to 2 September 1705 for extensive repairs to be made to the worm-eaten hull, before moving onto Calcutta, arriving there eleven weeks later. Tolson had managed to leave Grist behind through an unlucky accident that was nobody's fault. When Grist had gone ashore the day before the galley left Batavia he had been informed by Tolson that he intended to leave during the night. Grist, who had failed to return in time, tried to follow in a small boat. The *Mary Galley*'s own boat was sent to fetch him but the two missed each other. The crew neglected to inform Tolson until it was too late. Once

Grist was able to write home, he explained his going ashore at the last minute. He was passing some tea, lacquerwares and porcelain he thought Thomas' wife may like to the captain of a ship about to leave for England who had refused to deal directly with Tolson because of his bad reputation among his peers. Grist was forced to wait at Batavia until the *Mary Galley* returned the following April.

From Grist, Thomas learned the *Mary Galley* was, at the time, under charter to a local merchant. Tolson had been forced to accept this charter because they had been unable to purchase a satisfactory cargo at Batavia from the funds available. At Calcutta the *Mary Galley* met up with Thomas' *Rising Sun* which had been in India for two years. Tolson took the opportunity to send a letter to Thomas full of excuses about the cost of repairs and the poor trade he had been forced to carry out. After receiving Thomas' belated instructions, Tolson voyaged back and forth between Calcutta and Batavia, still under charter, throughout 1706 before leaving again for the Malay Archipelago a few weeks into the following year. News of this failure to trade on behalf of the galley's owners ensured Tolson would be returning to a hostile reception.

Her charter completed, the *Mary Galley* joined a returning Dutch East India Company fleet. During her voyage, the galley had lost seven crew members to death and desertion. Others had been taken on as replacements but most of these also left the ship for one reason or another before the end of the voyage. The convoy stayed at the Cape of Good Hope for four weeks, the *Mary Galley* losing another three crew members, before heading to the Dutch coast via the west of Ireland and the Shetland Isles to avoid the French in the English Channel.

West of the Shetlands, a fog came down. Before Tolson was able to re-establish contact with the convoy, a gale blew up. The convoy reached the Zuider Zee safely but without the *Mary Galley*. Now alone, Tolson wanted above everything to avoid the coast of Scotland and a fate similar to the *Worcester*. If anything, English-Scottish relations were even worse than three years earlier. Despite this, he was blown off course and into the Firth of Forth, the very place where the *Worcester* was seized. Fighting against the gale force winds, Tolson attempted to reach the safety of Newcastle but, yet again, met with French privateers. This time the tiny ship was engaged in a sea battle. One man on board the *Mary Galley* was killed and ten of the twenty-four crew, including Tolson himself, were injured. Command was taken over by Richard Griffin, the chief mate, and against the odds he managed to escape to the coast of Jutland. Spotting what he believed were two English men-of-war, Griffin appealed to them for aid before realising his grave error. They were actually yet more French privateers. Griffin's command was short lived. His ship was captured on 18 August 1707 and taken into Dunkirk. Her crew including the injured Tolson were imprisoned there. They would not reach England until early the following year.

It is unlikely that Thomas heard about the loss of yet another of his ships before the beginning of September. Yet, within nine days, he had made a claim against his insurance. That some of his loses were insured was not sufficient for Thomas. He had been distressed to receive the bad news from Batavia. Back in England, Grist wasted no time informing Thomas that Tolson and Griffin had surrendered the *Mary Galley* dishonorably. In Grist's opinion, Tolson had an excuse being wounded, but Griffin simply hid between decks and stopped others with him from emerging to engage with the attackers.

Egged on by Grist and Griffin, Thomas charged Tolson with breach of his contract and orders including a failure to keep an accounts book and ship's journal. As the ship's papers had been destroyed following her capture, this was difficult to prove as was the charge of Tolson carrying out private trade. Thomas had taken legal advice because he was concerned he may have been sued by some of his fellow owners who had been made insolvent by the loss of the ship. The advice received did not reassure him and he determined to recover as much as he was able from the captain. Tolson vehemently proclaimed his innocence of any wrong and, at his suggestion, they took the dispute to arbitration. When his friend, James Dolliffe, was appointed arbiter there can be no doubt Thomas believe the case would be found in his favour but he was to be disappointed. Dolliffe found in Tolson's favour and he was awarded one hundred and five pounds, eighteen shillings and nine pence. In a second case between Tolson and the other owners of the *Mary Galley* with a different arbiter, Tolson did not fare as well. It was claimed that he shared the diamonds on board with Griffin before the attack. This case went against Tolson who was orderd to pay a total of thirteen pounds and ten shillings. However, as the total losses amounted to £3,000, or about £480,000 today, these awards were relatively insignificant.

The case of the *Mary Galley* may have been resolved, however unsatisfactorily, but that of the *Worcester* would continue for years.

THE AFTERMATH OF THE *WORCESTER* AFFAIR

The remaining nine crew members were still under sentence of death. In the aftermath of the first hangings, the Scottish politicians were concerned about the threat posed by the strength of feeling of the mob. They did not want to experience a repeat of the hostility on the day the first executions. The remaining prisoners were quietly released the following autumn and given funds to enable them to return safely to London. Two of those released made affidavits outlining the pressure MacKenzie had applied to the accused in an attempt to obtain confessions.

The first the English public knew of the executions was the report in the *Post Man* newspaper of 14-17 April 1705:

> *Letters from Edinburgh say that there has been an uproar upon account of the execution of Captain Green, late Commander of the* Worcester, *tried and condemned for piracy, and that some of the chief ministers were insulted by the rabble, but we think fit to forbear mentioning any particulars till the next advices, which will bring a more certain account thereof.*

The editor correctly understood that, once the full details were known, they would provoke indignation at the miscarriage of justice and insult to both the Crown and the people of England. Generally, Scots continued to believe that Green was guilty of piracy, if not that of the *Speedy Return*, then of another ship. An extreme example of this survives in a letter dated 2 May 1705 from James, 4th Duke of Hamilton, to his wife Elizabeth Gerard. The letter comments that Green and the two others died maintaining their lies and made the sensational claim that the captain and Madder had ordered the surgeon to take blood from every member of the crew. The blood was mixed with wine before each man dipped bread into the mix as they swore to keep secret everything that happened on the voyage. It was further claimed that one of the crew who refused to do this was tied to a board and had the veins in his arm cut. As he slowly expired, each member of the crew stabbed him with their bayonets.

In contrast to the Scots, the majority of the English public believed Green to be innocent and, immediately after the news was known, English shipping avoided putting into Scottish ports with consequent further harm to Scottish trade. It was a major news story outside Scotland. Thomas received letters from John Evans, Bishop of Bangor, who he had known in the East Indies, sympathising about his losses and, even, from John Starke in Virginia which he described as the *fag end* of the world.

Unlike the crew, the *Worcester* was never released and the Scots auctioned off the ship and her cargo including the personal possessions of the crew. For Thomas, the executions changed little. He was still fighting to obtain compensation for the loss of the ship and cargo on behalf of her owners and freighters. He spent many years collecting evidence, making insurance claims and petitioning Queen Anne for compensation. It is possible he compiled *The Case of the Owners and Freighters of the Ship* Worcester *in relation to the seising ... of the said ship ... in Scotland, for reprisal of the Scots ship* Annandale, *seised ... in England. And also the case of the late Capt. Thomas Green* from those witness testimonies dismissed or unavailable at the time of the trial. This was published anonymously in London in 1705.

Thomas and a committee of the freighters of the *Worcester*

met with the Attorney General, Sir John Cooke, to discuss compensation at the end of November the same year. This meeting was probably the result of their petition to the queen earlier that month. At that stage, they had been unable to obtain the *Worcester*'s papers from the Scots and Thomas had already explored the possibility of taking legal actions against the Scots Company in the Scottish courts. The ship and cargo were insured but this would cover less than one-sixth of the original value. Subsequently, in August 1706, the owners petitioned the queen again. On 12 March 1707, a statement from the owners of the ship *Worcester* was read to the Lords at the Cockpit by Samuel Mears. Originally a cock-fighting venue and theatre and later a royal residence, at this time the Cockpit-in-Court or Royal Cockpit was used as offices by the Treasury. Damages were assessed at £27,971, valued at nearly £4.5 million today. This was going on as the political situation heightened. The Scots Company was closed down and MacKenzie lost his job within two years of the executions but the ramifications were much wider than this. It is generally accepted that the case of the *Worcester* brought about, or hastened, the Union of Scotland and England in 1707.

Opinion on the correctness of the verdict became polarised and linked to the question of the political Union. Those against the Union believed that Green and his crew were guilty. Supporters of Union believed that there had been a miscarriage of justice. The incident demonstrated to politicians on both side of the border the strength of Scottish public feeling about their overbearing neighbour. The two governments were shocked into trying to find a solution to the schism and, before the year was out, Queen Anne ordered her commissioners to start working on full Union between the two nations. On 6 March 1707, the queen gave her ascent to the Act of Union, one of the terms of which was the winding up of the Scots Company. It became clear to Thomas and his colleagues that they needed to speed up their efforts whilst there was still some chance that compensation could be obtained from the company.

Later, in 1707, Thomas despatched his relative, Henry Smith, to Edinburgh to make enquiries about the affair. This is the same man who was dismissed from his employment with the East India Company on more than one occasion and subsequently tried for piracy. As he had also criticised Thomas' Malay-English dictionary, Smith would seem to have been a strange choice but, in the prevailing political climate, there was not likely to be many people who would accept the task. He took the task seriously but encountered difficulties throughout starting with his mare scouring before he reached Doncaster on the outward journey. His troubles continued to the day he left Edinburgh when collecting his horse he was confronted by the difficult Barbara Binning and her lawyer. She had made life problematic for Smith and was now preventing him from leaving. He eventually got away from her but, rather than risk further trouble, slipped out of a back gate.

Arriving in Edinburgh on 2 August, Smith did not return to London until 1 October. Thomas set him the task of finding answers to eleven specific questions ranging from the fate of a gold cross and two diamond rings that had been in Green's chest of drawers to whether there was any rumour of embezzlement prior to the sale of the ship and cargo. A partial diary of his journey survives in Thomas' papers, as do twenty-three letters to his employer. Smith faced many obstacles during his stay in Scotland because feelings about the case still ran high. Whilst in Edinburgh, Smith witnessed the last reported sighting of the *Worcester*, as a convict ship departing for the West Indies. Overall, Smith's mission was not a success but he did succeed in obtaining the official, but incorrect, accounts of the auction sale of the *Worcester* and her cargo as well as other more important papers.

Despite his other commitments, Thomas continued to work tirelessly to obtain compensation for the losses for the rest of his life. The loss of the *Worcester*'s papers hampered his efforts. Despite various agreements to make compensation from the queen's share of the prize fund, the spoils of war at sea, all they ever received was £5,000. His fight continued until the end of his life. On 24 October 1712, less than five months before his death, he was given power of attorney by the freighters of the *Worcester* to receive the balance of the value of the ship due to them. With his death, and that of Queen Anne on 1 August 1714 with the resulting change in government, the affair of the *Worcester* finally came to an end, at least as far as legal action is concerned. The incident, however, continues to excite interest in certain quarters and is still being written about today. To a certain extent the indignation as well as the anger of the Scots has continued until the present day whereas English opinion remains that Green and his crew were innocent.

CHAPTER 10

The Final Projects
(1707-1711)

The saga of the *Worcester* had taken its toll of Thomas Bowrey. After the execution of Green, Madder and Simpson and the growing realisation he was unlikely to recover his losses on the voyage of the *Worcester*, he never invested in trading voyages again. The final two, those of the *Chambers Frigate* and the *John & Elizabeth*, departed in the spring of 1707. Their fate is unrecorded in Thomas' papers. That of others demonstrates the risks of such ventures: taken by pirates, privateers and the Scots; *cast away*; blown up, and lost. The *St George Galley* made a loss never having got any further than Portsmouth.

Although there is little concrete information, it is also likely that following the union between the old and new East India companies in 1708 the granting of licences for independent voyages ceased or reduced drastically. An unlicenced trading venture was considerably more risky. The news from his friends in the East was increasingly pessimistic about trade. Whatever his reason for ending his direct involvement, Thomas never lost his interest in the East Indies trade. However, for the remainder of his life, he restricted that interest to dreaming up schemes to improve it, and his fortune, without the risk associated with maritime ventures.

Thomas had, of course, for a long time invested in schemes unconnected with the East Indies trade. Alongside the King's Head Inn in Southwark, he had a number of houses built in the Goodman's Fields area close to Marine Square. This area was being newly developed with smart houses, taverns, coffeehouses and shops. His papers contain a wealth of information about these for students of vernacular architecture of the period. One was let rent free to his Davis relative with permission to sell tea, coffee, chocolate and muslins from the chamber. This was what Thomas described as the *China House* for which he drew up an inventory in October 1706. Queen Mary II had popularised blue and white Delftware, Chinese porcelain and oriental embroidered bedlinens. Alongside the tea, coffee, chocolate and textiles, fashionable customers of the *China House* could find everything needed to enjoy the beverages sold including the porcelain, canisters and jars, as well as pictures in frames he had especially lacquered, fans, toys and necklaces. The total valuation at the time was seventy-five pounds and two shillings, worth almost £12,000 today. This was not an entirely altruistic project for Thomas. Porcelain provided useful additional and modestly profitable ballast for ships returning from the East. Some of his other schemes would be considered unacceptable today but not his proposals for new coinage.

THOMAS BOWREY'S NEW COINAGE PROPOSALS

Today, we take the ready availability of cash – coins and notes – for granted but when Isaac Newton took up the post of Warden of the Royal Mint in May 1696, silver coinage had been disappearing from circulation for almost a decade. All denominations from the half-groat, worth two pennies, to the crown, worth five shillings, were made of silver. A pound of beef cost about three pence, a gallon of full-strength beer in a tavern cost no more than a shilling and a labourer earned just over a shilling a day. The small silver coins, needed for daily life and business, had become scarcer each year and were almost unobtainable. At a time when the modern consumer-led economy was in its infancy, shopkeepers were forced to give credit and, as receipts in Thomas Bowrey's papers show, often had to wait months or years for payment.

Newton's appointment was the consequence of his proposed solution to this shortage. A decade later, when there was still a problem, Thomas suggested a new copper coinage to compensate for the shortage of silver coins. His proposals were undated but, as they mention Great Britain, were probably written after the union in 1707. How did this coinage crisis arise?

From around the beginning of the reign of William and Mary in 1689, one could buy more gold in the rest of the world with a given lump of silver than the same weight of English minted silver coins could purchase in London. The difference in price equated only to one and a half pence per ounce of silver but this was more than sufficient to make it worthwhile for people to melt English silver coins into ingots and take them across the Channel to purchase gold. They returned to England, sold the gold for silver coins and started again. It is not known who these entrepreneurial people were but at one point it is estimated ten percent of the previous five year's production of silver coinage from the Mint had been shipped out of London in just six months. Five years' production was about £500,000. Ten percent, or £50,000, was worth the equivalent of over £8.5 million today.

This situation was worsened by two other factors. The first was the shipping of silver to the East Indies to pay for spices and other exotic goods demanded at home. There was little market for English manufactured goods which could be sold to raise funds there. If merchants wished to purchase these luxuries, they had to carry silver from England. The other was the existence of two parallel coinages: the old, hand-struck, pre-1662 coins and the newer, precisely weighted, machine-made ones. These machine-made coins had milled edges to prevent clipping. Older coins contained less silver after years of having small pieces of silver clipped off but had the same face value as the newer ones. Thus, the public held onto the new coins and used only the debased, older ones. Not only did this result in a shortage of silver coin but also a shortage of silver from which to mint new coins.

The shortage became so great that any business had to be on trust that payment would eventually be made. As this went on, the mood of the nation approached panic. In July 1696, Edmund Bohun, the former official press censor, described the desperate mood in the country saying people were discontented; there were many suicides and a fear it would take little to incite a riot. Counterfeiters responded to the shortage. It was estimated more than ten percent of the coins in circulation were fake. Finally, although the populous paid their taxes in the debased coinage they were reluctant to accept the same coins, at face value, from the government in payment for goods and services, such as the victualling of navy ships. The Treasury consequently retaliated by stopping accepting the old coins as payment for taxes.

A parliamentary investigation into the problem was launched in 1690. One of the people proposing solutions was Isaac Newton. He argued there should be a complete recall of the country's silver money, both old and new. The recalled coins would be melted down and used to make new coins, a re-coinage. Alongside this, there should be a devaluation of the currency so the face value of the new coins matched the intrinsic value of their silver content. He was appointed to the Royal Mint but devaluation was unacceptable to Parliament who, in January 1696, approved only the re-coinage. By the autumn, this was underway twenty hours per day, six days per week. Most of the available silver had been used to make new coins by the end of 1697 and the work was completed six months later. The production of silver coinage was now more difficult to counterfeit and clip. Newton was rewarded by being promoted to Master of the Mint. However, the failure to devalue the currency meant silver continued to leave the country. The only solution to the intrinsic value of silver coins being greater than their face value would be their replacement by paper money – but that is another story.

Thomas returned to England at the height of the crisis and, as a merchant, cannot have failed to have been severely affected by it. Not only was it almost certain his business in London was made more difficult but it is likely the shortage of silver affected his East Indies trade too. After the failure to devalue the currency and another decade of silver coins leaching from the country, there was a shortage of lower value copper coins to fill the gap. Thomas had his own solution. He wrote that the shortage of halfpenny and farthing (worth a quarter-penny) coins could only be rectified by the issue of new. He requested a ten-year patent to produce new copper coins to the standard of those last minted during the reign of King William III. The queen would benefit from the taxes on the import of the copper and the public would benefit from the increased availability of coins. No mention was made of what the patentee would receive other than it would be the same as for similar patents. It is certain Thomas saw an opportunity for profit.

His scheme came to nothing. No copper farthing and halfpenny coins were minted during Queen Anne's reign (1702-1714). The authorities claimed there was a glut from previous years but the evidence does not support this. Shopkeepers and others felt the need to produce tokens to cover shortages. Later, in the mid-eighteenth century, local half-pennies and farthings were still being produced. Later still, in 1787, employers even used tokens to pay their employees. In effect, the re-coinage was being undertaken by the public at no cost to the government.

THOMAS BOWREY'S ANTI-PIRACY PROPOSALS

He may have changed his focus from shipping but Thomas Bowrey had not reduced the complexity of his affairs. As he applied his mind to the shortage of coinage he still had at least five ships at sea and was dealing with the aftermath of the seizure of the *Worcester* and the *Mary Galley*. Consequently, safety at sea was never far from his thoughts, and one of the greatest risks was piracy. In view of the losses he sustained and his personal experience, it is understandable that one of the schemes Thomas worked on was for reducing piracy, specifically the risk from pirates based on Madagascar.

Piracy has existed at least as far back as the middle ages and probably as long as ships have traded around the world. People were only too willing to put the loss of any ship down to this and with good reason. During the period of Bowrey's life, more ships were lost to piracy than shipwreck. In the 1680s, a number of conditions in the West Indies forced Caribbean buccaneers out of the area. Voyages by their main targets, Spanish treasure galleons, had become less frequent. In addition, piracy was becoming less tolerated there by the English and French authorities. These changes resulted in piracy in the region being less profitable. It had previously existed in the Indian Ocean but these pirates were of local origin preying on local shipping, particularly those carrying pilgrims on their way to Mecca.

Now, European pirates moved to the region, basing themselves on Madagascar, especially St Mary's Isle. The Caribbean buccaneers were mostly French and English concentrating on raiding both the Spanish colonies and Spanish shipping serving them. English shipping was relatively safe. Once they moved to the Indian Ocean, the pirates became less discriminating although it has been said they would avoid attacking English shipping unless in need of provisions or alcohol. However, there are many examples of such attacks on English shipping taking place when both the ship, and at least some of the crew, were taken.

Following the move to the Indian Ocean, a support infrastructure was developed at St Mary's Isle with ships from the English colonies in America supplying arms, alcohol and other necessaries for sale to the pirates. These supply ships would return to North America with cargos of slaves. Samuel Burgess, who had been a member of infamous pirate William Kidd's crew, commanded one of the supply vessels. On his return to New York, he carried a number of other pirates who, having made their fortune, wanted to retire.

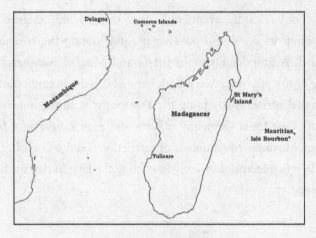

Mozambique and Madagascar.

The nuisance of piracy in the India Ocean came to a head in 1695. Early that year, Henry Avery arrived at the Comoros Islands between Mozambique and Madagascar as commander of the *Fancy*. He had started his career in the Royal Navy serving during the Nine Years' War (1688-1697). On discharge from the navy, he worked as a mariner on slave ships. In 1693, he had become first mate on a ship commissioned by the Spanish as a privateer against the French in the West Indies. When the Spanish failed to deliver the promised letter of marque granting the ship the status of privateer, the crew mutinied and elected Avery as captain. By the time the *Fancy* reached the Comoros Islands, they had already attacked and plundered five ships off the West African coast.

The *Fancy* attacked a French ship off the Comoros but was almost captured by an East Indiaman. Avery and his crew then turned their attentions to the large and heavily armed *Ganj-i-sawai* returning in convoy from Mocha, the Red Sea port for Mecca. Together with several other pirate ships, Avery attacked the convoy and, eventually, overpowered the pilgrim ship savaging its crew and passengers, and looting the treasure on board. A granddaughter of the Grand Mughal Aurangzeb was one of the pilgrims. Avery took her as his wife. In retaliation, the Mughal turned his rage on the Europeans in India, imprisoning many East India Company officers and even executing a few of them. He imposed a number of restrictions on the English, Dutch and French factories severely impacting the East Indian trade with Europe.

Indian Ocean, Red Sea and Persian Gulf.

In an attempt to pacify the Mughal, the East India Company offered to provide armed escorts to the Mocha fleets. The Governor of Bombay also commissioned Captain Alexander Hamilton to root out indigenous pirates on the Malabar Coast and Persian Gulf. With the French and Dutch, he worked to raise the huge compensation Auranzeb demanded, valued in the region of £70m in today's money. The East India Company escalated the issue to King William and on 18 August 1696 a royal proclamation was issued for apprehending Avery and other pirates and offering a reward of five hundred pounds for information leading to Avery's arrest plus fifty pounds for each of his crew. The East India Company had previously offered a similar reward in rupees.

In a further attempt to deal with the problem, the East India Company pressured the English colonial authorities in the Americas to cut off trading connection with Madagascar thus starving the trading post on St Mary's Isle of supplies. It was estimated at the time there were over one thousand pirates on Madagascar, mostly originating in the English colonies in America. Without the necessities previously supplied from the trading post, the pirates were forced to take refuge among the indigenous population.

The irony of the East India Company's reaction to Avery's attack on the Mughal's ships was that, in the previous decade, it had licenced some of its ships as privateers. Robert Knox, one of the Company's captains, was commission to make war against the Mughal and his subjects, and to take all the ships belonging to them. His ship, the *Tonqueen Merchant*, was equipped for the task by increasing the number of guns to twenty-four and adding thirty soldiers to his crew.

As was seen from Thomas' concerns about the return voyage in the story of the *Worcester*, North African corsairs and another danger awaited an East Indies trading voyage. During times of war, which accounted for most of the periods of Thomas' life, privateers licenced by enemy governments were a great risk in the English Channel and the other waters around the British Isles. During the four years of the Second Dutch War (1664-1667), three hundred and sixty English merchantmen were taken by Dutch privateers. A similar number were taken during the third war (1670-1672) and, it has been estimated than between 5,000 and 7,500 English ships were taken by the French privateers between 1695 and 1713. The captured ships and cargos would be taken as prizes shared between the crews and their government. Crew of merchantmen were encouraged to resist attack by pirates and privateers by withholding their wages until the ship and cargo had safely returned to the home port. Thus, capture by privateers would result in the crew of the captured ship losing their wages, their sea chests and, often, their liberty.

Within Thomas' surviving papers, there are a number of draft proposals dated between 1707 and 1710 for the redeployment of pirates. They would be used to seize a French East Indies island. The island in question was Mauritius to where a number of wealthy pirates had retired. In 1705 others, from Muscat, had attacked an East India Company ship. Since 1700, these pirates had also taken thirty Englishmen into slavery. Thomas was as concerned about the Muscat pirates as those from Madagascar and Mauritius. His suggestion was to send a small armed fleet to Madagascar and offer the English pirates there a pardon in return for surrendering their enormous fortune and providing their assistance in attacking poorly defended Mauritius. The wealth of the Mauritian pirates would be confiscated. Finally, the pardoned Madagascan pirates would help destroy those at Muscat before returning home.

On 21 May 1707, Thomas sent this paper to Peregrine Osborne, Marquess of Carmarthen, Royal Navy vice-admiral and Tory politician. He sent it again in July the same year; it would appear to no effect but he would not let it drop. In 1710, he showed the proposal to Samuel Sheppard and John Hungerford. Thomas had sold some cargo from the *St George Galley* to Samuel Sheppard. John Hungerford of Lincoln's Inn Fields was involved with another of Thomas' ships, the *Rising Sun*. Nothing else is known about these two people, who they were or why they were asked to review the document but Sheppard responded it was not the right time because of the war then current.

Thomas' attitudes to piracy were complex. He had personally been attacked by pirates and had suffered losses as a direct result of their actions. He had also planned to trade with them and was prepared for them to be offered pardons if the rewards were high enough. He had dealings with the known reformed pirate William Dampier. It is possible his leniency was because he understood how easy it was for his fellow mariners to find themselves with no real choice other than to become pirates. However, the attitude to pirates within society generally was also ambiguous. Dampier was fêted after his return to England. He was granted an audience with Queen Anne and was reported as kissing her hand. Robert Callant, supercargo of the *Worcester*, wrote to Samuel Burgess, another pirate, for information on whaling at Mozambique.

If Thomas was empathetic it was not only based on the experience of his step-uncle, Henry Smith. He was aware that it was a common experience for mariners to be sucked into piracy. The story of Henry Avery was fairly typical in that it involved him losing his career in the Royal Navy at the end of a war. Such men would often be owed a great deal of back pay with no likelihood of seeing any of it in the foreseeable future. It was essential for them to find new work as soon as possible at a time the market was flooded with candidates. Considering himself to have been *bred to the* sea, Avery looked for work as a sailor and turned to the slave trade.

Conditions on board these ships were by far the worst and the mortality rate for slave ship crews was roughly equal to the extremely high infant mortality rates in eighteenth-century London. On average, between twenty and twenty-five percent of the crew of a slaver would die during a voyage. As slavers needed larger crews to compensate for these high rates of loss and to guard the human cargo, a displaced mariner was more likely to find a berth on one than on a more desirable vessel. To escape these conditions, Avery quickly transferred to a privateer. Here conditions were generally better but there was a high risk of death or injury whenever they attacked an enemy vessel. When the letter of marque authorising their privateering for his new ship failed to arrive, the promise of lucrative rewards for the crew disappeared and they mutinied. Now outside the law, there was little choice left to the men on board but to starve or *turn pirate*. It has been estimated about one third of mutineers during Thomas' lifetime subsequently became pirates.

Thomas Bowrey's proposals to some extent echoed a general, time-limited pardon for pirates in the East Indies issued by William III in 1698. Not only was piracy having a negative effect on merchant shipping but pirates were believed to have huge wealth which they would bring home to England. This earlier amnesty specifically excluded Henry Avery, but others refused to trust that the authorities would honour it. This caution may well have been justified. At least one crew carrying a copy of the declaration were arrested on their voyage to retirement in New York. They eventually secured a pardon and most pirates who took advantage of the amnesty were not brought to trial once they reached England but their concern was understandable.

Whatever the reason for his scheme not being taken up, it remained important to Thomas for a number of years but not to the exclusion of his other projects.

THOMAS BOWREY AND THE SLAVE TRADE

One of Thomas Bowrey's schemes involved a business equally as old as piracy: the slave trade. Two authors, Bialuschewski and Lincoln, have suggested Thomas sought a licence to ship slaves from Madagascar to Brazil as compensation for the loss of the *Worcester* intending to establish a regular route taking advantage of the gold recently discovered there. I have been unable to confirm this claim either in the quoted source or elsewhere but it would not have been out of character: he never gave up trying to obtain compensation; had an interest in the commercial potential of South America and a number of his proposals involved the transportation of slaves.

One of his earliest was for the setting up of sugar and indigo plantations in Jamaica. He estimated such plantations required a thousand acres of good land near a market plus one hundred African slaves, fifteen European servants and craftsmen, and seventy-five cattle, horses and mules. Together with materials and tools for building the sugar-works and a mansion house, Thomas included the cost of provisions for the first two years. At this time, the triangular Atlantic trading system was in its infancy. Thomas' proposal may have been realised if Jamaica had not experienced a devastating earthquake in 1692 when a part of Port Royal collapsed into the sea and thousands were killed. It was one of the reasons the Caribbean buccaneers migrated to the Indian Ocean and may have been why Thomas did not take the scheme any further.

This proposal like those for new coinage and the reduction of piracy had two things in common with all Thomas' schemes: they were not only opportunities for increasing his profits through new or improved business opportunities but he thought them through in great detail. He may not always have been correct or successful but he approached each of them in great earnest. This also applied to his complex plans for a settlement on the east coast of Africa.

While still in the East Indies, Thomas had played a minor role in a lesser known area of the slave trade prevalent at the time. East African slaves were imported and used by the East India Company and Thomas was involved in transporting them within the region. It is estimated that that there are at least 20,000 people of African-ethnic origin living in India today, most of them the descendants of slaves, and known as Siddis. Back in England, Thomas looked for ways of becoming more involved. He began collecting information about Madagascar and the East African coast in 1707. It was probably from this time he formed his ideas about a trading settlement in Africa and it seems he may have tried to interest the East India Company in such a scheme in January 1708.

Thomas continued to work on his proposals and sent a copy to Charlwood Lawton the following April requesting him to review the document and make any corrections he considered necessary. Lawton was an English lawyer and pamphleteer with government connections. He replied that the proposal needed little improvement before publication. From this it is clear Thomas had plans to publish this work during 1708 but there is no record of anything coming of it at that time. Like so many of his schemes, this raised its head again a few years later.

The fourth of June 1712 was a day of great anticipation for Thomas. He had been called to appear before the House of Commons again, this time to present his proposal for settlements on the east coast of Africa. He was becoming impatient with the lack of trading ambition of the English East India Company in Africa. Although they had the monopoly of English trade within the Indian Ocean, they had done nothing to exploit the east African coast. Unfortunately, having failed to interest Parliament, Thomas needed to look yet further afield.

The Germans had interests in West Africa. Two small settlements on the Gold Coast in present-day Ghana were established in 1682 by the Brandenburg African Company. Their purpose was to supply the transatlantic market for slaves. The area was later renamed the Prussian Gold Coast but during the early eighteenth century the Prussians were losing their influence there. One of the two settlements had been occupied by the Dutch and they were both sold to the Dutch in 1721. Since 1701, Prussia and England, after 1707 Great Britain, were allies in the War of Spanish Succession and Thomas believed the Prussians could be persuaded to regain their advantage in the slave trade by transferring their interests to the opposite coast where demand was lower and Africans could be purchased more cheaply. Thomas was joined in this venture by Jacob Mears. The son of Thomas' agent in Amsterdam, Mears was a member of a prominent American Jewish family who had lived in Jamaica from 1698-1701. He travelled to Berlin, carrying their joint proposal intended to increase Prussian trade and revenue. Of course, it was also to be of advantage to Thomas and Mears but, for once, Thomas may not have been the driving force. Mears complained bitterly about the lack of response from him frequently both before and after he left England.

The proposal was detailed, covering the finances of setting up a new colony; the allocation of land to settlers and the military; and the transportation of criminals to the colony. The scheme also included the conditions to be imposed on pirates who wished to become settlers. The negotiations between Mears and the King of Prussia's representatives lasted two months. Proposals were delivered, commented on and revised. Eventually, an order was issued for a contract to be drawn up whereby Thomas would receive the enormous sum of £1,000 a year, an income worth over £142,000 today. Unfortunately for their ambitions one of the king's forts in Guinea was attacked by English and Dutch forces. These events on the west coast by their countrymen had reflected badly on their proposal. Mears was told the Prussians would not proceed. If he believed the proposal would be accepted, Thomas' disappointment would have been great. His correspondence shows no sign of this. Perhaps his lack of engagement with Mears throughout the process was a sign that he thought it was unlikely to succeed.

It is debatable whether Thomas should be judged by the attitudes of today for his willingness to be involved in slavery but can he be exonerated because of the prevailing beliefs of his day? In ancient Rome, slavery was considered the natural way of the world. From the age of ten, Thomas was raised in close contact with the employees of the East India Company and many of his values were formed at this time when each Company ship was required to carry to India ten African slaves. Back in London, the question was much more multifaceted and Thomas was exposed to a wide range of beliefs. One of his acquaintances, Daniel Defoe, frequently condemned Africans who sold slaves to Europeans; not for the act but for bad business. They sold them too cheaply. If Thomas knew that conditions for the crew of slavers were bad, he also knew that it was much worse for their human cargo. There were conflicting Christian attitudes to slavery. Many used the Bible to justify the practice but, by the late seventeenth century, Christian abolitionism had begun with Quakers who believed everyone was equal in the sight of God. By 1696, the Quakers of Pennsylvania officially declared their opposition to the slave trade. Thomas had returned to Wapping, an area with a strong Quaker community. He had at least one Quaker acquaintance in Peter Briggins. Charlwood Lawton, who reviewed Thomas' proposals in 1708, had previously acted as the agent in England for Quaker and founder of Pennsylvania, William Penn. It is probable Thomas was well aware of the abolitionist viewpoint. Some decades later, Thomas Clarkson was to discover that much of the population of Bristol expressed great loathing for the concept of slavery but yet did not consider its abolition. Thomas, who kept abreast of news and prevailing attitudes, made an informed and conscious decision to deal in human lives. That he was not unusual in this cannot excuse his actions.

THOMAS BOWREY AND THE SOUTH SEAS COMPANY

Whatever modern opinion may be of Thomas Bowrey's attitudes to slavery, his correspondence with Daniel Defoe demonstrated that he had a good reputation in his own time. Defoe is probably best known today as the author of *Robinson Crusoe*. He was, however, prolific at planning and setting up projects and schemes.

Much of his writing reflects his great interest in piracy. In 1708, Defoe wrote two letters to Thomas. The first, probably dated 9 March, acknowledged Thomas' request for a meeting but asked for more details because he needed to be sure he was not one of his many enemies. Alternatively, they could meet in a public place. Given Thomas' risk-adverse nature and Defoe's very public difficulties in relation to both debt and political matters over many years, it is unlikely Thomas took any offence on receipt of this letter. Defoe was intrigued because his second letter was written just five days later. He had made enquiries and was assured of Thomas' good character. Having learned he was unwell, he was prepared to call on Thomas at home. When they met, there is a strong likelihood they discussed a settlement in the South Sea, a long-standing interest of both of them. In February 1699, Thomas had presented his proposals to the Court of Directors of the East India Company in London. This came to nothing.

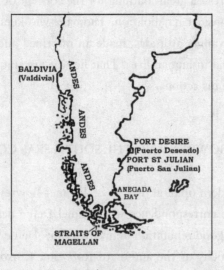

South America.

Defoe, like Thomas, had been interested in South Sea settlements for some years by the time they met. Defoe claimed he had proposed a settlement on the Pacific coast of Chile to William III shortly before his death in March 1702 and, if the king had not died, it would have been implemented. Thomas, too, saw the advantages of a trading settlement on the Pacific coast of South America to facilitate the East Indies market. Was this what they discussed and did they remain in contact, refining their proposals, over the following years? Comparison of their respective schemes strongly suggests that they did.

Defoe had been working for Robert Harley since he had rescued him from the pillory in 1703. At the time, Harley was Speaker of the House of Commons but was shortly to become Secretary of State. Having succeeded in securing his loyalty, Defoe promoted Harley's foreign and domestic policies in *The Review*. By August 1710, Harley had advanced to the post of Chancellor of the Exchequer. This followed a decade of the War of Spanish Succession and he had inherited a massive government debt of £9 million, over £1 billion today. His solution was to set up a new joint stock company linked to opening up commerce with Spanish America. This South Sea Company was, in name, to be similar to the East India Company having the monopoly of British trade in the South Sea. In reality, the government's debt was to be repaid by giving its unsecured creditors the equivalent value in shares in the Company in return for paying them six percent interest. The Company was set up by a bill which received royal assent in June 1711.

The passing of the bill in Parliament was the starting signal for the many people who had for years worked on schemes for settlements in the South Sea to make their submissions. Had

Harley read all of these, he would have been the best informed man in England - even if many presenting their proposals had never been to the region. Thomas, for example, never visited the Americas and appears to have based his proposals on the account of the region by his old associate William Dampier, who had a great deal of experience there. It was this knowledge that led to him being taken as navigator for Woodes Rogers' voyage on the *Duke* and the *Duchess*. It was during this voyage Alexander Selkirk, said to be the model for Defoe's *Robinson Crusoe*, was rescued. There is some evidence that Thomas and Dampier had been in touch in London when Thomas may have given Dampier a copy of Abel Tasman's map of his voyage round the coast of Australia.

Defoe had put his scheme to Harley in three letters in July 1711. He proposed setting up colonies in Chile and on the Atlantic coast of South America. He reasoned these were well away from the main centres of Spanish power in the region and safe from Spanish interference. With its temperate climate, friendly indigenous population, fertile land and gold mines, the Chilean colony would provide trading opportunities for the British despite the Spanish refusing to open their ports and markets to them. Like others who had clearly not experienced the region, Defoe suggested an English trading post in Chile should be connected to a colony in Patagonia by a route across the Andes.

It is unlikely Harley consulted Defoe about his proposal. Defoe's correspondence indicates the two men never met between early March and early August 1711 and there is a gap in Defoe's letters to Harley for three months from early March the same year. Later that summer, Defoe publically attacked Harley's South Sea scheme, regretting the combining of the floatation of the national debt with the opening of the South Sea trade. From this, it can be deduced Harley did not respond positively to Defoe's proposals. In view of the number of documents Harley was sent, it is possible he never considered them at all. Thomas, who kept up to date with current affairs, most likely had read Defoe's views published in both the *Review* and in his *Essay on the South Sea Trade*. In September 1711, Thomas presented his own proposals to Harley possibly in response to Defoe's failure. Thomas suggested a commercial settlement at Valdivia, Chile, plus a support settlement and harbour at Anegada Bay in Patagonia on the Atlantic seaboard. These were remarkably similar to those of Defoe except considerably more detailed.

Unlike Defoe, Thomas appears to have received a response from Harley because he started a follow-up letter *In obedience to your Lords Commands*. As there is nothing in writing in Thomas' papers, it is likely the request had been made, in person, possibly via Defoe. In his response, Thomas supplied a list of those captains he knew to have been to Rio de Janerio. He lists five names who visited between 1697 and 1708. He also *presumed* to include his own notes on the region. According to Thomas, Valdivia was the closest port to the Straits of Magellan on the Pacific coast and, consequently, the closest to Britain. In his view, because the rival French and Spanish naval forces in the region were of similar size and balanced each other out, the way was clear for a small British force to take the port. Spanish reinforcements were sixteen hundred miles away in Lima and the intervening territory was hostile. There were one thousand Spaniards at Valdivia but these had been exiled from Peru. He also believed the sizeable indigenous population around Valdivia, Chile were enemies of the Spanish. Thomas reasoned both the Spanish in Valdivia and the indigenous population were likely to side with the British.

The countryside around Valdivia was healthy with plentiful natural resources. It had a good harbour and could be provisioned from Juan Fernandez only three or four days sail away. Again similarly to Defoe, Thomas reasoned Valdivia was only five hundred miles overland from Anegada Bay clearly demonstrating he had no actual experience in the region. The distance is more like seven hundred and sixty miles as the condor flies and anyone who had seen the Andes was unlikely to suggest crossing them regularly as an alternative to sailing through the Straits of Magellan. However, the overriding reason for selecting this port over any other in the South Sea was that Valdivia produced the most gold.

The proposals continued with detailed instructions for setting up the settlements in both Anegada Bay and Valdivia. Thomas set a deadline for the first ship to depart from Britain by the end of November 1711. He followed up these proposals with a letter stressing the need to set the scheme in motion as soon as possible and a further, seventeen-page *Essay* setting out precisely how the South Sea trade should be carried out. On 28 February 1712, Thomas wrote to his friend James Dolliffe, one of the committee of directors of the South Sea Company, following up on his proposals he had sent to the Company. He was concerned about the time it was taking for an expeditionary force to be sent to establish the first settlement.

Thomas backed his belief in his proposition by investing £810, 6 shillings and 2 pence, worth over £115,000 today, in the new South Sea Company. His investment is shown on the receipt as covering the *Victualling Bill* of Francis Holloway dated 31 March 1708 plus the interest at 6% per annum due on the bill.

This demonstrates how each purchase of shares in the company went to repay a very specific government debt. Despite Thomas' efforts, as well as those of Defoe and others, no attempt was ever made by the South Sea Company to set up settlements on either coast of South America. Less than a decade later but long after Thomas' death, the South Sea Bubble crashed spectacularly. After the Bubble had burst, a contemporary observer commented the project was *a gross, palpable illusion*. Defoe was correct in his belief that the floatation of the national debt should not be linked to the formation of the Company. Thomas did not share his doubts but died before his short-sightedness resulted in a huge loss to himself.

CHAPTER 11

Preparing for Mortality (1710-1713)

The London to which Thomas Bowrey returned to just two decades earlier had changed and, in the main, it was due to merchants such as him. Increasing overseas' trade, despite all the challenges reported by his friends, was bringing greater wealth to the capital, benefiting the rising middle classes. The middling sort now had status as well as wealth and London provided the opportunities to spend it in venues such as the China House set up for Thomas' Davis relative. But there is little evidence that Thomas took advantage of the new consumerism beyond the coffee house and the spa. He remained prudent with his wealth.

As Thomas moved towards the end of his life, did he have an increasing sense of failure? A high percentage of his shipping ventures had ended in that way but, with all his experience, Thomas understood the risk before he embarked on them. He had repatriated his wealth from the East slowly, over a number of years, using many different ships. It was a fortune large enough for him to retire but he chose not to. Eventually he changed tack from shipping and diverted his energies into his projects with their twin objectives of improving his country's trade and recovering his own losses. It is easy to imagine his mounting disappointment as each one floundered whether from his lack of influence, the lack of political will or simply because they were ahead of their time. But he never stopped trying just as he never stopped fighting for compensation for the loss of the *Worcester*. This relentless activity started after Thomas' loss of nerve on the *St George Galley* in 1696. Having almost lost friends and reputation, perhaps he never wanted to be seen to quit again.

THE KING'S HEAD INN

Despite Thomas' multiple concerns he retained his compassion towards family, friends and associates until the end of his life. He had been renting the King's Head Inn, a coaching inn in Southwark since shortly after his return to England, initially from Thomas Lowfield for nineteen pounds per half year. In turn he sublet the inn. By 1706, ownership of the inn had transferred to Peter Briggins, a prominent Quaker who kept a diary in which he recorded details of the Friends' meeting he attended and brief notes about his business affairs. Briggins recorded searching for Thomas each half-year as the rent became due, sometimes not finding him for many days. Whether Thomas was deliberately avoiding Briggins is not clear but he was often late in paying. There is no record of who Thomas was subletting the inn to until 1 November 1709 when a Thomas Gillotts signed a statement admitting he was unable to pay the quarter's rent due the previous Lady's Day. He agreed to pay the arrears due at the rate of one shilling a day. The statement was witnessed by Joseph Noden, Thomas' servant.

Gillotts appears to have struggled to make a success of running the inn because he signed similar promises in April 1711,

April 1712 and the following July. Gillotts' rent was one shilling a day or eighteen pounds, five shillings a year – about twenty-five thousand pounds per annum in today's values and he again agreed to pay the arrears at one shilling a day until it was repaid. Thomas was now only paying Briggins thirty pounds and five shillings per annum but it is difficult to understand the economics of the Kings Head for him. He was making a loss of twelve pounds per year or over seventeen hundred pounds in today's values and yet was still willing to be lenient about late payment of rent. As Thomas was usually ruthless in his business dealings except with people known to be family members, perhaps Gillotts was a retired seamen from one of his ships.

DEATH OF ELIZABETH GARDINER

In November 1710, there was a tragedy in the family when Thomas Bowrey's sister-in-law, Elizabeth Gardiner, died aged just 42. Although Thomas married Mary rather than her elder sister, they had all lived together in the same house almost continually for fourteen years. Elizabeth was more sophisticated and literate than Mary with a much steadier signature and he chose her, rather than Mary, to assist him in his business affairs.

Elizabeth died of *rumetis*. This was probably a form of rheumatic illness all of which cause inflammation and chronic pain in joints or connective tissue. Even today the complications from rheumatoid arthritis can be fatal as can be rheumatic fever and rheumatoid endocarditis, all of which are associated with a higher risk of vascular diseases such as stroke and heart attack, respiratory diseases and certain types of cancer. Whatever form

Elizabeth's disease took, there was no effective treatment at the time and consequently she suffered a great deal of pain, over many years, with associated compromised mobility. She had written her will two years earlier when she was already *weak in body* and had, perhaps, contemplated her death for some time. Her will included detailed instructions for her funeral.

On 3 December, Elizabeth was buried in the chancel of St Katherine by the Tower parish church as she directed. If her instructions were carried out in full, this was under the communion table, which probably meant in the vault beneath the chancel. Her body was carried to the church in a hearse drawn by six horses and attended by as many relations and friends as her executor thought suitable in up to three coaches also drawn by six horses each. Puritans had opposed lavish funerals and there was still an understanding that, although sufficient ceremony was needed for propriety, additional pomp was indecent. Compared to other funerals of the time, Elizabeth's was decent rather than vulgar. Hundreds of people may have processed to the church in dozens of coaches at an extravagant funeral intended to impress the neighbours with the deceased's importance.

Also in her will, Elizabeth left her mother, Frances, her lifetime use of some of her property in Great Clacton, Essex, plus all her jewellery, plate and household goods. Eventually, this property was to be sold to provide education for fifty poor children. Elizabeth's remaining property in Great Clacton was bequeathed to her sister. The following March, Frances Gardiner sold Thomas all Elizabeth's household goods, silver, jewellery and books that may have included her half share of the household goods left by her late father. The contract for this sale additionally provided Thomas with an annuity of £25 per annum (worth about £3,000 today) to be paid out of the rents from Frances' property in Great Clacton. This annuity had been bequeathed to Frances by her late husband. It was possibly intended to provide an income to cover the cost of maintaining the household at Well Close Square and its transfer to Thomas may have marked his taking over that responsibility. From this date there are more household bills in his surviving papers.

Shortly after Elizabeth's death, Thomas approached the lawyer, John Hungerford, with questions about her estate. He was concerned that her debts to him be settled from the sale of her chattels and that both her mother, Frances Gardiner, and her sister, Mary Bowrey, should retained the full value of their inheritance for their own use. Whilst it is difficult to be certain what was in his mind after all this time, it does seem that Thomas was concerned to protect Frances' and Mary's financial independence at a time when a woman usually lost this on marriage. The law in England in this respect was harsher than in any other European country. He had lived among men from countries where married women were more financially independent. He had witnessed the total dependence of his English female friends on men in India where a widow had no choice but to remarry so that she and her children could survive. His experience had shaped his enlightened views.

SEARLE FAMILY MEDIATION

There is a further example of Thomas' standing among his friends when, on 23 July 1712, Captain Andrew Searle wrote to Thomas. He was helping to resolve a conflict between Searle and his son, also called Andrew, concerning his son's debts. The Searles were a prominent family from the Epping area of Essex and the son was facing debtors' prison. The father was concerned the son's debts were greater than the value of Chambers, their house in Essex. There is a separate listing of the debts showing they amounted to £991, 10 shillings, the equivalent of over £140,000 today. A little over a half were described as *old debts* and the rest *new debts*. There is no indication of how the son incurred such a large debt but, as he owed smaller amounts to Thomas, his father and another Searle relative, perhaps, he had already borrowed to pay off the most urgent.

Thomas had previous experience of helping to resolve the debts of his Middleton uncle and in September, he wrote to the son with the proposed resolution to this dispute. Searle had generously agreed to settle his son's debts and would also pay £200 or £300 *ready money* to his son. In addition, his grandson, yet another Andrew, would be sent to university to enable him to earn his own living. All the son was expected to do was to sell his house in Duck Lane. Thomas wrote to Searle at the same time saying he believed the offer to be kind and reasonable. What is puzzling is why Thomas needed to intervene to persuade the captain's son to accept his father's offer and why he felt it necessary to point out that his wife and children would become destitute if he did not accept it.

THOMAS BOWREY'S HEALTH & DEATH

Thomas spent nineteen years in the East Indies, a part of the world harmful to the health of Europeans. Most were lucky if they survived two monsoons. Alcohol, diet and the heat all took their toll. Cholera, typhoid and malaria, contributed to the death rate and as many as a third of the East India Company's overseas personnel died each year. At the time, malaria was endemic in swampy areas of England and people living in those areas acquired some resistance not present in the rest of the population. No doubt, the local population in the East Indies also acquired such immunity.

The only record of Thomas suffering ill-health whilst in the east was during the period December 1683 to January 1684. At that time, he was experiencing fever and ague, and there was some concern he may not survive. *Ague* was the term used for intermittent fever and usually referred to malaria. Transmitted by the bite of an infected mosquito, in Thomas' day ague was believed to be caused by the bad air in areas of marsh and stagnant water. Because of this, in many areas it was considered healthier to remain on board a ship than live ashore. It is known Thomas ignored this wisdom in Fort St George, Achin and Porto Novo.

The symptoms of malaria began a week or two after being bitten by a mosquito when the parasites escaped from the liver and started attacking the red blood cells. The first signs of having contracted the disease were pain in the head and loin, weariness in the limbs, coldness in the extremities and vomiting. Next came shivering and shaking and then the fever or ague. If not successfully treated, the parasites remained in the blood system and the destruction of the red blood cells eventually resulted in major organ failure and death. In Thomas' day, the only known treatment was quinine, also known as Jesuit bark, which could prevent the development of malaria parasites in the blood if it was taken early and for long enough but, today, it is usually reinforced with other medication.

After Thomas had returned to England, various correspondents commented on his being unwell, the first time in December 1696 and then during various summers between 1702 and 1712. There were probably other unrecorded periods of sickness. Thomas' visits to Bath and Tunbridge Wells may have been for health reasons. In January 1713, Thomas paid Dr James Sherard's bill for medicines supplied in December 1711 and October 1712. Sherard was an apothecary who had served his apprenticeship at the Chelsea Physic Garden and was a neighbour of Thomas' friend, Nathaniel Long, in Mark Lane. He became wealthy through his practice and supplied the Bowreys with *Lung Potion*, spa water and *Histerick Water*, used for treating problems associated with the womb. He also supplied *Elixir Proprietatis*, a useful medicine claimed to be effective against everything from wind to the plague, and *Cordial Julep*, for depression. *Electuary*, a sweet syrup, was used for making medicines palatable. *Jesuit Bark*, or quinine, was known to be effective against ague but tasted bitter to some people.

On 11 March 1712, Thomas Bowrey wrote his final will and was *at this present in health of Body and of Sound and perfect memory and mind*. He was also in good health when he drafted an earlier will in April 1706. In this draft, he planned to leave £1,000 to be used to purchase land within one hundred miles of London to produce an annual income of £1 to pay for a sermon to be preached on 7 September each year, his birthday, in the Parish Church of St Johns Wapping. This bequest was not included in his later will although his friend, John Russell, was still the minister at Wapping at this time.

Thomas' first two bequests in his final will were of his *Manuscript Book in a Green Cover* to the East India Company and his *Manuscript book of draughts and descriptions of the Coast of America* to the South Sea Company. I have been unable to trace either of these books. He bequeathed his clothes, sword, remaining books, journals and maps Mary did not wish to keep for herself to his cousin Thomas Studds. In December 1711, Thomas had catalogued his books, presumably as part of getting his affairs in order but useful in providing further insight into his character and interests. Ever ready to expand his knowledge and skills, when local publisher Jeremiah Seller published a new volume of John Seller's *Practical Navigation* in 1699, Thomas purchased a copy. It sat alongside Grenville Collins' *Great Britain's Coasting Pilot* and George St Lo's *England's Safety, ... a Sure Method for Encouraging Navigation, and Raising Qualified Seamen* ... He also owned instructional works on agriculture, brewing, distilling, glass making, smithing, joinery, carpentry, farming and bricklaying ensuring that he could speak with some authority to the tradesmen he dealt with. Alongside acts of Parliament and volumes on trade, travel, history, philosophy and religion, there were books that looked back to his time in the East Indies including Edward Tyso's *Orang-Outang* and Robert Knox's *An Historical Relation of the Island of Ceylon.* For a man who published the first English-Malay dictionary, it is unsurprising that Thomas possessed English, Dutch-Malay and French-English dictionaries as well as a French-English grammar and New Testaments in Dutch, French and Malay.

It is impossible to estimate Thomas' wealth from his will. He made cash bequests to friends and charity amounting to one hundred pounds, the equivalent of over £14,000 today, leaving the residue to his widow. However when Mary died two years later, she left the interest on her estate for the benefit of her mother for the remainder of her life and, after her death, the estate was to be used to set up an almshouse for poor men who had been *bred up to the Sea and past their labour* and widows of seamen. The almshouse was to bear an inscription in her and Thomas' memory. With no close family members surviving after the death of Frances Gardiner, Thomas' mother-in-law, in 1720 there was no one to oversee the trustees and the parish of Stepney was forced to take action in the Court of Chancery. The case was won in 1740 and, four years later, land purchased and eight almshouses built, one for each of the hamlets in the parish, plus a committee room. In the centre of this room, a tablet was installed bearing the inscription:

These Almshouses were built A.D. 1744 Under the will of Mrs Mary Bowrey The relict of Captain Thomas Bowrey for poor Seaman and their Widows of Ratcliff, Poplar, Bethnal Green, Mile End Old Town, Mile End New Town, St George, St Anne, Christ Church.

In 1878, the site of the almshouses was sold for £2,700, almost a quarter of a million pounds today, the money invested and the income administered by the parish of Stepney for the benefit of eight widows. The charity lasted another one hundred and twenty years before being removed from the register of the Charity Commission because the funds had been spent up.

By 5 March 1713, Thomas may have been aware that he was close to death and unable to venture out. He met with Peter Briggins that morning before the next half-year's rent was due on the King's Head Inn. They discussed insurance, whether this was on the inn is not recorded in his diary, but Briggins visited the insurance office on Thomas' behalf later that day. No meeting between the two men is recorded after this date so it is not known when Thomas died but, on 13 March 1713 aged just fifty-three, his body was sent from St John Wapping, where his friend John Russell was the minister, to the church where he and Mary married, St Margaret Lee Kent. He was buried the following day in a vault in the churchyard. Unlike his sister-in-law, he left no written instructions for his funeral and burial. In his 1706 draft will he had specified: *My Body I commit to be Decently Buried by my Executors ... in yᵉ Parish Church of Lee in Kent near Blackheath* but there was no such clause in his final will. It is likely he and Mary had discussed where they both wanted to be laid to rest and in her will she left £200 for a monument to be erected in her remembrance to be placed on or near the vault. If there was a memorial to Thomas, it has long since disappeared. Only the old church tower at Lee still stands. A new church was built on the other side of the road. Many of the monuments in the old churchyard are listed, including that of Edmund Halley who died in 1742, but there is not one for Thomas among them.

His memorial is his writing: his Malay-English Dictionary, his posthumously published *Bay of Bengal* and his papers distributed through a number of repositories. When a standard Romanised spelling system for Malay was developed in 1972, it was in part based on that developed by Thomas. His *Bay of Bengal* manuscript remains an important historical source for India, Malaysia and Indonesia. Thomas' papers are still studied by academics and other researchers in a number of areas of the early-modern period from letter-writing to marine insurance. But, even today, the strongest emotions are still stirred up by the one incident that Thomas never let drop, the saga of the *Worcester*.

It can still divide the Scots and the English and the union of the two countries is as much a contentious topic today as it was in Thomas' day. If he could reflect on his legacy he may be surprised but he would probably be satisfied. After all, he has not been forgotten.

Old Churchyard St Margaret Lee.

The Story that Refuses to Die

One day in 2005, a Wootton man walked into a Bonhams' valuation day at Cowes with a pair of volumes written between 1689 and 1695. According to a report i
n the *Isle of Wight County Press* the following March, he claimed to be the last descendant of the Bowrey line and the books had been passed down to him through the family. The manuscripts, a mixture of log book, memoranda and reminiscence including a journal of a two-year voyage from England to Bengal and an account of islands and bays in the East Indies, were to be sold at the Bond Street auction house a few weeks later. Someone compared handwriting samples and, before the volumes came under the hammer, a notice had been appended to the catalogue entry advising the lot appeared to be a mid-eighteenth-century family transcript, and not in Thomas Bowrey's hand. As a result, the original estimate of up to £15,000 was reduced to £5,000-£6,000. Despite this, the two manuscript books excited a great deal of interest and were purchased on behalf of a major American university library for an extraordinary £40,800, including fees.

When I discovered reports of this sale many years later at the start of my research into Thomas' life, I experienced the same excitement. The auction catalogue entry repeated the biographical details contained in the volumes. Was this the answer to Thomas' origins? A little more research uncovered that they were considered of such national importance that, before an export licence could be granted for the two books, copies had to be made by the British Library. The logbook, which contained the biographical details, also included two drafts of Thomas' will similar enough to his final will to confirm it purported to relate to the same person but my excitement was not to last long. Once I was able to study the manuscripts, I quickly understood something was not right. The style and content simply were not consistent with that of the man I had come to know. The volumes contained tales of purposeless exploration and gratuitous violence. It was impossible to understand which locations were visited. Having studied thousands of his papers I had some confidence in my judgement but further analysis was required.

In his will, Thomas left his books and journal to his cousin, Thomas Studds, with the exception of his manuscript book of the description of the coast of Africa in a green cover and a similar one of the coasts of America. He wished these to go to the East India Company and the South Sea Company respectively. Although there is evidence his widow, Mary, was preparing the second and intended to send it to James Pym, the secretary of the South Sea Company, if they have survived no trace of them remains of them in any catalogue and their descriptions do not fit the Isle of Wight Journal and Logbook.

ANALYSIS OF THE ISLE OF WIGHT
JOURNAL & LOGBOOK

There are four ways in which two collections of manuscripts can be compared to determine whether they have been created by the same person: provenance, handwriting, writing style and content. The handwriting had rightly been questioned before the volumes were sold.

Provenance: Despite a number of requests, I have been unable to establish what due diligence, if any, was carried out by the major American university library that purchased the manuscripts. In view of this, I have attempted to establish their provenance myself. The vendor of the Isle of Wight Journal and Logbook claimed to have been *last descendant of the Bowrey line* and that the volumes had been bequeathed to him. Thomas Bowrey and his wife, Mary, had no children. He was predeceased by his parents and siblings. None of his Bowrey uncles had children. Although there may be descendants from Thomas' Middleton cousins, there is no Bowrey line descending from Thomas or his close relations. In my opinion, the provenance of the manuscripts is at least questionable.

Writing Style: Subjectively, the writing style in the two books is in no way similar to that of the *Bay of Bengal* manuscript or the papers discovered at Cleeve Prior. More formally, stylometry is *the statistical analysis in literary style between one writer or genre and another*. It is what has been used to examine texts believed possibly to have been written by Shakespeare and other writers. Unfortunately, I found the material available was not suitable to apply these techniques.

Content: A number of the entries in the Journal and Logbook conflict with known events in Thomas Bowrey's life and these are set out in Appendix II.

In my opinion, there can be no doubt the Logbook and Journal are forgeries. That someone believed it worth the considerable effort required to produce them, is some measure of the continued interest in Thomas Bowrey's life. If his story has not been told in full before, there are elements of the story that refuse to die.

THE CONTINUED INTEREST IN THOMAS BOWREY

Although very much a man of his times, Thomas Bowrey remains capable of inciting excitement even today. This is even truer of the subjects that interested him most: piracy, slavery and globalisation. He remains relevant today. The auction was not the only recent press excitement concerning Thomas Bowrey. If you search for him on the Internet, you will quickly find reports of the Wellcome Trust's *High Society* exhibition between 11 November 2010 and 7 February 2011 at which Thomas' handwritten description of his experiment with *bhang* was displayed. The same story has been published in a number of works about recreational drugs. Hot debate about the case of the *Worcester* continues in certain circles. J. Irvine Smith's lecture on *The Trial of Captain Green* to the Annual General Meeting of the Stair Society in Edinburgh in 1998 is just one example. Thomas' dictionary is still studied and, with the emergence of India as a major economic power, so increasingly is his posthumously published *Bay of Bengal* book.

There is no sign of interest in Thomas' life and work dying out.

Notes

PREFACE

DATES
Ancestry 1: St. Margaret Lee Burial
    Register 14 March 1712/13
Blanchard: page 10
Waller: page xxiii
WDYTYA: Issue 116, Summer
    2016. Pages 77-78

MONETARY VALUES
Bowrey (1927): pages 114-115
Measuring Worth

MEASURES
Bowrey (1927): page 116

POLITICS OF PRE-COLONIAL
INDIA
Wikipedia (Aurangzeb)
Wikipedia (Mughal Empire)
Wikipedia (Nawab)
Wikipedia (Princely States)

EAST INDIA COMPANY
Encyclopaedia
Farrington (2002): pages 10, 23,
    29, 44, 48
Keay: locations 3405, 3979
Prakash: page 2
Theodora
Wikipedia (East India Company)

INTRODUCTION: THE PAPER TRAIL

THE BOWREY PAPERS
BL (D1076)
BL (E192)
Bowrey (1927): General
    Introduction, page 3
Christies
Healey: pages 253-254
Humphreys
LMA (24176)
LMA (3041)
Quaker House: D1-5 folios 4, 7
Stanford
Temple (1930)
TNA (Wills): PROB 11/578/249
    Will of Frances Gardiner,
    widow of Stepney, Middlesex
TNA (Wills): PROB 11/578/193
    Will of Robert Bushell of
    Cleeve Prior, Worcestershire

THE BAY OF BENGAL
MANUSCRIPT
Anderson (1890): page 266
BL (D782)
Bowrey (1701)
Bowrey (1927): page 122
Bowrey (1997): pages xv, xlii, xliii-
    xliv
LMA (Briggins): 22 October 1706,
    18 & 25 April, 24, 25 & 28
    October & 1, 6 & 7 November
    1707, 16 April, 15 October,
    26 November & 30 December
    1708, 11 April & 15 October
    1712, 5, 11, 17 & 19 March
    1712/13, 25 & 28 March & 9
    April 1713

OED (Cheroot)
Wikipedia (Temple)
Yule: page clxxxiii (183)

THE ESSEX MANUSCRIPTS
ERO

THE SLOANE CHARTS
BL (3972B): folio 390
BL (5222): Add Ms 5222.6, Add
    Ms 5222.7, Add Ms 5222.8,
    Add Ms 5222.9, Add Ms
    5222.10, Add Ms 5222.11,
    Add Ms 5222.12, Add Ms
    5222.13, Add Ms 5222.14,
    Add Ms 5222.15, Add Ms
    5222.16, Add Ms 5222.17
Delbourgo
Gill: locations 200-204
Jones: pages 38-40, 51
Madden: Preface, page 55
TNA (Wills): PROB 11/532/176
    Will of Thomas Bowrey of
    Stepney, Middlesex
Williams (1997): page 120

THE IDENTITY OF THOMAS
BOWREY
BL (D1076): folios 97-98, 259
Bowrey (1701): Preface
Bowrey (1997): pages xviii-xxiii,
    1-2
LMA (24176): folio 1588

THE LIFE OF THOMAS BOWREY
Wikipedia (Temple)

CH.1: EARLY LIFE

THE BEGINNINGS
Ancestry 1: St. Dunstan and All
    Saints Burial Register 13 March
    1712/13
Ancestry 1: St. John Wapping
    Baptism Register October 1660
Ancestry 1: St. John Wapping
    Baptism Register September
    1661
Ancestry 1: St. John Wapping
    Baptism Register 17 March
    1664/65
Ancestry 1: St. Margaret Lee Burial
    Register 14 March 1712/13
Ancestry 1: St. Margaret Lee
    Marriage Register 17
    September 1691
Bastable: page 48
Blanchard: pages 115-128
Bowrey (1927): pages xxix-xxx
Bowrey (1997): pages xxiv-xxv
British History (Interregnum)
Capp: pages 155-159
Davies (2008): locations 451-454,
    2323, 2449-2435, 2985-2986,
    3216-3218
Green (1860): page 269
Green (1880): pages 595-596
Green (1881): page 572
Green (1882): pages 399-400, 486
Green (1883): pages 469, 472
Green (1884): pages 406, 459, 462,
    466, 502, 511, 523
Green (1885): pages 289, 297, 302-
    303, 305, 426, 439-455, 489,
    516, 529, 542, 560, 563
Green (1886): pages 450, 478, 484,
    491, 492, 514
Herber: pages 125-128
Hunt (2004)
Lambeth Palace: Marriage licence
    allegation for Thomas Bowrey
    and Mary Gardiner 14
    September 1691

Laurence: pages 28, 76-77, 78-79

LMA (3041): 9(i) & (ii) doc 8 Draft
    will dated 13 April 1706 (no
    folios)

Pepys 1

FAMILY

Ancestry 1: St. John Wapping
    Baptism Register 25 June 1626

Ancestry 1: St. John Wapping
    Baptism Register 12 February
    1629/30

Ancestry 1: St. John Wapping
    Baptism Register 7 March 1635

Ancestry 1: St. John Wapping
    Marriage Register 27
    September 1657

Ancestry 1: St. Mary Whitechapel
    Marriage Register 14 July 1640

Ancestry 1: St. Nicholas Deptford
    Baptism Register May 1624

Ancestry 1: St. Nicholas Deptford
    Marriage Register 16 June
    1623

Ancestry 2: Will of Elianor Bowrey
    30 April 1669 MS72/60 Will
    number 158

Bowrey (1997): page xxv

British History (Interregnum)

Herber: pages 125-128

LMA (3041): 9(i) & (ii) doc 6
    Affidavit of Elizabeth Smith (no
    folios)

CHILDHOOD

Ancestry 1: St. Dunstan and All
    Saints Stepney Baptism Register
    25 January 1662/63

Ancestry 1: St. John Wapping
    Baptism Register 19 June 1664

Ancestry 1: St. John Wapping
    Baptism Register 17 March
    1664/65

Ancestry 1: St. Mary Whitechapel
    Burial Register 10 September
    1665

Bowrey (1997): page xxv

Davies (2008): locations 3019,
    3077-3091

Earle (1991): pages 65, 238-239

Green (1886): pages 450, 478, 484,
    491, 492, 514

Lindsay: page 13

PLAGUE

Ancestry 1: St. Mary Whitechapel
    Burial Register 10 September
    1665

Bastable: pages 169-207

Bowrey (1997): Administration
    Book, 1670 and 1672, at
    Somerset House quoted page
    xxv

Harvey

Porter (2005): pages 189-251

Porter (2011): pages 110-113

UNCLE JOHN

Ancestry 1: St. Peter Cornhill
    Marriage Register 12 February
    1649/50

Anglo-Dutch Wars

Bowrey (1997): page xxiv

Capp: pages 159, 379

Daniell (1902): pages 1-110

Gardiner: page 19

Green (1861): pages 331, 452, 523

Green (1864): page 510

Green (1877): page 617

Green (1879): page 439

Green (1882): pages 486, 498, 502,
    505, 510, 514, 519

Green (1883): page 421

Green (1884): pages 213, 417, 467,
    500, 520

Green (1885): pages 110, 301, 503,
    506, 511, 523, 562

Hearth Tax (1666)

Measuring Worth

Pepys 2

FIRE
Bastable: pages 208-248
Blanchard: pages 178-181
Channel 5 a
Channel 5 b
Channel 5 c
Hanson: pages 3-14, 17-34, 73-89
LMA (3041): 2 petition dated
    March 1696 (no folios)
Pickard: pages 25-27
Tomalin: pages 227-235

THE END OF CHILDHOOD
BL (H49): folios 91-96, 107, 114,
    129, 143, 183-189, 218-237,
    383-390, 991
Bombay:
Bowrey (1977): page 2
Davies (2008): locations 2974-
    2977, 4294-4297
Davies (2017): locations 444-446,
    1853-1859, 4615-4616
Earle (1998): pages 19-20, 22, 24-
    25
Farrington (1999): page 732
Foster (1927): pages 105, 111, 113,
    126, 138, 157, 158
Fryer (1909): pages 159-182
Gokhale: pages 7-9, 95, 101
LMA (3041): Ms3041/2 (no folios)
LMA (3041): 9(i) & (ii) doc 6
    Power of attorney Elizabeth
    Smith 17 February 1669 (no
    folios)
LMA (3041): 9(i) & (ii) doc 7
    Power of attorney Samuel
    Smith 27 December 1666 (no
    folios)
Pepys 3
Sandes: pages 17-19
Weapons and Warfare

CH.2: LEARNING HIS TRADE

1669
BL (H49): folios 91-96, 107, 114,
    129, 143, 183-189, 218-237,
    383-390, 991
Bowrey (1701): Preface
Bowrey (1997): pages 2-4, 6, 158-
    160
Delbourgo: location 3906
Farrington (1999)
Farrington (2002): page 30
Foster (1925): pages 313-323
Foster (1927): pages 99-118, 221-
    244
Fryer (1698): page 36
Fryer (1909): pages 103-108
Love: page 268
Mukherji: page 299
Prakash 2: page 214
Reid: pages 1-7

1670
BL (D1076): folios 300-303, 335-
    336, 351-352, 358-359
Bowrey (1997): pages 50-51
Bulley: location 60, 360-363
Earle (1998): pages 22-24
Encyclopaedia
Farrington (2002): pages 10, 25, 34,
    51, 64, 72-76
Gaastra: pages 50-51
Keay: locations 155, 2496, 2625,
    3193, 4010
Lenham: pages 101-102, 106
LMA (24176): folios 326, 338, 445
LMA (3041): Ms03041/4A copy
    letter 10 January 1705 (no
    folios)
LMA (9172): Ms9172/60 will
    number 158, Elianor Bowrey
    written 21 April 1669 proved
    30 April 1699
Love: page 269

Measuring Worth
Prakash: pages 1-3, 4
Reddy: locations 29, 1547
Rittman: pages 1-2
Theodora
Wikipedia (East India Company)

1672
Banerjee: pages 202-205, 211-213
BL (Blogs): Thomas Bowrey's Cloth
    Samples, http://blogs.bl.uk/
    untoldlives /2017/06/thomas-
    bowreys-cloth-samples.html
BL (D782)
BL (D1076): folios 364, 365-366
Bowen (2011): page 41
Bowrey (1997): pages 9, 14, 36-40,
    53-59, 100, 181, 203-204, 251
Chaudhuri: page 201
Crill: pages 9, 16-57, 244
Dijk: page 163
Encyclopaedia
Farrington (2002): page 39
Foster (1921): pages 102, 104, 185,
    391
Fryer (1698): page 152
Fryer (1909): page 256
Hall: pages 62-63, 78-81, 83
Harris: pages 42, 104-105
Hawley: pages 3-12
Hedges: volume 2, pages 199-200
Love: volume 1, page 202
Mentz: pages 165, 248
Nayar: pages 52-52, 59
Prakash: pages 3-6
Prakesh 3: page 245
Rittman: pages 4-5
Sen: pages 14-23, 253-255
Sharma: pages 1-6, 19-24
Shodhganga
Wikipedia (Machilipatnam)

1674
Bowrey (1997): pages 6. 9, 10, 11,
    12, 14, 15, 18, 24, 25, 26, 27,
    29, 32-34, 35, 37, 38, 41, 76,
    88, 94-96, 98, 129-130, 141,
    152-164

Holberg: page 410
Hunter: page 283
Mishra: pages 301-310
OED (Cheroot)
Shodhganga
Thornton: pages 249-250
Tripathy: pages 55-56, 59-62, 64

1675
Barnett
BL (D782)
BL (D1076): folio 121
Bowrey (1997): pages 235-255,
    311-321
Bulley: locations 62, 65-68, 70-72,
    87-90, 165-176, 177-179,
    189-190, 226-231, 276-277,
    287-288, 347-352, 1157-1162,
    1459-1463
Chaudhuri: pages 201-203, 208-209
Coates: pages vii, 12, 20
EIC Ships
Farrington (2002): pages 24, 54,
    77, 79
Graf: page 3
Hedges: Volume I page 118
Keay: locations 413, 2340
Lahiri: pages 169-170
Love: page 270
Marshall: pages 229-230
Measuring Worth
Murphy
Ovington: page 280
Prakash: pages 4-5
Quiason: pages 64-65, 70, 79
Reddy: location 394
Rittman: page 3
Shodhganga
Theodora
Wikipedia (Phuket)
Wikipedia (Taj ul-Alam)

1676
BL (5222): chart 8
Bowrey (1997): pages xix, 78-81,
    159, 172-178
Davenport-Hines: page 1786

Duvall:
Frank: locations 2077, 2079, 3298, 4640
Hugli-River
Kowl
Master: pages 322-324
Ulak
Wikipedia (Flyboat)
Wikipedia (Hooghly River)

1677
Ahmed: pages 292-293
BL (D782)
Bowrey (1997): pages 255-260
MacKay: chapter 14
Smith (2011): page 85

CH.3: BRANCHING OUT

Bowrey (1997): pages xvii-xxiii
BL (D782)
BL (D1076)
BL (E192)

1680 LETTER OF S ADDERTON DECEMBER
BL (D1076): folios 1-2, 14-16, 17
BL (G3-19): 14 April 1670
ERO: folio 10
Farrington (2007): pages 423-424, 438, 472-473
Fawcett (1936): pages 39, 51, 90, 91, 95, 100, 107, 115, 156, 184
Fawcett (1954): pages 16, 20, 44, 52, 53, 60, 72, 84, 89, 125-127, 130-137, 169, 170, 179, 205, 207, 289, 333, 335, 337
Forrest: pages 142-143
Strackey: pages 15, 67, 70, 71-74, 82, 92, 93, 94, 95, 96, 161

1682
Anderson (1890): pages 220-221

BL (D1076): folios 18-32, 33, 34-36, 37, 38, 39-40
BL (5222): chart 8, 13, 14, 15, 16, 17
Bowrey (1997): page 37
Bulley: locations 347-352, 1459-1463
Chaudhuri: pages 202-203
Cotton: pages 5, 8
Factory Records
Marshall: pp 229-230
Measuring Worth
Ovington: p 280
Winterbottom (2016): page 123

1683
BL (D1076): folios 18-32, 33, 41-44, 45, 46, 47, 48, 49-50, 51, 52-53, 54-55, 56, 57
BL (G24-2): page 43
Bowrey (1997): pages xxvii, 100, 167-170, 277
Factory Records
Measuring Worth
O'Connor: page 87
Pringle (1894): page 111
Shodhganga

1684
BL (D1076): folios 58-59, 60, 61, 62-63, 64, 65, 66-67, 68-69, 70, 73, 74, 76-77, 80-81, 82-83, 86
Bowrey (1997): pages xxvii, 123, 246
Farringdon (2002): pages 26, 76
Frank: locations 2077, 2079, 3298, 4640
Grundy: page 13
Measuring Worth
OED (Orangutan)
Pringle (1895 1): pages 89, 92-93, 101, 110, 150
Wikipedia (Bay)
Wikipedia (Ennore Creek)
Wikipedia (Monsoon)
Wikipedia (Monsoon of South Asia)

1685
BL (D1076): folios 75, 87-88, 89-95, 96, 99-106, 110, 111-112, 114, 117, 119
BL (G24-1): pages 5-7
Bowrey (1997): pages xxvii-xxviii
Ling: page xxii
LMA (24176): folios 1518, 1520
Pringle (1895 2): pages 5, 135, 137, 164
Shodhganga

CH.4: MOVING ON

1686
BL (D1076): folios 118, 120, 121
Bowrey (1997): pages xxviii-xxix
Dodwell (1913): pages 10, 14, 75, 81, 94, 104
Geni.com
Skeel

1687
Amrith: page 59
BL (D1076): folios 121, 122, 123, 124, 125, 126, 144, 154-157, 168, 169-170, 171-172, 175-176, 178-179, 180-181, 184, 185-186, 187-202, 203, 204-205, 207-229, 231-232. 236-237, 240-255
BL (G19-20): pages 144-146
BL (V27-36): pages 153-154
Bowrey (1997): pages xxix-xxxvii
Dodwell (1916 1): pages 6, 72, 76, 79, 94, 152
Francis: pages 49, 99, 128
Measuring Worth
Thornton: pages 212-213

1688
BL (D1076): folios 126, 127, 128, 129, 187-202, 207-229, 236-237, 238, 239, 240-255, 256, 258, 259

BL (L-AG-1-1-9)
Bowrey (1997): pages xxxvii-xl, 115, 135, 217, 226
Crill: page 106, 167,]244
Dampier (1937): locations
Dodwell (1916 2): pages 41, 47, 147
Earle (1991): page 115
Harris: pages 102-113
LMA (24176): folio 1516
Siam Records: pages 50-54
Wikipedia (Pulicat History)
Wikipedia (Pulicat)

CH.5: STARTING OUT AGAIN

Guillery: pages 70-73
Waller: pages 14-15, 27, 37, 40, 43, 44-45, 47, 64, 80-81, 92, 108, 134, 143, 144, 157-158, 183-186, 189-205, 206, 209-212, 213-230, 231-239, 251-256, 257, 273, 275-276
Wellclose

1689
Ancestry 1: St. John Wapping Baptism Register 13 March 1672/73
BL (D1076): folios 97-98, 125, 127, 129, 184, 234-235, 256, 261, 263, 264, 265, 267-268, 273, 298-299, 328, 362, 370
Earle (1991): pages 13-14
Farrington: pages 57, 734
LMA (24176): folios 1278, 1370, 1371-1373, 1588
Measuring Worth
1690
BL (D1076): folios 267-268, 317-318
Bowrey (1927): page 86
FEP

LMA (24176): folios 451, 453, 471

LMA (3041): 6(ii) receipted bills dated 1 May 1690, 28 October 1690, 16 January 1691 (no folios)

LMA (3041): 7(i) receipted bills relating to rental properties (no folios)

1691

Ancestry 1: St. Margaret Lee Marriage Register 17 September 1691

Earle (1998): pp 150, 180-185, 194-198

ERO: folio 10

Lambeth Palace: Marriage licence allegation for Thomas Bowrey and Mary Gardiner 14 September 1691

Lloyds Bank

LMA (24176): folios 928, 939, 980

LMA (30324): Printed list of Younger Brothers of Trinity House, 7 May 1691 Thomas Bowrey of Wapping, Master (no folios)

LMA (3041): 5 certificates for the purchase of Linen Company Shares 24 January 1691, statement from Thomas Bowrey dated 16 June 1693, receipted bill dated 16 September 1691 (no folios)

LMA (3041): 6(ii) receipted bill dated 10 July 1691 (no folios)

LMA (3041): 9(i) & (ii) Bill of sale Frances Gardiner to Thomas BOWREY 19 March 1711, Marriage Settlement between Thomas Bowrey and Phillip Gardiner dated 11 September 1691 (no folios)

LMA (9172): Ms9172/104 Will number 14, Elizabeth Gardiner written 26 September 1708 proved 12 January 1711

Worsley: locations 1283-1290

1692-1695

Aslet: pages 126-127, 134-135

BL (D1076): folios 146, 275-276, 278-279, 280-281, 282, 283, 284-285, 286-287, 288-289, 290-291, 292-293, 294-295, 296-297

BL (G20-2): December 1679

BL (G20-9): 10 January 1683

Chaudhuri: page 203

ERO: folio 4

Lloyds Bank

LMA (24176): folios 452, 472, 473, 474, 936, 941, 961, 1112, 1203, 1247, 1250, 1274, 1322, 1686, 1690

LMA (3041): 5 receipted bill dated 14 February 1693, draft statement dated 16 June 1693, assignment dated 27 November 1693, receipts dated 29 December 1693, 9 January 1694, 11 January 1694, 24 January 1694, 23 June 1694, 27 June 1694, 14 September 1694, 6 November 1694, 24 November 1694, 14 January 1695, receipted bill dated 14 January 1695, receipt dated 26 January 1695, 18 February 1695, 19 February 1695, 24 February 1695, 25 February 1695, 26 February 1695, 4 March 1695, 5 March 1695, 9 March 1695, 10 March 1695, 20 March 1695, 23 March 1695, 2 April 1695, 16 April 1695, 17 April 1695 (x2), 3 May 1695, 23 May 1695, 24 May 1695, 15 June 1695, 22 June 1695, 26 June 1695, 29 June 1695, statement of shares sold dated 7 July 1695, receipt dated 12 July 1695, 26 August 1695, receipted bill dated 31 August 1695, receipts dated 6

September 1695, 13 September 1695, 19 September 1695, 5 October 1695, 7 November 1695 (no folios)

LMA (3041): 6(ii) receipted bill dated 26 December 1692, bills dated 4 January 1695, 6 January 1695, receipted bill dated 21 August 1695, receipt dated 19 September 1695 (x2) (no folios)

LMA (3041): 7(v) statement dated July 1693 (no folios)

LMA (24176): folios 1278, 1370, 1371-1373, 1588

Measuring Worth

Wikipedia (Royal African Company)

6: THE *ST GEORGE* GALLEY

Encyclopaedia

Farrington (2002): pp 10, 23, 29, 44, 48

Keay: locations 3405, 3979

LMA (3041): Ms301/2 petition dated March 1696 (no folios)

Prakash: p 2

Theodora

Wikipedia (East India Company)

1696

BL (D1076): folios 269-270, 300-301, 302-303, 315-316, 317-318

Bowrey (1927): pages 224-225

LMA (24176): folios 961, 1121, 1138, 1139, 1141, 1156, 1160, 1161, 1169, 1179, 1182, 1183, 1188, 1191, 1192, 1193, 1195, 1204, 1208, 1213, 1231, 1233, 1691

LMA (3041): Ms301/9(i)&(ii) power of attorney dated 27 November 1696 (no folios)

Long Family

1697

Bowrey (1997): page 114

Earle (1998): pages 17-198

LMA (24176): folios 1125, 1139, 1142, 1159, 1160, 1166, 1176, 1179, 1187, 1190, 1196, 1215, 1254, 1255, 1256, 1257, 1279-1282, 1390, 1688

1698

BL (D1076): folios 315-316, 317-318, 328-329, 330-331

Bowrey (1927): pages 1-92

Defoe (1999): page xlvi

LMA (24176): folios 226-227, 1068, 1164, 1391

Wikipedia (Wars)

1699

Adams: locations 357-365

BL (B42): 22, 27 & 28 February 1699

BL (D1076): folios 306-307

Bowrey (1997): p xli

Chaudhuri: p 208

Dodwell (1913): page 30

Dodwell (1916 2): page 111

Dodwell (1918): pages 23-24

LMA (24176): folios 1388, 1399, 1401, 1583, 1660

LMA (3041): Ms3041/2 proposal dated February 1699 (no folios)

LMA (3041): Ms3041/6(i) butcher's account dated 15 June 1699, Bath account book dated 19 June to 15 July 1699 (no folios)

LMA (3041): Ms3041/6(ii) tailor's bill dated 29 July to 25 August 1699, receipt for rent dated 13 September 1699 (no folios)

Porter (2011): page 11

Smith (2015): pages 82-89

Waller: pages 11-12

CH.7: THE MALAY-ENGLISH DICTIONARY

LMA (24176): folios 1137, 1145, 1146, 1147, 1148, 1150, 1153, 1154, 1201, 1696

HENRY SMITH
BL (D1076): folios 300-301
BL (G3-2): 9 September 1680
Defoe (1999): page 676
Fawcett (1954): pages 20, 72, 84, 125-127, 130-137, 335, 337
Halleyslog
LMA (24176): folios 1, 2, 4
Marley: page 537
Strackey: pages 15, 67, 70, 71-74, 82, 92-96, 161
Thrower: page 189
TNA (1/14): folios 181-183, 185, 215, 216
TNA (1/29): folios 156, 167-169, 191, 192
TNA (1/53): folios 35-51, 72
Wheeler

COMPILING THE DICTIONARY
BL (D1076): folios 335-336, 337-338, 339-340
BL (E192)
Bowen: page 72
Bowrey (1701)
Bowrey (1997) page 32
Bowrey (1999): pages 25, 37, 306
Dagh
Farrington (2002): pages 35-36, 37
LMA (24176): folios 1139, 1140, 1393, 1583, 1594, 1595, 1596, 1597, 1598, 1630, 1631, 1632, 1692
Marsden (1): pages vii-viii
Marsden (2): pages xi-xlii
Miller
Omar (2002): pages iv, v
Omar (2004): pages 6, 13-14, 24, 25, 50, 60

Rost: pages 101-2
Tunbridge Wells 1
Tunbridge Wells 2
Wikipedia (Tunbridge Wells)
Winterbottom (2009): pages 3, 64

BOWREY AND THE ORIENTALIST
BL (D1706): folios 343-344, 349-350
BL (E192): folios 4-30
Raven: page 158
Wikipedia (Hyde)

HENRY SMITH AND THE DICTIONARY
Kader: pages 84-88, 111
Marsden (2): pages xl-xlii
SOAS
Winterbottom (2016): pages 54-81

WRITTEN AND LITERARY MALAY
Bowrey (1701): Preface
LMA (3041): Catalogue of my Books Dec 1711 (no folios)
Mee: page 321
Miller
Omar (2002): page iv
Omar (2004): pages 6, 7, 9, 14, 22-23
Rahman
Rost: pages 101-102

THE IMPORTANCE OF THE DICTIONARY TODAY
Kader: pages 83, 111-112
Mee: pages 316, 321
Omar (2002): pages iv, v
Omar (2004): pages 14, 22, 24, 25
Rahman
Winterbottom (2016): pages 54-81

1701 – LATER LANGUAGE PROJECTS
BL (E192)

Lincoln College
LMA (3041): Catalogue of my
    Books Dec 1711 (no folios)
Rost: page 103
Timperley: pages 553-554
Townley: pages 350-351
Winterbottom (2009): p14

THOMAS BOWREY AND THE
HOAXER
BL (E192): folios 1-2, 3
Breen: page 402
TheAtlantic
Wikipedia (Psalmanazar)

CH.8: THE *PROSPEROUS*

BL (G36-8): 25 February 1703, 8
    March 1703, 27 March 1703,
    15 May 1703
Bowrey (1927): page 142
Crimson Pirate
Delbourgo: location 3912
Farrington (1999): page 597
Fuller: (no page numbers)
Hackman: pages 24, 31
HoC (1707): pages 382-384
LMA (24176): folios 1253, 1314-
    1321, 1583
LMA (3041): Ms03041/1 accounts
    (no folios)
LMA (3041): Ms03041/11 Lloyds
    List (no folios)
Measuring Worth
Treasury Books (1701): pages 198-
    214

THE STORY OF THE
PROSPEROUS
BL (G36-5A): 22 September
    1702, 17 November 1702, 8
    December 1702
BL (G36-7): 19, 22, 23, 24, 25, 26,
    29 & 30 September 1702,

BL (G36-8): 8 & 15 October 1702,
    24 November 1702, 20 March
    1703
Bruce: page 472
Crimson Pirate
Dampier (1937): location 7225
Davies (2008): locations 2477-2488
Defoe (1999): pages 459-460, 462,
    480, 492-494, 502, 522, 686,
    689
Farrinton (2002): page 77
Graham (2007): pages 152-153
HoC (1707): pages 382-384
LMA (24176): folios 52-53, 985,
    1013, 1037, 1063, 1069, 1070,
    1071, 1092, 1583, 1589-1593,
    1595-1597, 1599-1650
LMA (3041): Ms03041/1
Temple (1930): pages 6, 110, 111,
    133, 134, 135, 436
Tuck: page 115

THE VOYAGE OF THE *SPEEDY
RETURN*
Graham (2007): pages 163-190

Hancock (2011)
Headsman
Irish (1924): page x
Kinnaird
Lang
MadderGenealogist
Prebble (1968): page 56
Smith (1998)
Temple (1930): pages 319-333

THE VOYAGE OF THE
WORCESTER
Anon2 (1705)
BL (H30): IOR/H/30 folios 2-15,
    35-43
Bowrey (1705)

Briggs (1976): pages 287-289
Carroll (2007)
Defoe (1720): locations 781-782,
    3452-3457

Farrington (2002): page 25
Graham (2007): pages 163-190

Hancock (2011)
Headsman
Howell (1816): case 438 pages
    1199-1328
Lang
LMA (24176): Ms24176 folios
    0001-0224, 1229, 1242-1244,
    1272-1273, 1284, 1296, 1299,
    1368, 1418, 1694-1695, 1699
MadderGenealogist
Measuring Worth
Prebble (1968): page 56
Smith (1998)
Temple (1930): pages 1-152
TNA (34/8/33)
TNA (34/8/33A)
Wikipedia (Thomas Green)

CH.9: THE FATE OF THE WORCESTER

BL (1076): folios 360-361
Bowrey (1927): pages 229, 246, 248
Farrington (1999):
Hackman:
LMA (24176): folios 1320, 1583
LMA (3041): Ms03041/1 (no folios)
Measuring Worth

THE RISING SUN

BL (1076): folios 360-361
Bowrey (1927): pages 229, 246, 248
Defoe (1704): locations 382-498
ERO (Clacton): St. John the Baptist
    parish church Great Clacton
    Register 27 August 1704
Essex Review 59: page 20
Kinnaird
LMA (24176): folios 242, 343, 476-
    967, 1302, 1583
LMA (3041): Ms03041/4 1709 (no
    folios)
TNA (E134)
TNA (Wills): PROB 11/477/449
    Will of Philip Gardiner 28
    August 1704

THE ARRIVAL OF THE WORCESTER IN SCOTLAND

Anon1 (1705)
Anon2 (1705)
Bowrey (1705)
Lang
LMA (24176): Ms24176 folios
    0001-0224, 1229, 1242-1244,
    1272-1273, 1368, 1694-1695,
    1699
Temple (1930): page 153-170

THE ANNANDALE INCIDENT

BL (H30): IOR/H/30 folios 2-15,
    35-43
Graham (2007): pages 158-163,
    165, 176, 187
Irish (1924): page x
Temple (1930): page 171-181

THE FATE OF THE WORCESTER

Anon1 (1705)
Anon2 (1705)
Bowie (2007)

Bowie (2015)
Bowrey (1705)
Graham (2007): pages 163-190
Hancock (2011)
Hayton
Headsman
Howell (1816): case 438 pages
    1199-1328
Lang
LMA (24176): Ms24176 folios
    0001-0224, 755, 1229, 1242-
    1244, 1272-1273, 1368, 1583,
    1694-1695, 1699
LMA (3041): Ms03041/1 (no folios)
Smith (1998)
Temple (1930): page 182-318
Wikipedia (Thomas Green)

THE *MARY GALLEY*
Bowrey (1927): pages 113-362
Driver
LMA (24176): Ms24176 folios 229-
450, 1265-1270, 1583
LMA (3041): Ms03041/1 (no
folios);
LMA (3041): MS03041/4 (no
folios) 23, 26 & 30 May 1704,
8 June 1704, 2 August 1704;
LMA (3041): MS03041/6(ii) (no
folios) 29 July to 21 August
1704;
LMA (3041): MS03041/7(ii) (no
folios) 16 May 1704
Peyps (4)

THE AFTERMATH OF THE
WORCESTER AFFAIR
Bowie (2015)
Bowrey (1705)
Defoe (1799): pages 23-31
Graham (2007): pages 189-190
Lang
LMA (24176): Ms24176 folios
0001-0224, 1229, 1242-1244,
1272-1273, 1368, 1694-1695,
1699
Measuring Worth
NRAS: Entry for NRAS2177/
Bundle 1444
Temple (1930): page 334-452
TNA (34/8/33)
TNA (34/8/33A)
TNA (54/1/10A)

CH.10: THE FINAL
PROJECTS

Bowrey (1927): page 148
Cox: locations 5837-5842
LMA (24176): Ms24176 folios
1321, 1583
LMA (3041): Ms3041/1, 1-2
January 1706 accounts (no

folios)
LMA (3041): Ms3041/4, May 1705
notes, 24 June 1706 agreement
(no folios)
LMA (3041): Ms3041/6(ii), 4 July
1705 bill (no folios)
LMA (3041): Ms3041/7(i), 23 May
1704 receipt, 16 January 1705
receipt, October 1712 receipt
(no folios)
LMA (3041): Ms3041/7(iii), 1672-
1713 tradesmen's bills, 14
February–7 November 1705
account book, 12 September
1705 bills for china shop (no
folios)
LMA (3041): Ms3041/7(v), 13
January 1710 lease, 18 July
1706 agreement (no folios)
LMA (3041): Ms3041/9(i)&(ii),
20 October 1706 china shop
valuation (no folios)
Rittman: page 5
Waller: page 280

THOMAS BOWREY'S NEW
COINAGE PROPOSALS
Earle (1976): page 61
Earle (1991): pages xi-xiii
English History Authors
Levenson: locations 78, 1521, 1535,
1540, 1542, 1548, 1555, 1560,
1567, 1571, 1601, 1636, 1640,
1682, 1728, 1884, 1992, 1943,
2006, 3266, 3305, 3314, 3320
LMA (3041): Ms3041/2 undated
proposal (no folios)
Martin (2014): page 129
Measuring Worth
Wikipedia (Condor Token)
Wikipedia (Farthing)

THOMAS BOWREY'S ANTI-
PIRACY PROPOSALS
Bialuschewski (2007)
Business Today (2011)

Dampier (1937): locations 14-15, 273-283, 531-535, 813-815, 7129-7147

Defoe (1999): pp xvi-xxii, 3-7, 52-54, 117-118, 122, 124-128, 130-132, 435-436, 671, 676, 686-687, 691

Earle (1998): pp 36-37, 115-124

Fox (2014): locations 139-140, 155, 203-207, 525-534, 734-737

Frank: locations 4600-4605

Graham (2007): pp 135-154

HoC (1707)

London Gazette: 15 April 1703

LMA (24176): folios 41, 879, 1128, 1131, 1655

LMA (3041): Ms3041/2, 21 May 1707 proposal, 2 June 1710 proposal (no folios)

Measuring Worth

Pirate Realm

Risso (1989): chapter 1

Rule

Tinniswood (2011): locations 178-181, 355-357

Vallar

Wikipedia (Avery)

Wikipedia (Corsairs)

Williams (1997): pages 118-120

THOMAS BOWREY AND THE SLAVE TRADE

Abolition

Bialuschewski (2007): pages 35, 36, 38, 39, 40-41

Defoe (1999): page xxviii

Digital Histories

Earle (1976): pages 67-68

Fox (2014): locations 719-721

Headlam (1916): page 303

HoC (1707)

Honeck (2013): page 7

Knox (1681)

Lincoln (2014): pages 166, 171-2

LMA (24176): Ms24176 ff 0922, 0923, 0925, 0926, 0927, 0976, 0977, 1071

LMA (3041): Ms3041/2 undated Jamaica proposal, undated fragment (no folios)

LMA (3041): Ms3041/3(i) undated descriptions, undated notes (no folios)

LMA (3041): Ms3041/3(ii) undated notes (no folios)

LMA (3041): Ms3041/3(iii) all (no folios)

Only Artists: approximate location 24 minutes

Rosenbloom: pages 110-111

TNA (Slaves)

Vallangi

Wikipedia (Brandenburger)

Wikipedia (German Empire)

Wikipedia (Lawton)

Wikipedia (Triangular Trade)

THOMAS BOWREY AND THE SOUTH SEAS COMPANY

BL (28140): Mss 28140 folios 29-33

BL (5222): chart 12

BL (70163): Mss 70163 folios 136, 138

BL (70291): Ms70291 folios 19-24

BL (B42): 22, 27 & 28 February 1699

Bowrey (1997): page xli

Bradley: pages 510-511

Chaudhuri: page 208

Defoe (1697): locations 157-158, 219-228, 304-310

Defoe (1724); pages xxviii

Defoe (1999): pages xiii, xxvii-xxviii

Delbourgo: locations 2739-2745

Earle (1976): pages 13-21, 55, 299

Frank: location 2641

Gill

Graham (2007): page 129

Healey (1955): pages 253-254, 332-333, 334-335, 338-341, 343-

345, 345-349

Lincoln (2014): page 122

LMA (24176): Ms24176 folios 200, 948

LMA (3041): Ms 3041/2 undated proposals, undated fragment, February 1699 proposal, 10 September 1711 proposal, 11 September 1711 proposal, 28 February 1712 letter (no folios)

LMA (3041): Ms 3041/3(ii) undated Considerations (no folios)

LMA (3041): Ms 3041/5 2 November 1711 receipt (no folios)

Martin (2015): location 3774

McCarthy: page 7

Morgan (1928): page 143

N&Q

Rogers (2014): pages 26, 27, 76

Satsuma: pages 61-62

Williams (1997): pages 119-120, 134, 161-162, 164, 165, 168-170, 180

CH.11 PREPARING FOR MORTALITY

Adams: locations 306-341

THE KING'S HEAD INN

LMA (3041): Ms3041/7(i) receipts dated 2 November 1690, 22 October 1691, 22 August 1692, 15 November 1692, 22 November 1693, 7 August 1694, 3 May 1695, 27 November 1695, 16 June 1697, 25 January 1698, 15 August 1698, 24 May 1699, 7 October 1699, 3 June 1700, 16 April 1708, Declarations 1 November 1709, 16 April 1711, 15 July 1711, 15 April 1712, 15 July 1712

DEATH OF ELIZABETH GARDINER

Ancestry: St Katharine by the Tower Burial Register 3 December 1710

Earle (1991): pages 158, 311-323

Grundy: pages 36, 66-67

Hopkins

LMA (24176); Ms24176 folio 1655

LMA (3041): Ms3041/9(i)&(ii) 19 March 1711 bill of sale (no folios)

LMA (9172): Ms9172/104 will 14

Rheumatology Article

TNA (Wills): PROB 11/477/449

Wikipedia (Rheumatism)

SEARLE FAMILY MEDIATION

ERO: folios 0047, 0048, 0050, 0051

Measuring Worth

THOMAS BOWREY'S HEALTH & DEATH

Ancestry: St. Dunstan and All Saints Burial Register 13 March 1712/13

Ancestry: St. Margaret Lee Burial Register 14 March 1712/13

BL (D1076): folios 49-50, 54-55, 66-67

BL (E192): folio 0029 (0078)

Bowrey (1927); pages xviii-xix

Bowrey (1997): page xx, xxi-xxii, xxiii, xlii, xliii-xliv, xlv-xlviii

Buchan: pages 47, 705, 713

Earle (1998): pages 133, 135-137

Grundy: pages 13, 38, 51

Healey (1955): pages 253-254

LMA (Briggins): 5 March 1712, 11 March 1713

LMA (24176); folios 0243, 0098, 0099, 0243, 1163

LMA (3041): Ms3041/3(iii) 26 July 1712 proposal (no folios)

LMA (3041): Ms3041/9(i) & (ii) 13
    April 1706 draft will (no folios)
LMA (3041): Ms3041/9(iii)
    Catalogue (no folios)
Quaker House: D1-2 folio 0001,
    D1-5 folio 0008
TNA (Wills): PROB 11/532/176
Traded Goods
Wikipedia (James_Sherard)
Wilson: pages 269-271

EPILOGUE: THE STORY THAT REFUSES TO DIE

Bonhams: Lot 143
IoW Press

ANANLYSIS OF THE ISLE OF WIGHT JOURNAL & LOGBOOK

Kenny
IoW Logbook
IoW Journal
Morton
Yale

THE CONTINUED INTEREST IN THOMAS BOWREY

Davenport-Hines
Kowl
Smith (1998)
Wellcome Trust

APPENDIX I

The Paper Trail

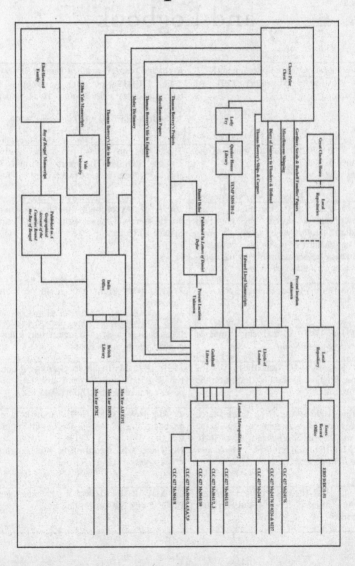

Analysis of the Journal
and Logbook

Yale Library Osborn Collection fc 177	Event and Journeys in life of Thomas Bowrey
14 July to 5 November 1701: At Kedgeree. *Volume 1 12081843-12081880*	7 Feb 1701-17 Nov 1702: At Wapping in correspondence with Thomas Hyde, except for: 16 Jul to 8 Sep 1701: At Tunbridge Wells. *British Library Mss Eur A33 E192* *LMA CLC 427 Ms03041/6(ii)*
22 June 1702: Three diagrams of the transit of Venus *Volume 1 12081881-120818885*	There was no Transit of Venus during Thomas' lifetime. There were two in 1631 and 1639, then the next two were 1761 and 1769. *https://en.wikipedia.ord/wiki/Transit_of_Venus*
1675-1692: Autobiographical note describing a career on an East Indiaman followed by over two years as commander of a ship on a voyage to America before returning to the *India Service* on the *Royall Henry*. *Volume 1 12081893-12081895*	1669-1688: According to his *Introduction* to his *Dictionary* Thomas spent nineteen years in the East Indies. *Bowrey (1701)*
4 Jan 1661: Thomas Bowrey born. *Volume 2 Title Page*	7 Sep 1659: From 1706 draft will and baptism *LMA CLC 427 Ms03041/9(i) & (ii) 13 Apr 1706* *St John Wapping Baptisms Oct 1660 & sep 1661*
10 Jun 1703: Visited churchyard at *Luddington in Spain* *Volume 2 page 8*	It has been impossible to identify any village called Luddington in Spain.
11 Dec 1689-14 Dec 1691: Voyage from England to the East Indies on the *Worcester*. *Volume 2 pages 10, 12, 37-122*	17Sep 1691: Married Mary Gardiner at Lee NB *Worcester* not chartered until 1701 and never commanded by Thomas Bowrey
10 jun 1695-1 Aug 1697: Commanded the *Four Friends* ona voyage to the *great Spanish South Seas*, arrived there in May 1696 and left *these islands near the Italian coast* *Volume 2 page 187*	29 Aug 1696-13 Jan 1697: Thoma bOwrey on board the *St George Galley* in English waters NB There is no record of the *Four Friends* in his papers. *LMA CLC 427 MS24176 1165-1213* *Temple (1930) page 70*
5 Jan 1698-16 May 1699: ... *left the arbs* ... sailed for England, arriving London *Volume 2 pages 189-191*	28 May-12 Jul 1698: In Flanders and Holland with Nathaniel Long. *Bowrey (1927) pages 10-72*

Timeline

Thomas Bowrey's Life in Context	
Jan 1649	Charles I executed
Feb 1649	Rump Parliament votes to abolish monarchy
Oct 1651	English Civil Wars end
Oct 1651	Navigation Act, all English trade to be carried on English ships
Apr 1652	Dutch East India Company founds Cape Town
Jul 1652	First Anglo-Dutch War starts
Apr 1653	Oliver Cromwell takes power
Dec 1653	Cromwell sworn in as Lord Protector
Apr 1654	First Anglo-Dutch War ends
Dec 1654	Anglo-Spanish War starts
Apr 1657	Cromwell declines English crown
Sep 1657	**Thomas Bowrey's parents marry**
Sep 1658	Death of Oliver Cromwell, succeeded as Lord Protector by son, Richard
May 1659	Richard Cromwell forced to resign as Lord Protector
Sep 1659	**Thomas Bowrey born at Wapping**
Oct 1659	End of Anglo-Spanish War
Jan 1660	**Thomas Bowrey senior part of Lawson's blockade of the Thames**
Ar 1660	Charles II issued Declaration of Breda
May 1660	Charles II returns from exile
Sep 1660	James Duke of York marries Anne Hyde
Nov 1660	Thames bursts its banks flooding from Westminster to Limehouse
Nov 1660	Royal Society founded
Jan 1661	Oliver Cromwell's corpse "executed"
Apr 1661	Charles II crowned & marries Catherine of Braganza by Proxy
Apr 1661	Charles II receives Bombay in Catherine of Braganza's dowry
Feb 1662	Major storm affects southern England
Apr 1662	Mary Stuart, daughter of James Duke of York and Anne Hyde, born
Dec 1663	Tidal surge floods Whitehall
Feb 1665	Anne Stuart, daughter of James Duke of York and Anne Hyde, born
Sep 1665	**Thomas Bowrey's senior dies at peak of Great Plague**
Sep 1666	Great Fire of London
Jan 1667	***Little Charles* commanded by Samuel Smith departs Thames**
Feb 1667	Thames freezes
Apr 1667	***Little Charles* departs England**
Jun 1667	Dutch ships attack the English fleet on the Medway
May 1668	***Little Charles* arrives Surat**
Jan 1669	**Walter Clavell arrives Fort St George**
Apr 1669	**Eleanor Bowrey, Thomas' grandmother, dies**
Oct 1669	**Samuel Smith dies at Bombay**
Feb 1670	**Elizabeth Smith departs London for Bombay**

Thomas Bowrey's Life in Context	
Mar 1671	Anne Hyde, 1st wife of Duke of York, dies
Jul 1672	French take San Thoma near Fort St George from English
Feb 1683	**Mary Gardiner born**
Sep 1672	Royal African Company with monopoly of African trade created
Sep 1673	James Duke of York marries Mary of Modena in Catholic ceremony
Nov 1673	Duke of York marries Mary of Modena in Protestant ceremony
June 1675	Foundation laid for the new St Paul's Cathedral
Nov 1675	Charles II closes London coffee houses
Nov 1677	Mary of Mary Stuart to Prince William of Orange
Aug 1678	Titus Oates conspiracy to replace Charles II by Duke of York
Jul 1679	Exclusion Bill to exclude James Duke of York from throne
Dec 1679	**Elizabeth Adderton dies at Bombay**
Oct 1680	English St Mary's church consecrated at Fort St George
Sep 1683	Battle of Vienna ends expansion of Ottoman Empire into Europe
Dec 1683	Keigwin's Rebellion at Bombay
Dec 1683	Thames freezes for months
Feb 1685	Charles II dies and is succeeded by James II
Apr 1685	Coronation of James II
Jun 1685	Duke of Monmouth and army lands at Lyme Regis
Sep 1685	**Stephen Adderton dies**
May 1687	**Thomas Bowrey imprisoned at Porto Novo**
Jul 1687	Elihu Yule becomes Governor of Fort St George
Aug 1687	Start of Anglo-Siamese war
Feb 1688	London Gazette publishes first reference to Lloyd's Coffee House
Jun 1688	**Thomas Bowrey entertains William Dampier at Achin**
Jun 1688	James Francis Edward (*Old Pretender*) son of James II born
Oct 1688	**Thomas Bowrey departs Fort St George for England**
Nov 1688	William of Orange lands near Torbay
Nov 1688	Start of Nine Years War between France and Dutch Republic
Dec 1688	James II makes first attempt to flee the country
Dec 1688	William of Orange arrives London
Dec 1688	James II flees England and renounces throne
Jan 1689	William of Orange becomes William III reigning jointly with Mary
Jan 1689	England joins Nine Years War
Mar 1689	James II lands in Ireland in attempt to invade England
Apr 1689	Coronation of William and Mary
Jul 1689	*Bengal Merchant* **arrives Portsmouth**
Dec 1689	Bill of Rights basis of Constitutional Monarchy
Sep 1691	**Thomas Bowrey marries Mary Gardiner at Lee**
Dec 1691	Lloyd's Coffee House moves to Lombard Street

Thomas Bowrey's Life in Context	
Sep 1692	Major earthquake in Belgium causes damage in Kent and East Anglia
Jul 1694	Bank of England created
Nov 1694	Million Lottery proposed and begins during 1695
Dec 1694	Queen Mary dies
Feb 1696	Failed attempt to assassinate William III
Nov 1696	**St George Galley departs from the Thames**
Sep 1697	Nine Years War ends
Dec 1697	First service in new St Paul's Cathedral
Jan 1698	Fire destroys Palace of Whitehall and Banqueting House
Jan 1698	Tsar Peter the Great visits Roya Dockyards at Deptford
May 1698	**Thomas Bowrey and Nathaniel Long tour Flanders and Holland**
Sep 1698	New (English) East India Company formed
Jul 1700	Prince William, last of Queen Anne's 13 children dies
1701	**Thomas Bowrey's Malay-English dictionary published**
May 1701	Captain Kidd executed at Execution Dock, Wapping
Jun 1701	Act of Settlement securing Protestant succession
Sep 1701	James II dies in exile
Jan 1702	War between England and France starts
Mar 1702	William III fatally injured when his horse stumbles in a mole hill
Sep 1702	Union of Old and New East India Companies
Nov 1703	The Great Storm
Feb 1704	First edition of Daniel Defoe's *The Review*
Aug 1704	**Death of Philip Gardiner**
Jan 1705	Greenwich Palace becomes hospital for sailors
Apr 1705	**Green, Madder and Simpson of the *Worcester* executed at Leith**
Mar 1707	**Thomas Bowrey meets Daniel Defoe**
Mar 1707	Grand Moghul Aurangzeb dies and Moghul Empire collapses
May 1707	Act of Union of England and Scotland
Oct 1708	St Paul's Cathedral completed
Nov 1710	**Death of Elizabeth Gardiner**
Mar 1711	South Sea Company founded
Apr 1713	Treaty of Utrecht ends War of Spanish Succession
Feb 1713	Edward Lloyd, founder of Lloyd's Coffee House, dies
Mar 1713	**Thomas Bowrey dies**
Aug 1741	Queen Anne dies and succession of George I
May 1715	**Mary Bowrey dies**
1744	**Mary Bowry's Almshouses built**

Bowrey Family Tree

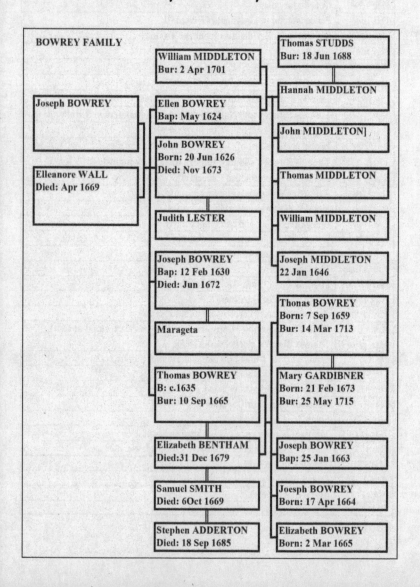

BOWREY FAMILY

Thomas STUDDS
Bur: 18 Jun 1688

William MIDDLETON
Bur: 2 Apr 1701

Hannah MIDDLETON

Joseph BOWREY

Ellen BOWREY
Bap: May 1624

John MIDDLETON]

John BOWREY
Born: 20 Jun 1626
Died: Nov 1673

Thomas MIDDLETON

Elleanore WALL
Died: Apr 1669

Judith LESTER

William MIDDLETON

Joseph BOWREY
Bap: 12 Feb 1630
Died: Jun 1672

Joseph MIDDLETON
22 Jan 1646

Thonas BOWREY
Born: 7 Sep 1659
Bur: 14 Mar 1713

Marageta

Thomas BOWREY
B: c.1635
Bur: 10 Sep 1665

Mary GARDIBNER
Born: 21 Feb 1673
Bur: 25 May 1715

Elizabeth BENTHAM
Died:31 Dec 1679

Joseph BOWREY
Bap: 25 Jan 1663

Samuel SMITH
Died: 6Oct 1669

Joesph BOWREY
Born: 17 Apr 1664

Stephen ADDERTON
Died: 18 Sep 1685

Elizabeth BOWREY
Born: 2 Mar 1665

Bushell Family Tree

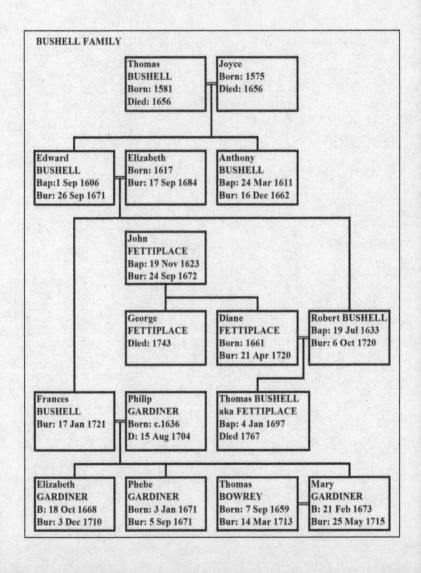

Bibliography

The resources listed are those which have been consulted in writing this book and include those referred to in the Notes. For printed books, the date in parentheses is the edition consulted. For Internet documents, the date is that the document was consulted. For Kindle editions, locations rather than page numbers are given,

Abolition: www.bbc.co.uk/history/british/abolition/church_and_slavery-article_01.shtml (12 November 2017)

Adams: J E Adams, The Painter, the Laundress and the Murders at the Inns of Court – The Most Notorious Crime of Walpole's Britain, Createspace, Kindle Edition, 2011

Ahmad: Abu Talib Ahmad and Tan Liok Ee, New Terrains in Southeast Asia History, Singapore, 2003

Amrith: Sunil S. Amrith, Crossing the Bay of Bengal: The Furies of Nature and the Fortunes of Migrants, Harvard University Press, Cambridge, MA, 2013

Ancestry 1: London Metropolitan Archives, Clerkenwell, London, England London, England, Church of England Baptisms, Marriages and Burials, 1538-1812 collection at http://www.ancestry.co.uk

Ancestry 2: London Metropolitan Archives and Guildhall Library Manuscript Section, Clerkenwell, London, England collection at http://www.ancestry.co.uk

Anderson (1890): John Anderson, English Intercourse with Siam in the Seventeenth Century, Routledge, Trench & Trübner, London, 1890

Anglo-Dutch Wars: http://anglo-dutch-wars.blogspot.co.uk/archives/2005_5_01_anglo-dutch-wars_anglo-dutch wars-archice.html (26 March 2018)

Anon1 (1705): (Possibly Daniel Defoe), A Letter from Scotland, to a Friend in London: Containing a Particular Narrative of the Whole Proceedings Against the Worcester and her Crew from her First Arrival in Leith-Road, to to 20th April 1705 ..., London, 1705

Anon2 (1705): The Case of Captain Green, Commander of the Ship

Worcester and his crew Tried and Condemned for Pyracy and Murther in the High Court of Admiralty of Scotland, John Nutt, London, 1705

Aslet: Clive Aslet, The Story of Greenwich. The Book People Ltd., St Helens,

Banerjee: Pompa Banerjee, Burning Women: Widows, Witches, and Early Modern European Travelers in India, Palgrave MacMillan, New York, 2003

Barnett: Len Barnett, The 'Honourable' East India Company (1600-1857) – A Realistic Guide to What is Available to Those Looking into the Careers of Seagoing Servants (1600-1834) at http://www.barnettmaritime.co.uk/mainheic. htm (3 July 2016)

Bastable: Jonathan Bastable, Inside Pepys' London, David & Charles, Newton Abbot, 2011

Bialuschewski (2007): Arne Bialuschewski, Thomas Bowrey's Madagascar Manuscript of 1708, in History in Africa, volume 34, 2007

BL (28140): British Library: Add Ms28140 Memoirs and Proposals on the South Seas

BL (3972B): British Library: Sloane Ms 3972B Catalogue of Printed Books, Manuscripts, Charters, Rolls, Hori Sicci, Maps, Miniatures, Prints, Periodicals

BL (5222): British Library: Sloane Add Ms 5222 Maps and Charts of the East Indies

BL (70163): British Library: Add Ms70163 Proposals for South Sea Trade

BL (70291): British Library: Add Ms70291 Letters to Lord Oxford from Daniel Defoe

BL (Blogs): British Library Untold Lives Blogs: http://blogs.bl.uk/untoldlives

BL (B42): British Library: B/42 (Rough Court Book)

BL (D782): British Library: Mss Eur D782 – Bay of Bengal Manuscript

BL (D1076): British Library: Mss Eur D1076 Thomas Bowrey's Papers in India

BL (E192): British Library: Mss Eur A33 E192 Papers Relating to Thomas Bowrey's Dictionary

BL (G3-2): British Library: IOR/G/3/2 Bombay Factory Diaries and Consultations 1674-1681

BL (G19-20): British Library: IOR/G/19/20 Fort St George Letters Despatched

BL (G20-2): British Library: IOR/G/20/2 Hugli Factory Diaries and Consultations 1678-1680

BL (G20-9): British Library: IOR/G/20/2 Hugli Factory Diaries and Consultations 1682-1683

BL (G24-2): British Library: IOR/G/24/2 Madapollam Letters Despatched 1683

BL (G3-19): British Library: IOR/G/3/19 Letters to Bombay to Surat 1669/70-1682

BL (G36-5A): British Library: IOR/G/36/5A Factory Records Surat 1702-1704

BL (G36-7): British Library: IOR/G/36/7 Factory Records Surat 1701-1702

BL (G36-8): British Library: IOR/G/36/8 Surat 1702-1704

BL (H30): British Library: IOR/H/30 Petitions Relating to the Annandale

BL (H49): British Library: IOR/H/49 State Papers

BL (L-AG-1-1-9): British Library IOR/L/AG/1/1/9 Fort St George Accounts

BL (V27-36): British Library: IOR/V/27/36/2 Press Lists of Ancient Records of Fort St George 1685-1689

Blanchard: Gill Blanchard, Lawson Lies Still in the Thames: The Extraordinary Life of Vice-Admiral Sir John Lawson, Amberley, Stroud, 2017

Bombay: The Seventeenth Century at theory.tifr.res.in/Bombay/history/c17.html (5 April 2018)

Bonhams: Auction 13809: Printed Books and Manuscript Including the Hooke Folio, 28 March 2006 at https://www. Bonhams.com/auctions /13809/lot/143/category=list

Bowen (2011): Huw V. Bowen, John McAleer & Robert J. Blyth, Monsoon Traders: The Maritime World of the East India Company, Scala, London, 2011

Bowen (2015): Huw V. Bowen, Margarette Lincoln & Nigel Rigby, editors, The Worlds of the East India Company, Boydell Press, Woodbridge, 2015

Bowie (2007): Karin Bowie, Scottish Public Opinion and the Anglo-Scottish Union, 1699-1707, Boydell Press, Woodbridge, Surrey

Bowie (2015): Karin Bowie, Newspapers, the early modern public sphere and the 1704-5 Worcester affair in Benchimol, A., Brown, R. and Shuttleton, D. (eds) Before Blackwood's: Scottish Journalism in the Age of Enlightenment Series, Pickering & Chatto, London, 2015

Bowrey (1701): Thomas Bowrey, A Dictionary English and Malayo, Malayo and English, Samuel Bridges, London, 1701

Bowrey (1705): Thomas Bowrey, The Case of the Owners and Freighters of the Ship Worcester in relation to the seising ... of the said ship ... in Scotland, for reprisal of the Scots ship Annandale, seised ... in England. And also the case of the late Capt. Thomas Green, Publisher, London, Date

Bowrey (1927): Thomas Bowrey, The Papers of Thomas Bowrey (1669-1713) – Diary of Six Week Tour in 1698 to Holland and Flanders, also The Story of the *Mary Galley* (1704-1710), Hakluyt Society, London, 1927

Bowrey (1997): Thomas Bowrey, A Geographical Account of Countries Round the Bay of Bengal 1669-1679, Munshiran Manoharlal, New Delhi, 1997

Bradley: Peter T Bradley, British Maritime Enterprise in the New World from the Late 15th to the Mid-18th Century, Edwin Mellen Press, Lewiston, 1999

Breen: Benjamin Breen, No Man Is an Island: Early Modern Globalization, Knowledge Networks, and George Psalmanazar's Formosa in Journal of Early Modern History 17 (2013)

Briggs (1976): Katharine Mary Briggs, An Encyclopaedia of Fairies: Hobgoblins, Brownies, Bogies, and Other Supernatural Creatures, Partheon Books, New York, 1976

British History (Interregnum): Acts and Ordinances of the Interregnum 1648-1660, HMSO, London, 1911 http://www.british-history. ac.uk/no-series/acts-ordinances-interregnum/pp715-718 (22 March 2017)

Bruce: John Bruce, Annals of the Honorable East-India Company from their Establishment by the Charter of Queen Elizabeth 1600, East India Company, London, 1810

Buchan: William Buchan, Domestic Medicine; Or, A Treatise on the Prevention and Cure of Diseases, London, Strahan & Cadell, 1798

Bulley: Anne Bulley, The Bombay Country Ships 1790-1833, Abingdon, 2013, Kindle Edition, Routledge, 2013

Business Today (2011): The French Connection in Business Today (Oman's No.1 Business Magazine) published 29 November 2011, http://www.businesstoday.co.om/Issues/A-big-leap-forward/The-French-connection (29 June 2016)

Capp: Bernard Capp, Cromwell's Navy: The Fleet and the English Revolution 1648-1660, Clarendon Paperbacks, Oxford, 1989

Carroll (2007): Rory Carroll, The Sorry Story of How Scotland Lost its 17th Century Empire in The Guardian: https://www.theguardian. com/uk/ 2007/Sep/11/britishidentity.past (19 June 2016)

Channel 5 a: The Great Fire – 1: London Burns, broadcast Wednesday 31 May 2017

Channel 5 b: The Great Fire – 2: Death & Destruction, broadcast Thursday 1 June 2017

Channel 5 c: The Great Fire – 3: A City Rebuilt, broadcast Friday 2 June 2017

Chaudhuri: K. N. Chaudhuri, The Trading World of Asia and the English East India Company: 1660-1760, Cambridge University

Press, Cambridge, 2006

Christies: Lot 51, Dale 7411, 3 July 2007 http://www. christies.com/ LotFinder/lot_details.aspx?from=sale summary&intObjectID=4939673

Coates: W. H. Coates, The Old 'Country Trade' of the East Indies, Cornmarket Press, London, 1911

Cotton: Julian James Cotton, List of Inscriptions on Tombs & Monuments in Madras, volume 1, Government Press, Madras, 1945

Cox: Jane Cox, Old East Enders: A History of Tower Hamlets, Kindle Edition

Crill: Rosemary Crill (editor), The Fabric of India, V&A Publishing, London, 2015

Crimson Pirate: The Crimson Pirate's Pirate Information – Pirate Places: Madagascar, http://thecrimsonpirate.com/crimsonpirate.us/ historical pirates/pirateplaces/madagascar.html (15 January 2015)

Dagh: Batavia Dagh-Register, Dagh-Register Gehouden int Casteel Batavia ... [available at www.sejarahnusantara.anri.go.id/daily_ journals].

Dampier (1937): William Dampier, A New Voyage round the World, Kindle Edition (N.B. This edition is also available from the Gutenberg Project at Gutenberg.net.au/ebooks05/0500461h.html but this edition has no page numbers.)

Daniell (1902): F H Blackburne Daniell, editor, Calendar of State Papers, Domestic Series, 1673, Longman, London, 1861

Davenport-Hines: Richard Davenport-Hines, The Pursuit of Oblivion: A Social History of Drugs, Weidenfeld & Nicolson, London, 2001

Davies (2008): J. D. Davies, Pepys's Navy: Ships, Men and Warfare 1649-1689, Kindle Edition, Seaforth Publishing, 2008

Davies (2017): J. D. Davies, The Devil Upon The Waves, Kindle Edition, Endeavour Press, 2017

Defoe (1697): Daniel Defoe, An Essay Upon Projects, Kindle Edition,

Defoe (1704): Daniel Defoe, The Storm, Kindle Edition

Defoe (1720): Daniel Defoe, The Life, Adventures and Piracies of the Famous Captain Singleton, Kindle Edition, Trajectory Classics, 2014

Defoe (1724): Daniel Defoe, A Tour thro' the Whole Island of Great Britain, Kindle Edition, Houseshop, 2011

Defoe (1799): Daniel De Foe, The History of the Union Between England and Scotland. To which is added the Articles of Union, &c., John Exshaw, Dublin, 1799

Defoe (1999): Daniel Defoe, A General History of the Pyrates and also Their Policies, Discipline and Government, From their first Rise and Settlement in the Island of Providence, in 1717, to the present

Year 1724, London in Dover Edition, Schonhorn, Manuel editor, Dover Publications, New York,1999 (N.B. This edition is published with Defoe as the author but it is probably by another, unknown, author)

Delbourgo: James Delbourgo, Collecting the World: The Life and Curiosity of Hans Sloan, Kindle Edition, Penguin, 2017

Digital Histories: digitalhistories.yctl.org/2014/11/01/elihu-yale-was-a-slave-trader (26 November 2017)

Dijk: Wil O Dijk, Seventeenth-century Burma and the Dutch East India Company, 1634-1680, Singapore, 2006

Dodwell (1913): H Dodwell, editor, The Diary and Consultation Book of the Agent Governor and Council of Fort St. George 1686, Government Press, Madras, 1913

Dodwell (1916 1): H Dodwell, editor, The Diary and Consultation Book of the Agent Governor and Council of Fort St. George 1687, Government Press, Madras, 1916

Dodwell (1916 2): H Dodwell, editor, The Diary and Consultation Book of the Agent Governor and Council of Fort St. George 1688, Government Press, Madras, 1916

Dodwell (1918): H Dodwell, editor, The Diary and Consultation Book of the Agent Governor and Council of Fort St. George 1694, Government Press, Madras, 1918

Driver: Christopher Driver and Michelle Berriedale-Johnson, Pepys at Table, Bell & Hyman, London, 1984

Duvall: Chris Duvall, Cannabis, Reaktion Books, London, 2014

Earle (1976): Peter Earle, The World of Defoe, Weidenfeld and Nicolson, London, 1976

Earle (1991): Peter Earle, The Making of the English Middle Class: Business, Society and Family Life in London 1660-1730, Methuen, London, 1991

Earle (1998): Peter Earle, Sailors, English Merchant Seamen 1650-1775, Methuen, London, 1998

EIC Ships: http://www.eicships.info/help/shiprole.html (3 July 2016)

Encyclopaedia: http://www.enclopaedia.com/topic/British_East_India_Company.aspx (3 July 2016)

English History Authors: http://www.englishhistoryauthor.blogspot.co.uk/ /2011/10/currency-in-secod-half-of-18th-century.html (1 July 2016)

ERO: Essex Record Office D/DC

ERO (Clacton): Essex Record Office, register of Great Clacton Church 1560-1710 D/P 179/1/2

Essex Review 59: Essex Review, Volume 59, 1950

Factory Records: List of Factory Records of the Late East India Company, London, 1896 @ http://www.archive.org/details/

cu31924023223757 (13 November 2016)

Farrington (1999): Anthony Farrington, Catalogue of East India Company Ships' Journals and Logs 1600-1834, British Library, London, 1999

Farrington (2002): Anthony Farrington, Trading Places: The East India Company and Asia 1600-1834, British Library, London, 2002

Farrington (2007): Anthony Farrington & Dhiravat na Pombejra, The English Factory in Siam 1612-1685 volumes 1 & 2, British Library, London, 2007

Fawcett (1936): Sir Charles Fawcett, The English Factories in India Volume I 1670-1677, Clarendon Press, Oxford, 1936

Fawcett (1954): Sir Charles Fawcett, The English Factories in India Volume III 1678-1684, Clarendon Press, Oxford, 1954

FEP: F.E.P., List of Marriages at Fort St George Madras, William Pollard, Exeter, 1907

Forrest: George W Forrest, Selections From the Letters, Despatches and other State Papers Preserved in the Bombay Secretariat, Home Series Volume II, Government Central Press, Bombay, 1887

Foster (1921): Sir William Foster, The English Factories in India 1655-1660, Clarendon Press, Oxford, 1921

Foster (1925): Sir William Foster, The English Factories in India 1665-1667, Clarendon Press, Oxford, 1925

Foster (1927): Sir William Foster, The English Factories in India 1668-1669, Clarendon Press, Oxford, 1927

Fox (2014): E. T. Fox, editor, Pirates In Their Own Words Eye-witness accounts of the Golden Age of Piracy, 1690-1728, Kindle Edition, Lulu.com, 2014

Francis: W. Francis, Frederick Nicholson, C. S. Middlemas, C. A. Barber, E. Thurston & G. H. Stuart, Gazetteer of South India, Volume 1, Mittal Publications, New Delhi, 2002

Frank: Katherine Frank, Crusoe: Daniel Defoe, Robert Knox and the Creation of a Myth, Pimlico, Kindle Edition, Vintage Digital, 2011

Fryer (1698): John Fryer, A New Account of East India and Persia in Eight Letters being Nine Years' Travels Begun 1672 And Finished 1681, Chiswell, London, 1698

Fryer (1909): John Fryer, A New Account of East India and Persia being Nine Years' Travels 1672-1681 Volume 1, Asian Educational Services, New Delhi, 1992

Fuller: Tony Fuller, East India Company Ships 1600-1833, 2000

Gaastra: Femme S. Gaastra, War, Competition and Collaboration: Relations between the English and Dutch East India Company in the Seventeenth and Eighteenth Centuries, in Bowen (2015): The Worlds of the East India Company

Gardiner: Samuel Pawson Gardiner & Christopher Thomas Atkinson,

Letters and Papers Relating to the First Dutch War 1652-1654, Navy Record Society, 1912

Geni.com: https://www.geni.com/people/Axel-Juel/60000000128499 80461 (19 October 2016)

Gill: Anton Gill, The Devil's Mariner, A Life of William Dampier, Pirate and Explorer, 1651-1715, Kindle Edition, Sharpe Books, 2018

Gokhale: Balkrishna Govind Gokhale, Surat in the Seventeenth Century: A Study in Urban History of pre-modren India, Curzon Press, London, 1979

Graf: Amdt Graf, Susanne Schroter & Edwin Wierings, Aceh: History, Politics and Culture, Institute of Southeast Asian Studies, Singapore, 2010

Graham (2007): Eric J. Graham, Seawolves: Pirates & the Scots, Birlinn, Edinburgh, 2007

Green (1860): Mary Anne Everett Green, editor, Calendar of State Papers, Domestic Series, 1660-1661, Longman, London, 1860

Green (1861): Mary Anne Everett Green, editor, Calendar of State Papers, Domestic Series, 1661-1662, Longman, London, 1861

Green (1864): Mary Anne Everett Green, editor, Calendar of State Papers, Domestic Series, 1666-1667, Longman, London, 1864

Green (1877): Mary Anne Everett Green, editor, Calendar of State Papers, Domestic Series, 1651-1652, Longman, London, 1877

Green (1879): Mary Anne Everett Green, editor, Calendar of State Papers, Domestic Series, 1653-1654, Longman, London, 1879

Green (1880): Mary Anne Everett Green, editor, Calendar of State Papers, Domestic Series, Interregnum 1654, Longman, London, 1880

Green (1881): Mary Anne Everett Green, editor, Calendar of State Papers, Domestic Series, 1655, Longman, London, 1881

Green (1882): Mary Anne Everett Green, editor, Calendar of State Papers, Domestic Series, 1655-1656, Longman, London, 1882

Green (1883): Mary Anne Everett Green, editor, Calendar of State Papers, Domestic Series, Interregnum, 1656-1657, Longman, London, 1883

Green (1884): Mary Anne Everett Green, editor, Calendar of State Papers, Domestic Series, 1657-1658, Longman, London, 1884

Green (1885): Mary Anne Everett Green, editor, Calendar of State Papers, Domestic Series, Interregnum, 1658-1659, Longman, London, 1885

Green (1886): Mary Anne Everett Green, editor, Calendar of State Papers, Domestic Series, 1659-1660, Longman, London, 1886

Grundy: Joan E Grundy, A Dictionary of Medical & Related Terms for the Family Historian, Swansong Publications, Rotherham, 2006

Guillery: Peter Guillery, The Small House in Eighteenth-Century

London, Yale University Press, London, 2004

Hackman: Rowan Hackman, Ships of the East India Company, World Ship Society, Gravesend, 2001

Hall: David George Edward Hall, Early English Intercourse With Burma 1587-1743 and the Tragedy of Negrais, Longmans, Green and Company, London, 1928

Halleyslog: https://halleyslog.wordpress.com/2014/07/08/hallwy-writes-from-bermuda/ (9 February 2018)

Hancock (2011): Christine Hancock, John Madder Englishman or Scot? in the Journal of the Guild of One Name Studies volume 10 number 9 Jan-Mar 2011

Hanson: Neil Hanson, The Dreadful Judgement: The True Story of the Great Fire of London 1666, Doubleday, London, 2001

Harris: Jennifer Harris, editor, 5000 Years of Textiles, British Museum Press, London, 1993

Harvey: Ian Harvey, The Bacteria Behind London's Great Plague, https://m.thevintagenews.com/2016/09/14/ bacteria-behind-londons-great-plague-positively-identified (23 May 2017)

Hawley: John Stratton Hawley, Sati, the Blessing and the Curse – The Burning of Wives in India, Oxford University Press, New York, 1994

Hayton: D Hayton, E Cruickshanks & S Handley (editors), The History of Parliament: the House of Commons 1690-1715, Boydell & Brewer, 2002

Headlam (1916): Cecil Headlam, editor, America and West Indies: November 1704, 1-15 in Calendar of State Papers Colonial, America and West Indies, Volume 22, 1704-1705, British History Online @ http://www.british-history.ac.uk/cal-state-papers/colonial/America-west-indies/Vol22/ (15 June 2016)

Headsman: Headsman, 1705: Captain Thomas Green and two of his crew on the Worcester @ http://www. executedtoday. com/2011/04/11/1705-captain-thomas-green-worcester/ (15 October 2014)

Healey (1955): George Harris Healey, editor, The Letters of Daniel Defoe, Oxford University Press, Oxford, 1955

Hearth Tax (1666): Hearth Tax: Middlesex 1666, Stepney, Shadwell Hamlet (2 of 2) in London Hearth Tax: City of London & Middlesex 1666, 2011 @ British History Online http://www. british-history.ac.uk/london-hearthtax/ london-mddx/1666/stepney-shadwell-hamlet-2 (15 January 2017)

Hedges: William Hedges, The Diary of William Hedges Esq. During his Agency in Bengal; As Well As On His Voyage and His Return Overland (1681-1687) in 3 volumes, Burt Franklin, New York, 1887

Herber: Mark Herber, Ancestral Trails: The Complete Guide to British Genealogy and Family History, Second Edition, Sutton Publishing, London, 2004

HoC (1707): House of Commons Record Office HC/CC/JO/I, no. 114, journal of the House of Commons, 8 April 1707

Holberg: Dale Holberg, editor, Students' Britannica India: Select Essays, Encyclopaedia Britannica (India) Private Limited, New Delhi, 2000

Honeck (2013): Mischa Honeck, Martin Klimke & Anne Kuhlmann (editors), Germany and the Black Diaspora – Points of Contact, 1250-1914, Berghahn, New York, 2013

Hopkins: www.hopkinsmedicine.org/healthlibrary/conditions/cardiovascular_diseases/rheumatic_heart_disease_ 85,P00239 (17 October 2017)

Howard: Eliot Howard, Eliot Papers Volume no. 1-2, E Hicks, London, 1895

Howell (1816): Thomas Bayly Howell, A complete collection of State Trials and Proceedings for High Treason and other Criteria and Misdemeanours from the earliest period to the year 1783, 1700-1708, Longman, Rees. Orme, Brown & Green, London, 1826 @ https://books.google. co.uk

Hugli-River: https://www.britannica.com/place/Hugli-River (29 September 2016)

Humphreys: John Humphreys, Cleeve Prior, Trans Birmingham Archaeological Society (Birmingham and Midland Institute), Vol. 61 (1916), pp 22-44

Hunt (2004): Margaret R Hunt, Captain Thomas Bowrey in Oxford Dictionary of National Biography, Oxford University Press, Oxford, 2004

Hunter: Sir William Wilson Hunter, A Statistical Account of Bengal, volume xviii, Truer & Co., London, 1877

IoW (Logbook): Osborn Collection fc 177 volume 1

IoW (Journal): Osborn Collection fc 177 volume 2

IoW Press: Isle of Wight County Press, 13 March 2006

Irish (1924): George Pratt Irish, editor, Papers relating to the Ships and Voyages of the Company of Scotland Trading to Africa and the Indies, 1696-1707, Scottish History Society, Edinburgh, 1924

Jones: Peter Murray Jones, A Preliminary Check-List of Sir Hans Sloane's Catalogues, British Museum, London, 1988 @ http://www.bl.uk/ebji/ 1988articles/article3.pdf

Kader: Mashudi Kader, Some Aspects of Seventeenth Century Malay via Thomas Bowrey's Bilingual Dictionary, Published 1701, Kemanusiaan, 2009

Keay: John Keay, The Honourable Company, Kindle Edition, Harper Collins, 2010

Kenny: Anthony Kenny, The Computation of Style: An Introduction to Statistic for Students of Literature and Humanities, Pergamon Press, Oxford, 1982

Kinnaird: http://www.kinnaird.net/darien.htm, (20 March 2016)

Kowl: Andrew Kowl & Robert Lemmo, editors, Encyclopaedia of Recreational Drugs, 1978

Knox (1681): Robert Knox, An Historical Relation of the Island of Ceylon, Richard Chiswell, London, 1681

Lahiri: Shompa Lahiri, Contested Relations: the East India Company and Lascars in London, in Bowen (2015): The Worlds of the East India Company

Lambeth Palace: Lambeth Palace Library, Vicar General of the Archbishop of Canterbury Marriage Licence Allegations.

Lang: Andrew Lang, The Case of Captain Green in The Select Works of Andrew Lang @ http://online-literature.com/andrewlang/historical-mysteries/9/ (15 October 2014)

Laurence: Anne Laurence, Women In England 1500-1760: A Social History, Phoenix Giant, London, 1996

Lenham: Bruce P. Lenham, The East India Company and the Trade in Non-Metallic Precious Materials from Sir Thomas Roe to Diamond Pitt, in Bowen (2015): The Worlds of the East India Company

Levenson: Thomas Levenson, Newton and the Counterfeiter, London, 2010, Kindle Edition, Faber & Faber, 2011

Lincoln (2014): Dr Margarette Lincoln, British Pirates and Society, 1680-1730, Routledge, London, 2014

Lincoln College: https://www.lincoln.ox.ac.uk/The-Thoma-Marshall-collection-of-Civil- (11 March 2017)

Lindsay: Kenneth Lindsay, English Education, William Collins, London, 1941

Ling: Alex Ling, Golden Dreams of Borneo, Xlibris, 2013

Lloyds Bank: www.lloydsbankinggroup.com/Our-Group/our-heritage/our-history/bank-of-scotland/british-linen-bank/ (9 August 2017)

LMA (Briggins): London Metropolitan Archives: ACC/1017/0002 Peter Briggins Diary Volume 1 and ACC/1017/0002A Peter Briggins Diary Volume 2

LMA (24176): London Metropolitan Archives: CLC 427 MS24176 Lloyds of London Papers of Thomas Bowrey

LMA (30324): London Metropolitan Archives: CLC 526 MS30324, List of Younger Brothers of Trinity House

LMA (3041): London Metropolitan Archives: CLC 427 MS3041 Papers of Thomas Bowrey

LMA (9172): London Metropolitan Archives: MS9172 London Wills and Probate 1507-1858

London Gazette: https://www.thegazette.co.uk

Long Family: http://www.thepeerage.com/p19335.htm (8 September 2017)

Love: Henry Davison Love, Vestiges of Old Madras, 1640-1800: Traced from the East India Company's Records Preserved at Fort St George and the India Office and from Other Sources. Volume Index – Primary Source Edition, John Murray, London, 1913

MacKay: Colin MacKay, A History of Phuket and the Surrounding Region, Second Edition, Kris Books Company Limited, 2016

Madden: F Madden, Index to the Additional Manuscripts, with Those of the Egerton Collection Preserved in the British Museum and Acquired in the Years 1783-1835, British Museum, London, 1849

MadderGenealogist: http://maddergenealogist.wordpress.com/2013/04/11/start-of-the-voyage/ (15 October 2014)

Marley: David Marley, Pirates of the Americas (volume I: 1650-1685), ABC-CLIO, Santa Barbara, 2010

Marsden (1): William Marsden, A Dictionary of the Malayan Language In Two Parts, Malayan-English and English-Malayan, Samuel Bridge, London, 1812

Marsden (2): William Marsden, A Dictionary of the Malayan Language; To Which is Prefixed a Grammar with An Introduction and Praxis, Cox and Bayliss, London, 1812

Marshall: P. J. Marshall, Afterward: the Legacies of Two Hundred Years of Conflict, in Bowen (2015): The Worlds of the East India Company

Martin (2014): Felix Martin, Money: The Unauthorised Biography, Vintage, London, 2014

Martin (2015): John Martin, Beyond Belief – The Real Life of Daniel Defoe, Kindle Edition

Master: Streynsham Master, The Diaries of Streynsham Master 1675-1680, Volume I 1676-1677, John Murray, London, 1911

McCarthy: Dr M McCarthy, Zheng He and the Great Southland: the Context for the Belief that he may have Voyaged there, Department of Maritime Archaeology Western Australia Museum, 2005

Measuring Worth: https://www.measuringworth.com/ukcompare

Mee: R Mee, An Old Malay Dictionary in Journal of the Malayan Branch of the Royal Asiatic Society, volume VII, pp 317 to 326, 1929

Mentz: Søren Mentz, The English Gentleman Merchants at Work: Madras and the City of London, Museum Tusculanum Press, Copenhagen, 2005

Miller: George Miller, Malay Used By English Country Traders of the 18th Century, http://mcp.anu.edu.au/rtm/ country.html (16 April 2016)

Mishra: Patit Paban Mishra, Balasore Port-Town in Seventeenth

Century in Proceedings of the Indian History Congress Volume 59, 1998

Morgan (1928): William Thomas Morgan, The South Sea Company and the Canadian Expedition in the Reign of Queen Anne in The Hispanic American Historical Review, volume 8, number 2 (May 1928) pp 143-166

Morton: Andrew Quinn Morton, Literary Detection: How to Prove Authorship and Fraud in Literature and Documents, Bowker, Bath, 1978

Mukherji: Bimala Prasad Mukherji, The English Factory at Hooghly (1651-1690) in the Proceedings of the Indian History Congress Vol 19, 1956

Murphy: Howard Murphy, http://rootsweb_archives/ MARINERS/2000-06/0959982176 (20 June 2000)

NRAS: National Register of Archives for Scotland catalogue

Nayar: Pramod K. Nayar, English Writing and India, 1600-1920: Colonizing Aesthetics, Routledge, Abingdon, 2008

N&Q: R. C. Temple, Daniel Defoe and Thomas Bowrey, in Notes and Queries, Literary and Historical Notes, 17 January 1931

O'Connor: Daniel O'Connor, The Chaplains of the East India Company, 1601-1858, Continuum International Publishing Group, London, 2012

OED (Cheroot): Oxford English Dictionary @ http://www. Oed.com/ view/Entry/31339?rskey=TR5cUj &result=1#eid 7684308 (7 February 2015)

OED (Orangutan): Oxford English Dictionary @ http://www.Oed.com/ view/Entry/132186?redirectedFrom= orangutan#eid (3 November 2016)

Omar (2002): Zuraidah Omar, Pocket Malay Dictionary, Periplus, Singapore, 2004

Omar (2004): Prof. Dato' Dr Asmah Haji Omar, The Encyclopedia of Malaysia: Languages and Literature, Archipelago Press, Singapore, 2002

Only Artists: www.bbc.co.uk/programmes/b09dyxxt (16 November 2017)

Ovington: John S. Ovington, A Voyage to Suratt In the Year, 1689. Jacob Tonson, London, 1690

Pepys 1: http://www.pepysdiary.com/diary/1660/01 (27 May 2017)

Pepys 2: http://www.samuelpepystoday.com/?day=0121 (5 November 2016)

Pepys 3: http://www.pepysdiary.com/diary/1667/06 /13 (9 July 2017)

Pepys 4: http://www.pepysdiary.com/diary/1663/01 /13 (25 February 2018)

Pickard: Lisa Pickard, Restoration London, Phoenix Press, London,

2001

Pirate Realm: The Pirate's Realm, http://www.thepiratesrealm.com/Madagascar.html#.VpkHRJUrFwE (15 January 2016)

Porter (2005): Stephen Porter, Lord Have Mercy Upon Us: London's Plague Years, Tempus, Stroud, 2005

Porter (2011): Stephen Porter, Pepys's London: Everyday Life in London 1650-1703, Amberley, Stroud, 2011

Prakash: Om Prakash, The English East India Company and India, in Bowen (2015): The Worlds of the East India Company

Prakash 2: Om Prakash, Cultural History of India, New Age International, New Delhi, 2005

Prakash 3: Om Prakash, European Commercial Enterprise in Pre-Colonial India Volume 2, Cambridge, 1998

Prebble (1968): John Prebble, The Darien Disaster, Pimlico, New York, 1968

Pringle (1894): Arthur T. Pringle, editor, The Diary and Consultation Book of the Agent Governor and Council of Fort St. George 1683, Government Press, Madras, 1894

Pringle (1895 1): Arthur T. Pringle, editor, The Diary and Consultation Book of the Agent Governor and Council of Fort St. George 1684, Government Press, Madras, 1895

Pringle (1895 2): Arthur T. Pringle, editor, The Diary and Consultation Book of the Agent Governor and Council of Fort St. George 1685, Government Press, Madras, 1895

Quaker House: Quaker House Library, A Ruth Fry Papers, TEMP MSS 373 (1621-1937)

Quiason: Serafin D. Quiason, The English "Country Trade" with Manila Prior to 1708 at http://asj.upd.edu.ph/ mediaox/archive/ASJ-01-01-1963/Quiason.pdf (3 July 2016)

Rahman: Nor-Afidah Abdul Rahman, The First English and Malay Dictionary, http://www.nlb.gov.sg/2016/ 01/22/the-first-english-and-malay-dictionary/ (16 April 2016)

Raven: James Raven, Publishing Business in Eighteenth Century England, Boydell Press, Woodbridge, 2014

Reddy: V. M. S. Reddy, The Advent of the Europeans, Kindle Edition,

Reid: Douglas Muir Reid, A Story of Fort St George, Diocesan Press, Madras, 1945

Rheumatology Article: https://academic.oup.com/rheumatology/article/46/2/183/2289541/What_kills_patients_ with_rheumatoid_arthritis (17 October 2017)

Risso (1989): Patricia Risso, Oman and Muscat: An Early Modern History, Routledge, Abingdon, 1989

Rittman: Paul Rittman, Rise and Fall of the British East India Company at http://www .paulrittman.com/EastIndiaCompany.pdf (3 July 16)

Rogers (2014): Pat Rogers, Robinson Crusoe, Routledge, Abingdon, 2014

Rosenbloom: Joseph R Rosenbloom, A Biographical Dictionary of Erly American Jews – Colonial Times Through 1800, University of Kentucky Press, 1960

Rost: R Rost (editor), Miscellaneous Papers Relating to Indo-China (volume 1), Kegan Paul, Trench, Trübner & Company, London, 1886

Rule: Chris Rule, Piratical History of Madagascar, http://www.piratesinfo.com/cpi_Piratical_History_of_Madaggascar_543.asp, (15 January 2016)

Sandes: Lieut.-Colonel E.W.C. Sandes, The Military Engineer in India, Navy & Military Press, Dallington, 1996

Satsuma: Shinsuke Satsuma, British and Colonial Maritime War In the Early Eighteenth Century: Silver, Seapower and the Atlantic, Boydell Press, Woodbridge, 2013

Sen: Mala Sen, Death by Fire: Sati, Dowry Death and Infanticide in Modern India, Phoenix, London, 2002

Sharma: Arvind Sharma, Sati: Historical and Phenomenological Essays, Motilal Banarisdass, Delhi, 1988

Shodhganga: http://shodhganga.inflibnet.ac.in/bitstream/10603/16506/18/18_appendix.pdf (13 November 2016)

Siam Records: Records of the Relations Between Siam and Foreign Countries in the 17th Century, Volume 1688-1700, Bangkok, 1921

Skeel: http://skeel.info/getperson.php?personID=14533&tree=ks (19 October 2016)

Smith (1998): J Irvine Smith, The Trial of Captain Green lecture @ Annual General Meeting of the Stair Society, Edinburgh @ http://schooloflaw.academicblogs.co.uk (26 February 2016)

Smith (2011): Stefan Halikowski Smith, Creolization and Diaspora in the Portuguese Indies – The Social World of Ayutthaya, 1640-1720, Brill, Leiden, 2011

Smith (2015): F Andrew Smith, Misfortunes in English Trade in Sukadana at the End of the Seventeenth Century With an Appendix on Thomas Gullock a Particularly Unlucky Trader in Borneo Research Bulletin Volume 46, 2015

SOAS: School of Oriental and Africa Studies EB70.10 William Marsden's English-Malayo Dictionary

Stanford: https://web.stanford.edu/gropu/virus/adeno/ 2000/variola.html (13 April 2017)

Strachey: Ray & Oliver Strachey, Keigwin's Rebellion (1683-84) An Episode in the History of Bombay volume 6 in the Oxford Historical and Literary Studies, Clarendon Press, Oxford, 1916

Temple (1930): Lieut.-Colonel Sir Richard Carnac Temple, New Light on the Mysterious Tragedy of the Worcester 1704-1705, Ernest Benn, London, 1930

TheAtlantic: https://www.theatlantic.com/international/archive/2014/04/London-forgotten-aryan-asian-fraudster/ 361035/ (6 March 2017)

Theodora: http://www.theodora.com/encyclopedia/e/east_india_company. html (3 July 2016)

Thornton: Thomas Thornton, Oriental Commerce: Or the East India Trader's Complete Guide, Kingsbury, Parbury & Allen, London, 1825

Thrower: Norman J W Thrower, editor, The Three Voyages of Edmond Halley in the Paramore 1698-1701, Hakluyt Society, London, 1980

Timperley: C H Timperley, A Dictionary of Printers and Printing, H Johnson, London, 1839

Tinniswood (2011): Adrian Tinniswood, Pirates of the Barbary Coast: Corsairs, Conquests and Captivity in the 17th century Mediteranean, Kindle Edition version 1.0, Vintage Digital, 2011

TNA (1/14): The National Archives: High Court of Admiralty Oyer and Terminer Records HCA 1/14

TNA (1/29): The National Archives: High Court of Admiralty Oyer and Terminer Records HCA 1/29

TNA (1/53): The National Archives: High Court of Admiralty Oyer and Terminer Records HCA 1/53

TNA (34/8/33): The National Archives: SP 34/8/33 ff42, 44

TNA (34/8/33A): The National Archives: SP 34/8/33A f41

TNA (54/1/10A): The National Archives: SP 54/1/10A

TNA (E134): The National Archives: E134/9Anne/East 13

TNA (Slaves): The National Archives, leaflet: Britain and the Slave Trade

TNA (Wills): The National Archives online at discovery. nationalarchives.gov.uk

Tomalin: Claire Tomalin, Samuel Pepys: The Unequalled Self, Viking, London, 2002

Townley: Rev. James Townley, Illustration of Biblical Literature, (volume III), Lane & Sandford, London, 1821

Traded Goods: http://www.british-history.ac.uk/no-series/traded-goods-Dictionary/1550-1820/aqua-aqua-mirabilis (17 October 2017)

Treasury Books (1701): William A Shaw, editor, Calendar of Treasury Books, volume 16, 1700-1701, His Majesty's Stationary Office, London, 1938

Tripathy: Rasananda Tripathy, Crafts and Commerce in Orissa (in the Sixteenth-Seventeenth Centuries), Mittal Publications, Delhi, 1686

Tuck: Patrick J N Tuck (editor), Trade, Finance and Power volume IV in The East India Company 1600-1858, Routledge, London, 1998

Tunbridge Wells 1: https://www.britannica.com/place/Tunbridge-Wells-England (14 August 2018)

Tunbridge Wells 2: http://www.localhistories.org/tunbridge.html (14 August 2018)

Ulak: http://www.gettyimages.fr/detail/photo-d'actualité/model-rafts-dugout-canoes-and-plankbuilt-vessels-were- employed-on-the-picture-id90745383 (30 September 2016)

Vallangi: Neelima Vallangi, India's Forgotten African Tribe, http://www.bbc.com/travel/story/20160801-indias-forgotten-jungle-dwellers (10 April 2018)

Vallar: Cindy Vallar, Notorious Pirate Havens – Part 3: Madagascar, http://www.cindyvallar.com/havens3.html, (15 January 2016)

Waller: Maureen Waller, Ungrateful Daughters: The Stuart Princesses Who Stole Their Father's Crown, Sceptre, London, 2002

WDYTYA: Who Do You Think You Are? Magazine

Weapons and Warfare: https://wealonsandwarfare.com/2016/10/30/the-battle-of-the-medway-part-ii/ (9 July 2017)

Wellcome Trust: High Society Press Release, https://wellcome.ac.uk/press-release/high-society (9 December 2017)

Wellclose: http://www.stigitehistory.org.uk/precinctwellclose.html (20 August 2017)

Wheeler: http://www.wheelerfolk.org/keithgen/d913.htm (11 March 2017)

Wikipedia (Aurangzeb): https://en.wikipedia.org/wiki/Aurangzeb (23 August 2018)

Wikipedia (Avery): https://en.wikipedia.org/wiki/Henry_Every (22 March 2016)

Wikipedia (Bay): https://en.wikipedia.org/wiki/Bay_of_Bengal (17 August 2016)

Wikipedia (Brandenburger): https://en.wikipedia.org/wiki/Brandenburger _Gold_Coast (9 April 2016)

Wikipedia (Condor Tokens): https://en.wikipedia.org/wiki/Condor_token (1 July 2016)

Wikipedia (Corsairs): https://en.wikipedia.org/wiki/French_corsairs (22 March 2016)

Wikipedia (East India Company): https://en.wikipedia.org/wiki/East_India_Company (3 July 2016)

Wikipedia (Ennore Creek): https://en.wikipedia.org/wiki/Ennore_creek (21 August 2016)

Wikipedia (Farthing): https://en.wikipedia.org/wiki/History_of_the_British_farthing (20 October 2017)

Wikipedia (Flyboat): https://en.wikipedia.org/wiki/Flyboat (30 September 2016)

Wikipedia (George_Psalmanazar): https://en.wikipedia.org/wiki/

George_Psalmanazar (6 March 2017)

Wikipedia (German Empire): https://en.wikipedia.org/wiki/German_
colonial_empire (9 April 2016)

Wikipedia (Hooghly River): https://en.wikipedia.org/wiki/Hooghly_
River (29 September 2016)

Wikipedia (Hyde): https://en.wikipedia.org/wiki/Thomas_Hyde (6
March 2017)

Wikipedia (James Sherard): https://en.wikipedia.org/wiki/James_Sherard
(17 October 2017)

Wikipedia (Lawton): https://en.wikipedia.org/wiki/Charlwood-Lawton
(14 May 2016)

Wikipedia (Machilipatnam): https://en.wikipedia.org/wiki/
Machilipatnam (14 May 2016)

Wikipedia (Monsoon): https://en.wikipedia.org/wiki/Monsoon (17
August 2016)

Wikipedia (Monsoon of South Asia): https://en.wikipedia.org/
wiki/Monsoon_of_South_Asia (17 August 2016)

Wikipedia (Mughal_Empire): https://en.wikipedia.org/wiki/Mughal_
Empire (23 August 2018)

Wikipedia (Narasapram): https://en.wikipedia.org/wiki/Narasapuram_
West_Godavari_district (19 August 2016)

Wikipedia (Nawab): https://en.wikipedia.org/wiki/Nawab (23 August
2018)

Wikipedia (Phuket): https://en.wikipedia.org/wiki/Phuket_Province (5
April 2018)

Wikipedia (Princely States): https://en.wikipedia.org/wiki/Princely_
States (23 August 2018)

Wikipedia (Pulicat): https://en.wikipedia.org/wiki/Pulicat (30 October
2016)

Wikipedia (Pulicat History): https://en.wikipedia.org/wiki/History_of_
Pulicat (30 October 2016)

Wikipedia (Rheumatism): https://en.wikipedia.org/wiki/Rheumatism
(17 October 2017)

Wikipedia (Royal African Company): https://en.wikipedia.org/wiki/
Royal_African_Company (27 August 2017)

Wikipedia (Taj ul-Alam): https://en.wikipedia.org/wiki/Taj_ul-Alam (17
August 2016)

Wikipedia (Temple): https://en.wikipedia.org/wiki/Richard_Carmac_
Temple (9 June 2017)

Wikipedia (Thomas Green): https://en.wikipedia.org/wiki/Thomas_
Green (15 October 2014)

Wikipedia (Triangular Trade): https://en.wikipedia.org/wiki/Triangular_
trade (26 November 2017)

Wikipedia (Tunbridge Wells): https://en.wikipedia.org/wiki/Tunbridge_

Wells (14 August 2018)

Wikipedia (Wars): https://en.wikipedia.org/wiki/List_of_wars_ involving_England (24 June 2018)

Williams (1997): Glyndwr Williams, The Great South Sea, English Voyages and Encounters 1570-1750, Yale University Press, New Haven & London, 1997

Wilson: George Wilson, A Complete Course of Chymistry, London, J Osborn, 1736

Winterbottom (2009): Anna Winterbottom, Producing and Using the Historical Relation of Ceylon: Robert Knox, the East India Company and the Royal Society in the British Society for the History of Science doi:10.1017/ S0007087409002209. 2009

Winterbottom (2016): Anna Winterbottom, Hybrid Knowledge in the Early East India Company World, Palgrave MacMillian, London, 2016

Worsley: Lucy Worsley, If Walls Could Talk, Faber & Faber, Kindle Edition, 2011

Yale: Yale University Osborn Collection fc 177, volumes 1 & 2

Yule: Colonel Henry Yule, The Diary of William Hedges, Hakluyt Society, London, 1889

Glossary

ague: Fevers accompanied by aching limbs.
ambergris: A valuable waxy substance excreted by sperm whales and used in perfume production. This remains an extremely expensive material today.
arrack: A spirit made from the fermented sap of coconut flowers, sugarcane, grain or fruit.
asafoetida: Dried latex used as a condiment in food.
baleen: Also known as whalebone, baleen in the filter inside the mouths of whale used for filtering crill.
bangha: Mild form of cannabis grown locally in India.
batta peon: Armed guard.
betilles: Muslin.
bloody flux: Dysentery, including passing blood.
blunderbuss: A short musket with a wide barrel that scatters shot over a wide area.
boat: Technically a small vessel that could be carried on a larger one. In Bowrey's time, ships usually carried boats for use as a tender between ship and shore.
boatswain: Also bosun, the senior deck crew man responsible for the maintenance of the ship.
bottomry: Also bottomage. An agreement in which the master of a ship used the keel, or bottom, of the ship as security against a loan to finance a voyage. The lender lost their money if the ship sank. The master forfeited the ship if the money with interest was not paid at the appointed time following the ship's safe return.
bowsprit: Is the spar attached to the prow of a ship to which the front-most sail is attached and allows this sail to project in front of the prow.
Brahmin: Hindu priest.
brig or brigantine: A two-masted, square-rigged, wide-decked sea-going merchant vessel.
buccaneer: Another term for pirate. Usually refers to 17th century pirates who attacked Spanish ships in the Caribbean.
cash: A copper coin used in India the value of which varied by location. Eighty Fort St. George copper cash were worth a fantam.

chambray: A fabric, similar to denim in that the weave has a coloured warp and white weft but, unlike denim, it is woven in a twill construction. That is, in a chambray single warp and weft threads pass over each other. A denim's warp thread is passed over two weft threads and under one.

charter party: The contract between the owner of a vessel and the charterer of the vessel defining the conditions of the charter.

chief mate: The second-in-command of a vessel. The chief mate would usually deputise for the captain while he is off the ship or ill, and replace him if the captain dies on a voyage.

China root: A natural medicine.

Cockpit-in-Royal: Also Royal Cockpit. Originally a cock-fighting venue and theatre and later a royal residence, in Thomas Bowrey's time was used as offices by the Treasury.

Commonwealth: The period from 1649 to 1660 when England and Wales, later also Ireland and Scotland, was ruled as a republic following the execution of Charles I.

compass rose: Device used on maps to indicate north, outdated by the time Thomas Bowrey copied his surviving charts.

corsair: Another term for privateer. Usually used for French privateers working in the southern Mediterranean Sea.

country ships: Ships involved in the local, intra-Asian trade.

country trade: Local, intra-Asian trade.

Downs: An area of the southern North Sea near the English Channel of the east Kent coast. A sheltered anchorage for ships awaiting a favourable wind or escort convoy.

crown: Coin worth five shillings.

dugong: A marine, herbivorous mammal related to the manatee or sea cow.

Dutch (United) East India Company: Also known as the VOP or Vereenigde Oostindische Compagnie formed in 1602 from a number of smaller, regional Dutch companies.

East India Company: The Governor and Company of Merchants of London Trading into the East Indies was created under a Royal Charter from Elizabeth I on 31 December 1600 to pursue trade with the East Indies. Also known as the London East India Company and, between 1698 and 1708, Old East India Company.

East Indiaman: Any vessel hired or owned by the East India Company.

East Indies: According to the 1600 East India Company charter in all lands washed by the Indian Ocean from the southern tip of Africa to Indonesia in the South Pacific.

English East India Company: The English Company Trading in the East Indies was created in 1698 to challenge the monopoly of the London East India Company. It was also known as the New East India Company before it was merged with the London East India Company as the United East India Company.

escritoire: Writing desk.

fantam: A gold coin used in India the value of which varied by location. A Fort St. George fantam was worth 80 copper cash. Thirty-two Fort St. George fantam were worth one pagoda.

farthing: Quarter of a penny.

flux: Dysentery.

flyboat: A European light vessel used primarily as a cargo carrier. Derived from the Dutch vileboat, a boat with a shallow enough draught to be able to navigate a shallow river.

factory: A place where factors, representatives of a merchant company such as the East India Company, lived and traded.

fakīr: A Hindu ascetic.

foul: To foul (of a ship) means to collide or interfere with another vessel. Alternatively (in a nautical context), to become entangled or jammed.

free merchants: A merchant not employed by the East India Company. If operating without a licence, also an interloper.

frigate: A light ship of 20 to 38 guns usually with stepped decks.

galley: A low, flat-built, sailing vessel pierced for large oars which could be used in light winds requiring a comparatively larger crew.

gangah: Form of cannabis that was five times more expensive than bangha, considered more pleasant and much more addictive.

gingham: Originally striped cloth of mixed cotton and Bengal silk.

Glorious Revolution:
The largely peaceful revolution by which the protestant William of Orange overthrew James II.

godown: Warehouse.

Gregorian calendar: The calendar in used in Britain from 1752. The New Year started 1 January.

groat: Coin worth four (old) pence.

havildar: Indian military commander.

hubblebubble: Glass hookah pipe.

interloper: Independent English trader, or free merchant, in the East
                  Indies operating without a licence or in contravention of
                  the terms of their licence.

isthmus: A narrow strip of land between two larger land masses
                  with sea on each side.

jagt: A Dutch yacht.

Jawi: Arabic-based Malay script

Julian calendar: The calendar used in Britain before 1752. The New
                  Year started 25 March.

kalamkari: A technique by which designs are drawn on fabric by
                  hand, a mordant (fixing agent) is painted on and then
                  the fabric is dyed. To produce multiple colours, multiple
                  stages using different mordants and dyes are necessary.
                  Different mordants will produce different shades with the
                  same dye.

ketch: A vessel with a mainmast and mizenmast, usually
                  between 100 and 250 tons.

lading, bill of: Detailed list of a ship's cargo.

lateen sail: A triangular sail used on Indo-Arab vessels that
                  permitted sailing only before the wind.

lascar: A native East Indian sailor.

letter of marque: A legal document granted to a master to act as a
                  privateer in time of war.

Levelers: A political movement during the English Civil Wars that
                  emphasised rule by the House of Commons, extended
                  suffrage, equality before the law and religious tolerance.

licenced ships: Independent English ships operating in the East Indies
                  under licence from the East India Company.

lighter: A flat-bottomed barge used for loading and unloading
                  cargo from ships.

London East India Company: The Governor and Company of
                  Merchants of London Trading into the East Indies was
                  created under a Royal Charter from Elizabeth I on 31
                  December 1600 to pursue trade with the East Indies.
                  Also known as the East India Company and, between
                  1698 and 1708, Old East India Company.

longcloth: Long pieces of plain cotton cloth.

mace: A spice made from the skin of a nutmeg.

Malacca canes: A cane or walking stick made from the stem of a rattan
                  palm for in the imported from the Malacca region of
                  Malaysia.

manilloes: bracelets used for trade in parts of Africa, often to
                  purchase trade.

mast: A tall, vertical pole that from which the sails are suspended via yards on a sailing ship.

masula boat:	Flexible surf boat used for landing passengers and cargo.
matchlock:	A type of musket required a slow burning fuse (match) to fire the gun.
Mogul:	Or Moghal, Mughal
monsoon:	The changes in atmospheric circulation and precipitation associated with the asymmetric heating of the land and sea.
mulmuls:	Fine, soft, Indian cotton.
musk:	A greasy secretion with a powerful odour produced in a gland of the male musk deer and other animals, and used in the production of perfume. A recognised way of sending wealth to England.
naik:	Indian district officer.
New East India Company:	The English Company Trading in the East Indies created in 1698 to challenge the monopoly of the London East India Company. It was also known as the New East India Company before it was merged with the London East India Company as the United East India Company.
oud:	A wood with an aromatic resin used for incense and perfumes.
paddy:	Unhusked rice.
pagoda:	1: The generic name used for a temple. 2: A gold coin used in India, the value of which varied according to location. A Fort St. George pagoda was worth eight English shillings or thirty-two fanams.
palanquin:	A covered, wheel less passenger vehicle carried on two horizontal poles.
Papal Bull:	In Roman Catholicism, a legally-binding, official document issued by the Pope authenticated by a lead seal or bulla.
paun:	Box for keeping betel-leaf.
pilot:	A specialist mariner who manoeuvres ships through rivers or harbours.
pirate:	One engaged in acts of robbery or criminal violence at sea.
pomfret:	A small fish.
priest-codder:	Vigilantes who searched for and apprehended Roman Catholic priests
privateer:	A private person or ship authorised by a government by a letter of marque to attack foreign vessels during a time of war and to take them as prizes.
Prize:	A vessel and/or cargo legally taken in times of war by a

	naval commander or privateer.
Prize:	The Crown's fund from the prizes from war at sea.
Protectorate:	The period during the Commonwealth when England and Wales, Ireland and Scotland were governed by a Lord Protector.
reale:	Also known as a royal of eight or piece of eight. A Spanish silver dollar.
Restoration:	The Restoration of the English, Scottish and Irish monarchy under Charles II.
rhumb lines:	Lines used in navigation, which cross all meridians on the longitude at the same angle, outdated by the time Thomas Bowrey drew his surviving charts.
road:	A safe anchorage for ships in a river or harbour.
royal of eight:	Also known as a reale or piece of eight, a Spanish silver dollar.
Rumi:	Roman alphabet Malay script adopted in 1972
Rump Parliament:	The English Parliament following the purge of the Long Parliament during the English Civil Wars.
saltpetre:	Potassium nitrate used to preserve meat and in the production of explosives.
sarassa:	A patterned cloth used as a waist-cloth.
sati:	Ritual widow burning, in theory at least, voluntary practiced in Bengal and Rajasthan, a religious ritual that conferred a status similar to Christian sainthood on the deceased widow.
Scots Company:	The Company of Scotland Trading to Africa and the Indies, also called the Scottish Darien Company, was founded by an act of the Parliament of Scotland in 1695 as an overseas trading company with a monopoly of Scottish trade to India, Africa and the Americas.
seer:	Unit of weight equivalent of between ten and thirty ounces and varied both by location and according to the item being weighed.
ship:	In the 17th and 18th centuries, a "ship" was a square-rigged, decked vessel with three masts. In the 21st century, "ship" has a wider meaning of a large seagoing vessel and I have used this definition throughout.
Siddi:	Indian of East African ethnic origin. Siddis are mostly descended from slaves.
sloop:	The general term for single-decked vessels, usually single-masted, often used as a service boat to a larger ship.
spire:	Drinking glass with air-twist stem.
spoiling trade:	Perishable goods.
sumpitan:	Blowgun.

supercargo:	A person, usually with experience of stocktaking and bookkeeping, appointed by the owners of a cargo to trade on their behalf. While he had no say in the daily handling of the vessel, he usually decided which ports they would visit for trade.
toddy:	A spiced drink based on a mixture of spirits, hot water and honey or sugar.
toys:	Small decorative items.
trekschiat:	A Dutch towed passenger barge.
ulak:	(Olocko or Oolauk) small, clincher-built cargo vessel employed on the River Ganges and its tributaries.
VOP:	Vereenigde Oostindische Compagnie or Dutch United East India Company, also occasionally known as the United East India Company.
wherry:	A light, passenger-carrying rowing boat.
xebeck:	Type of fast, highly manoeuvrable galley used on the north African coast.
yard:	The cross beam attached to the mast from which the sails are suspended on a sailing ship.

Gazetteer

Achin: Also Achen, Acheen and Achene, now Aceh on the northern tip of Sumatra.

Aleppo: A city in Syria.

Amboina: Also Amboyna and Ambon, the capital of Ambon island, Maluku province, Indonesia.

Andaman Islands: An archipelago in the Bay of Bengal between India and Myanmar.

Anegada Bay: A bay in northern Patagonia, Argentina.

Anjengo: Now Anchuthengu in Kerala on the south west coast of India.

Balasore: Also known as Baleshwar, a town in present-day Odisha, India.

Banda Islands: A group of small islands, part of Indonesia, the centre of the Spice Islands.

Banjar: Banjarmasin, a town on the south coast of Kalimantan, Indonesian Borneo.

Bantam: Now Banten, a city and former sultanate, Java, Indonesia.

Barbary Coast: The term used by Europeans in the 16th to 19th century for the coast of northwest Africa.

Batavia: Now Jakarta, Java, Indonesia.

Bay of Bengal: The area of the Indian Ocean surrounded by the east coast of India, Bangladesh, Myanmar, Thailand and Malaysia.

Bencoolen: Town on the west coast of Sumatra.

Bengal: The region of India now made up of West Bengal, India and Bangladesh.

Bombay: Now Mumbai, a city in Maharashtra on the west coast of India. Bombay was included in the dowry of Catherine of Braganza when she married Charles II.

Borneo: A large island in the Malay Archipelago comprising Kalimantan (part of Indonesia), Sabah and Sarawak (part of Malaysia) and the Kingdom of Brunei.

Burgara: I have been unable to identify this port.

Cabo Corsa: Guinea, West Africa.

Cadiz: Port in southwestern Spain.

Calcutta: Now Kolkata, West Bengal, northern India.

Calicut: Now Kozhikode, Kerala, southern India.

Callequilon: On the coast of Kerala between Karunagappally and Kollan.

Cape of Good Hope: The southern tip of South Africa.

Cape Verde Islands: Island in the Atlantic about 1,500 miles west of the coast of Senegal, Africa.

Ceylon: Also Singala, now Sri Lanka.

Cochin: Now Kochi, Kerala, India.

Comoros Islands: A group of small islands between the north tip of Madagascar and Mozamique.

Coromandel Coast: South-eastern coast of India.

Cossimbazar: A town in West Bengal on the Hooghly River, also known as Kasim Bazar, where there were English and Dutch factories during Thomas Bowrey's time in the East Indies.

Cuddalore: City in the Indian state of Tamil Nadu.

Darien: Roughly equates to the Panama Isthmus of Panama separating the Caribbean Sea and Pacific Ocean.

Delagoa Bay: On the southern coast of Mozambique, east Africa.

East Indies: All lands washed by the Indian Ocean from the southern tip of Africa to Indonesia in the South Pacific.

Ennore Creek: A Chennai backwater.

Formosa: Island east of China, now Taiwan or Republic of China.

Fort St George: The East India Company fortified factory at what is now Chennai. Madras or Madraspatam was the name of the settlement that grew up around the Fort but the three names were used interchangeably during the life of Thomas Bowrey.

Fort William: The East India Company factory at Calcutta (now Kolkata).

Golconda: Also known as Golkonda and Golla Konda about 500 km north-west of Chennai.

Gold Coast: Coast of West Africa on the Gulf of Guinea.

Guinea: West Africa.

Hugli: Also known as Hugli-Chinsura, Hugly, Hughli and Hooghly, a city on the Hooghly River in West Bengal, India.

Isle Bourbon: Now Reunion off the east coast of Madagascar.

Jamaica: An island in the Caribbean Sea.

Java: Indonesian island between Sumatra and Bali.

Johanna: Probably Anjouan, one of the Comoros Islands.

Juan Fernandez: A small island in the Pacific Ocean approximately 670km west of Valparaiso, Chile. The island on which Alexander Selkirk, the supposed model for Defoe's Robinson Crusoe, was shipwrecked.

Junk Ceylon: Also Janselone, now Phuket Island, Thailand.

Lima: The capital city of Peru.

Madagascar: A large island off the east coast of Africa.

Madapollam: A village near, and now a suburb of, Narsapur, Andhra Pradesh, India.

Maderia: Island in the Atlantic.

Madras: See Fort St George.

Madraspollam: See Fort St George.

Mahim: Site of Islamic pilgrimage about eight miles north of Bombay, now a neighbourhood of Mumbai.

Malabar Coast: The south-west coast of India.

Malacca: On the southern tip of the Malay Peninsula, Malaysia, just north of Singapore.

Malacca Strait: The narrow stretch of water separating the Malay Peninsula, Malaysia and Sumatra, Indonesia.

Maldives: A group of islands in the Indian Ocean.

Maritan: Now Manantenina on the east coast of Madagascar.

Masulipatnam: Also Metchilipatam, now Machilipatnam a city in the Krishna district of Andhra Pradesh, India.

Mauritius: The French Republique de Maurice, an island group in the Indian Ocean off the south-west coast of Africa.

Mecca: Also known as Makkah in modern-day Saudi Arabia.

Mergui: An archipelago in what is now southern Myanmar or Burma.

Mocha: Also known as Mokha on the Red Sea coast of modern-day Yemen.

Morocco: Country on the north-west coast of Africa.

Mozambique: Country on the east coast of Africa, north of South Africa and south of Tanzania.

Muscat: Capital of Oman.

Naraspore: Narasaput, also Narasapuram, Andhra Pradesh, India.

Nicobar Islands: An archipelago in the eastern Indian Ocean.

Odisha: Eastern Indian state on the Bay of Bengal.

Palicatt: See Pulicat.

Passir: There are number of villages (Panjangs) called Pasir in Indonesia on Java, Sumatra and Borneo. It is not clear which Bowrey visited.

Patagonia: A region of Argentina.

Pattantecar: Padang Island off the west coast of the main island of Borneo to Sukadana (capital city of the North Kayong region).

Penang: An island on the northwest coast of Malaysia

Pernambuco: Now Recife, Brazil.

Persia: Now Iran.

Pettipolee: Also Petapouli, Pettipolle, Peddapalle and Peddapalli, now Nizampatam, then a coastal village, about 400km north of Fort St George.

Porto Novo: Now Parangipettai, Cuddalore, Tamil Nadu, India.
Prussia: Historically a state in the north-east of present-day
                Germany.
Pulicat: Also Palicatt, now Pazhaverkadu, a coastal town north
                of Chennai with a salt-water lagoon.
Queda: Now the state of Kedah, Malaysia.
Quilon: Now Kollan on the Malabar coast of India.
Rajapore: A coastal town in west Bengal. Now Rajapur.
Rangoon: Now Yangon, the largest city in Myanmar.
Sarawak: One of the two Malaysian states on the island of Borneo.
St Helena: A settlement of the East India Company and now a
                British overseas territory on a volcanic island in the
                South Atlantic about 4,000 km east of Rio de Janeiro.
St Mary's Isle: A small island off the east coast of Madagascar now
                known as Nosy Boraha.
Sambalpur: City in th western part of Odisha.
Siam: Also Syam, now Thailand.
Singala: See Ceylon.
South Seas: An imprecisely defined area usually referring to the South
                Pacific but sometimes meaning either the South American
                coast or the Indian Ocean.
Spice Islands: Malaku, Molucca or Spice Islands are a group of
                Indonesian islands situated between New Guinea and
                East Timor centred on Banda.
Straits of Magellan: A navigable sea route between the southern tip of
                mainland South America and Tierra del Fuego.
Sukadana: Sukadana, capital city of the North Kayong region.
Sumatra: An island in western Indonesia.
Surat: A coast town in present day Gujarat. The East India
                Company had a major factory here until they moved to
                Bombay.
Swally: Now Suvali, a village close to Surat.
Tellicherry: Now Thalassery, Kerala.
Tenasserim: Tanintharyi Region, Myanmar or Burma – the
                southernmost region of Myanmar north of Phuket.
Tierra del Fuego: Archipelago at the south of the South American
                mainland.
Tranquambar: Tranquebar, now Tharangambadi, a town in Tamil Nadu
                where the Danes had a fort.
Tristan da Cunha: An island in the South Atlantic about 1,500 miles
                west of modern South Africa.
Valdivia: A city in Chile, south of Valpariso.
Vizagapatam: An East Indian Company district in the Madras
                presidency – now Visakhapatnam.

Index

A

abolitionist. *See* slave, slavery

accounts
  accountant 69, 165
  account books 101, 104, 145, 269, 273
  household 101, 102, 103, 248
  merchants' accounts 46, 104
  slave 73, 97, 103, 152, 232, 233
  trading 101, 103

Aceh. *See* Achin

Achin, Sumatra, Indonesia 54, 57, 58, 60, 88, 89, 90, 91, 94, 95, 97, 99, 100, 104, 105, 116, 129, 170, 171, 250

acts of parliament. *See* parliament

Acts of the Apostles in Malay 167

Adderton, Elizabeth. *See* Bowrey

Adderton, Stephen, stepfather of Thomas Bowrey 67, 72

Admiralty 14, 24, 133, 203

affidavit 198

Africa xxi, 124, 125, 156, 170, 176, 185, 200, 211, 234, 235, 257
  East Africa 156, 170
  North Africa 157, 229
  South Africa 211
  West Africa 124, 235

ague. *See* sickness

ale. *See* beverage
  tax 124

Aleppo, Syria 105

Alford, Henry, Thomas Bowrey's business partner 74, 76, 79, 87, 90, 94, 96, 98, 99, 104, 105, 106, 113, 125

Allahabad, India 6

almshouse 253

ambergris 56, 87, 130

Amboina, Indonesia 43, 44, 310

America 55, 143, 151, 176, 177, 226, 229, 233, 238, 239, 240, 243, 252, 257
  South America 143, 176, 233, 238, 239, 240, 243

Amsterdam, Holland 140, 141, 191, 198, 235

anchor 57, 59, 79, 83, 87

anchovies. *See* food

Andaman Islands, Indian Ocean 78, 85

Andes 240, 242

Anegada Bay, Patagonia, Argentina 241, 242

Anglo-Dutch War 229, 263

Anglo-Spanish War 20

Anjengo, India 186, 189

Anjouan. *See* Johanna

Anne Stuart, daughter of James II, Queen of England xxi, 108, 109, 128, 205, 216, 217, 219, 225, 231

Antwerp, Belgium 142

apothecary 1, 119, 251

apprenticeship 45, 155, 251

Ap-Rice, John, previous owner of the *Annandale* 202

Arabic. *See* language

Armenian 103

arrack. *See* beverages

artichoke. *See* food

asafoetida 187, 303

Asia 43, 45, 50, 55, 63, 158, 159,

165, 266
astronomy 46, 51
Atlantic Ocean 29, 31, 125, 153,
    233, 240, 241
Attorney General. *See* Cooke, Sir
    John
auction 113, 218, 256, 259
  by candle 136, 198
Aurangzeb, Grand Mughal xx,
    84, 228, 261
Australia 240
Austria 44
Avery, Henry, pirate 227, 228,
    229, 231, 232, 274
Ayscough, Samuel, catalogue of
    manuscripts at British
    Museum 9
Ayscue, Sir George 24

B
bacon. *See* food
baker 102
Balasore, India 51, 52, 53, 60,
    89, 90, 115
baleen. *See* whalebone
Balliol College, Oxford 160
Banda, Spice Islands, Indonesia
    43, 44
Bangor, Bishop of. *See* Evans, John
Banjar, Borneo, Indonesia 78, 84,
    94, 161
Bank of England 124
Bantam, Java, Indonesia 44, 69,
    151
Banten, Indonesia. *See* Bantam
Barbary pirate. *See* pirate
barber 102
Barbon, Nicholas If-Jesus-Christ-
    Had-Not-Died-For-Thee-
    Thou-Hadst-Been-Damned
    110, 111
Barebone, Praisegod 110

barley. *See* food
Batavia, Java, Indonesia 44, 78,
    79, 84, 103, 143, 144,
    156, 191, 210, 211, 212,
    213
Bath, Somerset 145, 146, 147,
    154, 155, 207, 251, 269
batta peon 103
Bay of Bengal. *See* A Geographi-
    cal Account of Countries
    Round the Bay of Bengal
Bays, Captain 82
bazaar 61, 79, 88, 164, 165
beans. *See* food
Beavis, John 82
bedding 123
  curtains 123
  cushions 57, 123
  pillows 123
  quilt 99, 123
  valence 123
bedlinen. *See* textiles
beef. *See* food
beer. *See* beverages
  Nottingham 123, 130
  tax 124
Beg, Ismail 62
Beg, Mohammed 62
Bencoolen, Sumatra, Indonesia
    156, 211
Bengal, India 31, 47, 48, 53, 60,
    61, 76, 78, 79, 80, 81, 84,
    85, 87, 99, 106, 115, 123,
    130, 132, 190, 193, 200,
    210, 256
  Bay of Bengal xvii, 6, 7, 8, 9, 10,
    29, 31, 43, 48, 52, 53, 60, 63,
    74, 75, 79, 85, 123, 132, 138,
    189, 190, 254, 258, 259
Bentam, Mrs 72
Bentham, Elizabeth. *See* Bowrey
bequest 251
Berlin, Prussia (now Germany)
    235

betel leaf 209
Bethlehem Hospital 194
bettiles. *See* textiles
beverages
  ale 124, 208
  arrack 52, 78, 82, 102, 138
  beer 102, 123, 124, 130, 147, 222
    Nottingham 123, 130
    tax 124
  brandy 26, 81, 202, 208
  chocolate 221
  coffee 137, 147, 198
  tea 87, 89, 212, 221
  wine 25, 26, 73, 106, 147, 178, 202,
    208, 215
    Italian red 208
    Rhenish 208
bhanga. *See* cannabis
Bible 237
Bill of exchange 131
bill of lading. *See* lading
Bills of Mortality 22
Binning, Barbara 218
Birmingham Archaeological
    Society 4
Blackheath. Kent 254
Blaswell, John 89
Blewett, Captain of the *Aurengzeb*
    188, 189
blunderbuss. *See* guns
boatswain 151, 152, 173, 195
boatyard 117, 137
Bodleian Library, Oxford 149,
    160
Bohun, Edmund 223
Bombay 6, 32, 33, 34, 39, 66,
    67, 68, 69, 70, 71, 72, 73,
    109, 150, 151, 163, 228,
    264
Bonham's 256
Borneo, Indonesia 45, 76, 78,
    79, 80, 81, 82, 83, 84, 85,
    86, 87, 88, 90, 91, 93, 94,
    96, 98, 99, 100, 104, 123,

126, 144, 151, 161
Borough High Street, Southwark
    118
Boston, America 151
Botolph Lane. *See* London
bottomry, also bottomage 122,
    190
Bowcher, Mrs, of Surat 150
Bowen, John, pirate 178
Bowen, William 125, 130
Bowrey, Captain John, uncle of
    Thomas Bowrey 19, 20,
    23, 24, 25, 30
Bowrey, Captain Thomas junior
  baptism 16, 17
  birth 16, 17
  death 253, 254
  Freeman 41, 83, 84
  marriage 116, 120, 121
  sickness 249, 250, 251
  will 252, 253
Bowrey, Captain Thomas senior,
    father of Thomas Bowrey
    13, 14, 15, 16, 17, 18, 19,
    20, 23, 30, 51, 66, 129
Bowrey, Elizabeth née Bentham,
    mother of Thomas Bowrey
    13, 14, 16, 17, 19, 23, 25,
    26, 30, 71, 72
Bowrey, Elizabeth, sister of
    Thomas Bowrey 21
Bowrey, Ellen. *See* Middleton
Bowrey, Hellin née Wall, wife of
    Joseph Bowrey senior 19,
    20
  will 20
Bowrey, Joseph junior, brother
    of Thomas Bowrey 19,
    20, 23
Bowrey, Joseph senior, grandfa-
    ther of Thomas Bowrey
    19, 20
Bowrey, Judith, aunt of Thomas
    Bowrey 24

Bradish, Joseph, boatswain of the
    Adventure 151
Brahmin 51
Brandenburg African Company
    235
brandy. *See* beverage
Brazil 153, 233
bread. *See* food
Bridge, Samuel, publisher 162
Briggins, Peter 5, 7, 237, 245,
    246, 253, 261, 275
  diary 7, 245
Bristol, Somerset 237
British Indian Army 6
British Library, formerly British
    Museum iv, xiii, 5, 8, 49,
    66, 257
British Linen Company 118
Broudly, Charles, of the *Speedy
    Return* 178
Bruges, Belgium 141, 142
Bruntisland, Scotland 204
buccaneer. *See* pirate
buoy 82
Burdett, Francis 125
Burgara, Malabar Coast, India 71
Burgess, Samuel, pirate 226, 231
burial xvi, 17, 40, 206, 254
Burrish, Captain George Luke of
    the *Scipio* 155
Bushell, Anthony 3
Bushell, Francis. *See* Gardiner
Bushell, Thomas junior, nephew
    of Frances Gardiner 3
Bushell, Thomas senior 3
butter. *See* food

C
cabbage. *See* food
Cabo Corsa, Guinea, Africa 152
Cadiz, Spain 129, 132, 137, 310
Calais, France 139, 140, 141,
    142
Calcutta, India. *See* Fort William
Callant, Robert of the *Worcester*
    182, 183, 185, 187, 188,
    189, 200, 203, 231
Callaway, William 59
Calliquiloan, India 188
cambrays. *See* textiles
candles 136, 198
canister 221
cannabis 10, 61, 83, 90
Cannon Lane. *See* London
Cape of Good Hope, Africa 43,
    196, 200, 211, 212
capers. *See* food
Cape Verde Islands 210, 211
capital punishment 51, 58, 59,
    68, 151
cargo vii, 31, 37, 44, 46, 54, 59,
    60, 70, 76, 77, 78, 80, 84,
    86, 87, 88, 89, 90, 91, 97,
    113, 115, 123, 126, 129,
    132, 134, 135, 136, 137,
    138, 152, 156, 171, 172,
    183, 184, 186, 188, 189,
    193, 196, 198, 199, 200,
    201, 203, 209, 212, 216,
    217, 218, 219, 230, 231,
    232, 237
Caribbean 171, 176, 226, 233
carpenter, ship's 135, 153, 173,
    174, 178, 182, 195
carpet 57
carrot. *See* food
Case of the Owners and Freight-
    ers of the Ship *Worcester*
    216
Catchpole, Allen 123, 130
Catholic. *See* Roman Catholic
    Church
cattle 233
cavalry 42
Ceylon 43, 53, 54, 56, 58, 61,
    62, 63, 83, 94, 97, 100,

103, 198, 252
chamber pot, pewter 208
Chambers, Essex 220, 249
Chancellor of the Exchequer 239
Channel, English 200, 212, 229
chaplain 59, 68, 80
charity 107, 252, 253
  Commission 253
Charles II, king of England xxi,
    90, 140, 161
Charles I, king of England 14
Charleston, America 193
Charlton, William 137, 139
charter party 181
charts. *See* maps
Chatham, Kent 30
cheese. *See* food
cheesecake. *See* food
Chelsea Physic Garden 251
Chennai, India. *See* Fort St George
cheroot 50
chest, iron 1, 2, 3, 4, 218
chicken. *See* food
Chief of Affairs 50
children 16, 26, 34, 35, 37, 108,
    109, 117
Chile 239, 240, 241
China 94, 106, 115, 221, 244
China House. *See* shop
china root 102
Chinese 96, 99, 142, 158, 159,
    221
chintz. *See* textiles
chocolate. *See* beverage
cholera. *See* sickness
Christie's, auctioneers 5
Christmas 82
cinnamon. *See*
Civil Wars, English 24
claret 81
Clarkson, Thomas, abolitionist
    237
Clavell, Walter, East India Com-
    pany writer 31, 34

Cleeve Prior, Worcestershire 1, 2,
    3, 5, 10, 258, 261
clerk 152, 165
climate 39, 49, 77, 171, 176,
    218, 240
cloth. *See* textiles
clothing
  apron 146
  breeches 39, 117
  coat 117
  cravat 126
  drawers, pair of 208
  flannel 117
  gold-lace trimmed 117
  gown 117, 146
  hat 126, 172, 177
  jacket 39, 117
  neck cloth 123
  nightgown 117
  nightshirt 117
  petticoat 123
  ruffles 126
  shirt 117
  shoes 37, 177
  stockings 177
  suit 117
  waistcoat 117
cloves. *See*
coach 147, 155, 206
Cochin, India 186, 187, 189
  Governor 187
Cockpit-in-Court 217
cocount. *See* fruit
coffee. *See* beverage
coffeehouse 137, 147, 148, 198,
    221, 244
  Lloyd's 137, 147, 148
  Marine 198
coin
  copper 222, 224, 225
  crown 222
  farthing 73, 224, 225
  half-groat 222
  halfpenny 224, 225

silver 126, 129, 138, 186, 221, 222, 223, 224
Cole, George, business partner of Thomas Bowrey 132, 135
Coleroon Shoal 100
Collins, Grenville 252
Combes, Walter, London merchant 175
Commonwealth Navy 14, 20, 51
Commonwealth period 14, 19
Comoros Island, Indian Ocean 174, 227
compass 82
Content, companion to the Speedy Return 177, 178, 258
convoy 14, 15, 17, 24, 195, 196, 200, 210, 211, 212, 213, 227, 228
  convoy duty 15, 24
  Dutch convoy 200
cook 102, 208
Cooke, Sir John, Attorney General 216
copper xvii, 31, 78, 80, 89, 161, 167, 222, 224, 225
  plates 31
Cordial Julep. See medicine
Cornhill. See London
Coromandel Coast, India 41, 48, 91, 92, 95, 100, 103
cosair. See pirate
Cossimbazar, Bengal, India 123
counterfeiter 223
country trade 54, 55, 75, 76, 80, 143
Court iv, 143, 198, 201, 203, 217, 238, 253
  Court of Chancery 253
  of Exchequer 201
  of the Queen's Bench 198
Cowes, Isle of Wight 256
crab. See food
crew 14, 18, 24, 73, 74, 77, 78, 93, 94, 105, 106, 132,
133, 136, 139, 141, 143, 148, 151, 152, 156, 157, 172, 173, 174, 175, 179, 180, 181, 183, 185, 186, 187, 188, 189, 191, 194, 195, 196, 198, 200, 202, 203, 204, 205, 208, 211, 212, 213, 215, 216, 217, 219, 226, 227, 228, 229, 230, 232, 237
  poaching of 93
Cromwell, Oliver, Lord Protector 15, 45
Cromwell, Richard 15, 17
cucumber. See food
Cuddalore, India 92, 93, 97, 98
custard. See food
customs 63, 120, 208
Customs House 33
cutlery 172
cyclone 37

D
Dampier, William 9, 64, 105, 106, 231, 240, 267, 271, 274
Danes 52, 313
Darien 176, 177, 193
Davis, James, husband of Martha Bushell, aunt of Mary Bowrey 221, 244
Davis, James of the Speedy Return 178
Day, Francis 41
Deal, Kent 182
debt xiv, 138, 154, 238, 239, 241, 243, 249
Defoe, Daniel 5, 236, 237, 238, 239, 240, 241, 242, 243, 269, 270, 271, 272, 273, 274
Delagoa, East Africa 184, 185,

186, 187, 188, 204
river 186
Delft, Holland 142
Delftware 221
Denmark 44, 95, 161
Deptford, Kent 19, 121, 202, 263
diamond 53, 146, 218
ring 218
Dictionary of Printers and Print-
    ing 167
dishes 82, 102, 208
distilling 252
dog 84
Tiger 84
Dolliffe, James, friend of Thomas
    Bowrey, Director of the
    South Sea Company 214,
    242
Doncaster, Yorkshire 218
Dordrecht, Holland 142
Dover, Kent 18, 201, 202, 289
Downs, The 18, 133, 182, 183,
    209
Downton, Hendry of Tunbridge
    Wells 123
drawers, pair of. See clothes
Drummond, Captain Robert of
    the Speedy Return 177,
    178, 180, 187, 204
Drummond, Thomas, brother of
    Robert 177
duck. See food
dugong 186
Dunaway, John 71
Dunkirk, France 141, 142, 213
Dupuy, Elias owner of the Mary
    Galley 208, 210
Dutch 13, 24, 29, 30, 41, 43,
    44, 48, 53, 54, 57, 58, 80,
    102, 103, 139, 140, 141,
    142, 144, 159, 164, 187,
    196, 200, 209, 212, 228,
    229, 230, 235, 236, 252,
    263

colours/flag 209
soldiers 29
War, Second. See war
Dutch United East India
    Company 43
dyer 101
dysentery. See sickness

E

earthquake 233
East Africa. See Africa
East India Company xix, xx, xxi,
    7, 10, 31, 33, 34, 40, 41,
    43, 44, 45, 47, 48, 49, 50,
    52, 53, 54, 55, 58, 59, 60,
    63, 64, 66, 67, 69, 71, 76,
    77, 79, 80, 84, 86, 91, 93,
    95, 96, 97, 98, 99, 100,
    104, 105, 112, 124, 127,
    128, 131, 143, 144, 150,
    156, 158, 159, 160, 161,
    162, 163, 165, 166, 167,
    169, 170, 171, 174, 175,
    176, 186, 188, 190, 193,
    194, 197, 201, 202, 203,
    206, 209, 211, 212, 218,
    228, 229, 230, 234, 235,
    236, 238, 239, 250, 251,
    257, 261, 265, 269
charter 193
Council 6, 68, 69, 73, 87, 88, 92,
    93, 97, 98, 104, 150
Court of Directors 143, 238
employees 40, 45, 71, 73, 236
English xxi, 44, 127, 235
factory xix, 31, 41, 44, 50, 52, 53,
    58, 69, 73, 76, 80, 84, 88, 98,
    100, 144, 161, 188, 189, 190
Fort xvii, xix, 10, 29, 31, 32, 34, 36,
    38, 40, 41, 42, 43, 48, 50, 51,
    53, 54, 55, 60, 61, 74, 76, 77,
    78, 79, 80, 81, 82, 84, 85, 86,

87, 88, 90, 91, 92, 93, 94, 95,
96, 97, 98, 99, 102, 103, 104,
105, 106, 107, 108, 125, 126,
131, 144, 190, 197, 198, 250
New 190
United 43, 128
East Indies xvi, xvii, xx, xxi, 10,
29, 35, 36, 39, 41, 43, 44,
45, 49, 50, 51, 53, 54, 55,
63, 64, 66, 73, 75, 80, 82,
86, 89, 91, 92, 106, 108,
112, 113, 116, 119, 122,
123, 124, 127, 128, 130,
132, 138, 140, 141, 143,
144, 146, 149, 156, 157,
158, 160, 167, 170, 171,
172, 175, 176, 177, 178,
181, 187, 190, 195, 197,
204, 209, 216, 220, 221,
223, 224, 229, 230, 232,
234, 239, 249, 250, 252,
256
ebony 50
Eckings, Captain Thomas of the
Woolwich 196
eclipse (of moon) 51
Eddystone Lighthouse 193
Edinburgh, Scotland 66, 200,
202, 204, 205, 215, 218,
259
Castle 204, 205
Governor of 204
Old Parliament House 205
education xiv, 6, 21, 46, 50, 51,
164, 247
eggs 101
Egyptians 100
Electuary. See medicine
elephant 57, 186
Eliot-Howard, family 7
Eliot, John, surgeon on Mary
Galley 7
Elixir Proprietatis. See medicine
Elizabeth I 44, 145, 304, 306

England xv, xvi, xix, 5, 10, 13,
14, 15, 18, 21, 23, 24, 29,
33, 34, 39, 40, 42, 44, 45,
48, 49, 50, 51, 54, 55,
67, 68, 69, 73, 76, 80, 84,
89, 90, 91, 95, 96, 98, 99,
103, 104, 106, 107, 108,
109, 112, 117, 118, 119,
121, 122, 123, 124, 125,
126, 129, 130, 131, 132,
138, 139, 140, 143, 144,
148, 149, 151, 155, 160,
166, 168, 170, 173, 176,
180, 185, 186, 189, 190,
192, 196, 197, 204, 210,
211, 212, 213, 215, 216,
217, 222, 223, 224, 231,
232, 234, 235, 236, 237,
240, 245, 248, 250, 251,
252, 256
England's Safety 252
English ix, xv, xvi, xviii, xix, xx,
xxi, 3, 5, 6, 7, 9, 16, 17,
30, 33, 39, 40, 42, 44, 49,
50, 52, 53, 58, 63, 69, 76,
78, 80, 82, 84, 88, 100,
106, 107, 115, 118, 124,
126, 127, 128, 138, 141,
142, 144, 149, 153, 158,
159, 160, 162, 163, 164,
169, 174, 175, 176, 177,
189, 196, 197, 200, 201,
202, 204, 205, 206, 210,
212, 213, 215, 216, 218,
219, 222, 223, 226, 228,
229, 230, 234, 235, 236,
240, 248, 252, 254, 255,
270, 273
Channel 200, 212, 229
English East India Company.
See East India Company
Epping, Essex 249
escritoire 85, 99
Essex xiii, 8, 119, 197, 247, 249,

272
Essex Record Office xiii, 8
Etherington, Madam 161
Etherington, Richard commander
    of the *Redbridge* 123,
    138, 161
Europe xv, xvi, 14, 40, 43, 50,
    141, 168, 228
European xx, xxi, 39, 45, 50, 55,
    56, 75, 76, 80, 100, 102,
    157, 158, 165, 186, 226,
    233, 248
Evans, John, East India Company
    chaplain and Bishop of
    Bangor and Meath 80, 84,
    85, 87, 90, 216
explosion 27
exports 49

F
fabric. *See* textiles
factor 31, 41, 53, 57, 124, 159
factory xix, 31, 41, 44, 50, 52,
    53, 58, 69, 73, 76, 80, 84,
    88, 98, 100, 144, 161,
    188, 189, 190
fakïr 61
fan 99, 221
  Chinese 99
fantam xvii
Fettiplace, George 3
Fettiplace, Thomas 3
fever. *See* sickness
fire. *See* London
fire engine 111
first mate 173, 174, 210, 227
Firth of Forth, Scotland 200, 213
fish. *See* food
fishing 33, 70, 142
Fitzhews, Mr 90
Flanders, Belgium 5, 139, 140
Flemming, Thomas, commander

    of the *Borneo Merchant*
    95, 96
flour 102
Flushing, Belgium 141, 142, 194,
    195, 198
flux. *See* sickness
food
  anchovies 147
  bacon 146
  barley 52, 111
  beans 146, 207
  beef 146, 208, 222
    rump 146
    sirloin 208
    steaks 146
  bread 102, 147, 208, 216
  butter 82, 102, 147
  cabbage 147
  capers 147
  cheese 102, 172
  cheesecake 147, 208
  chicken 146
  crab 146
  custard 147, 208
  fish 101, 103, 146
    dried 103
  fowl 101, 208
  ham 208
  lobster 146, 208
  mutton 146
  oil 26, 102, 184
  peas 146, 207
  pork 101
  rice 52, 70, 71, 94, 101, 102, 103
  salmon 147
  shrimp 146
  sole 2, 44, 86, 116, 146
  tart 147, 208
  tongue 202
  trout 146
  veal 146
  vinegar 23, 147
fork 208
Formosa 168

Fort St George, Madras, India
xvii, xix, 10, 29, 31, 32,
34, 36, 38, 40, 41, 42, 43,
48, 50, 51, 53, 54, 55, 61,
74, 76, 77, 78, 79, 80, 81,
82, 84, 85, 86, 87, 88,
90, 91, 92, 93, 94, 95, 96,
97, 98, 99, 102, 103, 104,
105, 106, 107, 108, 125,
126, 131, 144, 250
  Charles Street 54
  Governor 55
fortune. See wealth
Fort William, India 60, 190, 197,
198
fowl. See food
France 44, 100, 124, 132, 139,
140, 168, 176, 197
Francis, Captain 107
Francis, Lucy, widow of Captain
Francis 107
Fraserburgh, Scotland 200
Freeland, Peter of the Speedy
Return 180, 205
Freeman, Mr 83
French 29, 132, 139, 156, 159,
196, 197, 200, 209, 211,
212, 213, 226, 227, 228,
230, 241, 252
  colours/flag 197
  soldier 29
fringe, silk 99
fruit
  cherries, Kentish 155
  coconuts 33, 37, 52, 101
  dish of 208
  guava 101
  limes 101, 156
  papaya 101
  strawberries 147
funeral 2, 197, 247, 254

G
Gammon, Captain Philip 138
gangah. See cannabis
Garden 19, 251
Gardiner, Elizabeth, sister-in-law
of Thomas Bowrey 246,
247, 248, 268
Gardiner, Frances, née Bushell,
mother-in-law of Thomas
Bowrey 2, 3, 247, 248,
253, 261, 268
Gardiner, Mary, wife of Thomas
Bowrey 116, 119, 120,
121, 122, 123, 127, 130,
131, 135, 145, 146, 154,
197, 207, 246, 248, 252,
253, 254, 257, 258
Gardiner, Phillip, father-in-law of
Thomas Bowrey 8, 96, 98,
129, 130, 268
Geographical Account of Coun-
tries Round the Bay of
Bengal, A 6
Gerard, Elizabeth, wife of 4th
Duke of Hamilton 215
Ghent, Belgium 142
Gifford, William 123
Gillotts, Thomas, Thomas Bow-
rey's tenant at the King's
Head Inn 245, 246
ginger. See spices
Gingham. See textiles
glass 25, 27, 82, 156, 209, 252
  spire 209
globalisation 44, 259
Glorious Revolution 109, 305
Gloucester, Gloucestershire 138,
139, 147
Glover, Samuel 126, 144
Goa, India 34, 71
godown 305
Golconda, India 45, 311
gold 44, 56, 78, 89, 90, 96, 99,
100, 101, 105, 106, 117,

119, 121, 146, 157, 218, 222, 233, 240, 242
cross 218
Gold Coast 235
Prussian 235
Golla Konda, India. *See* Golconda, India
gong 82
Goodman's Fields. *See* London
Gothenburg, Sweden 25
Gouda, Holland 141
government xxi, 16, 49, 68, 119, 124, 127, 128, 219, 223, 225, 230, 234, 239, 243
Gravesend, Kent 18, 20, 133, 136, 198, 209, 210
Great Britain's Coasting Pilot 252
Great Clacton, Essex 8, 197, 247, 248, 272
Great Fire of London. *See* London
Great Seal of State 109
Great Storm 192, 193
Green, Captain Thomas of the *Worcester* 182, 215, 216, 259, 272
Green, John, brother of Thomas 205
Greenwich, Kent xv, 120, 121, 122, 127, 139, 143
  Crescent 121
  East 121
  King's House 122
  Queen's House 121
  Royal Observatory 121
  West 121
Gregorian calendar xv
Griffin, Richard of the *Mary Galley* 210, 213, 214
Griffith, Endimion 144
Grist, Elias of the Mary Galley 208, 210, 211, 212, 213, 214
guava. *See* fruit
Guidott, Thomas 145

Guild of One-Name Studies 4
Guinea, Africa 152, 196, 236
Gujarat, India 50
Gullock, Captain Thomas 143, 144, 151, 156
  his crew 150
gunners 205
gunpowder 27, 31, 79, 83, 200
guns 15, 24, 33, 37, 42, 76, 134, 151, 156, 171, 172, 186, 188, 189, 196, 203, 209, 229

H
Hague, Holland 142
Hakluyt Society 6
Halley, Edmund 153, 254
ham. *See* food
Hamilton, Captain Alexander 188, 228
Hamilton, James, 4th Duke of 215
Hammond, Thomas, freighter of the *Worcester* 200, 208
Harbin, Robert, business partner of Thomas Bowrey 129
harbour master 116
harpooner 184
Harwich, Essex 15, 17
havildar 92, 97
Healey, George Harris 5, 261, 274, 275
heart attack. *See* illness
Hearth Tax 25, 263
Heath, Captain 136
hens. *See* poultry
Herron, George 59, 99, 115
High Society exhibition 259
Hilliard, Captain John of the *Prosperous* 171, 172, 174
Hilliard, Edward, investor in *Prosperous* on behalf of

John Hilliard 172
Hill, John 123, 130
Hindu xx, 51, 52
Historical and Geographical Description of Formosa, An 168
Historical Relation of the Island of Ceylon, An 252, 294
history xiv, 156, 262, 263, 267, 273
hogs 101
Holland 5, 27, 139, 140, 141, 154, 194
Hollar, Wenceslaus 31
  map 31
Holloway, Francis 242
honeymoon 122, 127
hookah pipe. See hubblebubble
horse 25, 111, 141, 142, 145, 147, 218, 233, 247
horseback 41, 46
hot spring 145
house 2, 3, 19, 20, 23, 25, 26, 33, 38, 39, 42, 45, 56, 58, 61, 74, 88, 89, 106, 110, 111, 116, 121, 122, 140, 147, 148, 155, 192, 193, 207, 221, 233, 244, 246, 249, 256
  mansion 233
House of Commons. See Parliament
Howard, Henry 4, 6, 8
Howard, Thomas 173, 175, 179
Howison, James 159, 166
hubblebubble 305
Hugli, Bengal, India 60, 76, 79, 80, 84, 85, 87, 89, 90, 99, 132, 190, 266
Hugli Hole, Hooghly River 80
Huguenot 100
Humphreys, John 4, 261
Hungerford, John, lawyer of Lincoln's Inn Fields 123, 130, 231, 248
Hutchins, Dr Henry C of Connecticut 5
Hybrid Knowledge in the Early East India Company World 166
Hyde, Thomas, Oxford orientalist 149, 160, 161, 162, 163, 164, 167, 270

I

India xvii, xix, xx, xxi, 5, 6, 7, 9, 10, 20, 29, 30, 31, 33, 34, 40, 41, 43, 44, 45, 46, 47, 48, 49, 50, 52, 53, 54, 55, 58, 59, 60, 62, 63, 64, 65, 66, 67, 68, 69, 71, 72, 76, 77, 79, 80, 83, 84, 85, 86, 89, 91, 93, 95, 96, 97, 98, 99, 100, 104, 105, 112, 113, 115, 116, 117, 123, 124, 125, 127, 128, 130, 131, 132, 133, 136, 138, 143, 144, 150, 155, 156, 158, 159, 160, 161, 162, 163, 165, 166, 167, 169, 170, 171, 174, 175, 176, 179, 185, 186, 188, 190, 193, 194, 197, 198, 199, 201, 202, 203, 206, 209, 211, 212, 218, 220, 227, 228, 229, 230, 234, 235, 236, 238, 239, 248, 250, 251, 254, 257, 259, 261, 265, 269
Indian Archipelago, charts of 8
Indian Ocean xxi, 49, 226, 228, 233, 235
India Office 9
Indonesian archipelago 55
insurance 7, 111, 213, 216, 253, 254

fire 111
interloper 54
interpreter 47, 158, 161
iron 1, 2, 57, 100, 147, 156, 172, 193
Isle Bourbon, off Madagascar 178
Isle of Wight County Press 256
Isle of Wight, Hampshire 134, 156, 196, 256, 257, 258
ivory. *See* elephant

J
Jackson, Ann 130, 131
Jackson, John 130, 131
Jackson, Mary 131
Jakarta, Indonesia. *See* Batavia
Jamaica 9, 233, 235, 274
James II, King 108, 119, 145, 161
Japanese 44, 99
jar 61, 221
Jawi 164
Jearsey, William 53, 54, 56, 62
Jenifer, Captain James 138
Jesuit 250, 251
  bark. *See* medicine
jewellery 1, 2, 99, 146, 247
  diamond 53, 146, 218
  necklace 221
  ring 68, 118, 146
Jews 45
Johanna, Comoros Islands 174
Jones, Captain Samuel, London merchant 198, 199, 262
Jordan, Clement 60
journal 104, 214, 256, 257
Juan Fernandez 242
Juel, Senor Axel 95
Julian calendar xv
Junk Ceylon, Thailand 53, 54, 56, 58, 62, 63, 94, 97

Justice of the Peace 125
Jutland 213

K
kalamkari 49
Kalimantan, Indonesia. *See* Borneo
Kedah, Malaysia. *See* Queda
Keigwin, Captain Richard 73, 74
Kepler, Johannes 51
ketch 14, 15, 17, 18, 70, 71, 74, 76, 77, 78, 79, 85
Kiddells, Madam 90
Kidd, William, pirate 151, 226
Killingworth, William, tailor 117
King's Head Inn, Southwark 7, 118, 221, 245, 253
knife 57, 82, 102, 208
Knox, Robert 61, 83, 167, 229, 252, 274
Kochi. *See* Cochin
Kolkata, India. *See* Fort William
Kollan. *See* Quilon

L
labourer 222
Lackie, Captain John of the *Constant Friend* 170, 171
lading, bill of 99, 107
Lambeth, Surrey 109, 262, 268
Landuk, Borneo 144
language 50, 51, 107, 141, 158, 159, 163, 164, 165, 166, 168
  Arabic 158, 159, 162, 164
  Asian 158
  contact 158, 165
  Latin 158, 159
  lingua franca 158, 164
  Malay ix, 5, 7, 9, 46, 49, 56, 57, 62, 84, 107, 141, 149, 157, 158,

159, 160, 161, 163, 164, 165, 166, 167, 210, 212, 218, 252, 254, 270

Persian 158

Latin. *See* language

launch dinner. *See Mary Galley*

Lawson, Vice-Admiral Sir John 17, 18, 20, 42

Lawton, Charlwood 234, 237, 274

lead 76, 80, 123, 172, 188, 193

Lee, Kent xiii, 2, 17, 121, 254, 255, 261, 262, 268, 275

Leghorn (Livorno), Italy 24

Leigh, Essex 27

Leith, Scotland 200, 202, 205, 206

Road 200

Sands 205

South Leith Church 206

lemon. *See* fruit

Lesley or Lesly, Robert (Robin), son of Philadelphia Masfen 46, 132, 155, 190

Lester, Judith. *See* Judith Bowrey

Letter of Marque 133, 201, 227, 232

Letters of Daniel Defoe, The 5

Levant 44

Levellers 15

Leyden, Holland 142

Leyden, John 166

librarian 149, 160

Libya, North Africa 157

lightermen 19, 26

Lima, Peru 241

limes. *See* fruit

Lincoln, Dr Margarette 167, 231, 233, 271, 274, 275

Linen Manufacture 118, 124

linen, table 118, 124, 125, 268

Linseed, Thomas of the *Worcester* 200

Litchfield, HMS 210, 211

Lloyd, Edward 147, 148

Lloyd's List 156

Lloyd, John 147

Lloyd's Coffee House. *See* coffeehouse

Lloyd, Thomas 147, 148

lobster. *See* food

London vii, xiii, xx, xxi, 2, 5, 9, 16, 18, 21, 22, 23, 24, 25, 26, 27, 28, 29, 31, 37, 39, 42, 44, 45, 53, 54, 66, 67, 69, 80, 108, 109, 110, 113, 118, 119, 120, 121, 125, 127, 129, 131, 135, 136, 137, 139, 141, 143, 144, 147, 156, 162, 170, 171, 175, 180, 182, 184, 187, 190, 193, 194, 196, 197, 198, 200, 201, 203, 205, 206, 207, 215, 216, 218, 222, 224, 232, 236, 238, 240, 244, 251, 274

Birchin Lane 198

Botolph Lane 27

Bridge 26, 118

Cannon Lane 27

City of 22, 24, 26, 28, 110, 111, 121, 127

Cree Church 131

Mayor and Aldermen 127

Cornhill 25, 263

Goodman's Fields 221

Great Fire 25, 26, 27, 28, 29, 30, 37, 111, 127

Lambeth 109, 262, 268

Lombard Street 137

Marine Square 2, 110, 221

Mark Lane 251

Mile End Green 28

Moorfields 27

Pudding Lane 27

Ratcliffe 28

riots 29

Southwark 7, 118, 207, 221, 245

St Dunstan's Hill 262
Three Cranes Wharf 27
West End 111
London East India Company.
      See East India Company
London Metropolitan Archives
      xiii, 5
long boat 152, 173
longcloth. See textiles
Long, Edward, probably son of
      Nathaniel Long 172
Longford, Captain 67
Long, Nathaniel, friend and busi-
      ness partner of Thomas
      Bowrey 129, 133, 134,
      135, 136, 139, 141, 142,
      143, 147, 154, 169, 207,
      251
long pepper. See
Long, Sarah, wife of Nathaniel
      207
Lord Protector. See Oliver
      Cromwell
Lowfield, Thomas 118, 245
Loyd. See Lloyd
Luckings, James 130, 131
Lung Potion. See medicine

M
MacClachee, John, of the Speedy
      Return 178
mace. See
Machilipatnam, India. See
      Masulipatnam
MacKenzie, Roderick, secretary of
      the Scots Company 201,
      202, 203, 204, 205, 215,
      217
Madagascar, Africa 156, 169,
      170, 171, 172, 174, 175,
      178, 180, 186, 225, 226,
      227, 229, 230, 233, 234

St Mary's Isle 178, 186, 226, 229
Madapollam, Andhra Pradesh,
      India 74, 76, 77, 78, 79,
      81, 83, 88, 91
Madder, John of the Worcester
      182, 183, 184, 204, 205,
      206, 215, 220
Madras, India. See Fort St George
Madraspatam, India. See Fort St
      George
Magellan, Ferdinand 159, 241,
      242
Mahim, Bombay, India 67
   pilgrimage 67
Malabar Coast, India 67, 70, 97,
      161, 179, 180, 185, 186,
      187, 189, 203, 211, 228
   pirates of 67, 70, 97, 179, 228
Malacca 54, 55, 56, 129, 133,
      143, 144, 171, 201
   cane 129
   Strait of 55
malaria. See sickness
Malay. See language
Malay Archipelago 49, 163, 164,
      210, 212
Malay-English dictionary xviii, 5,
      7, 9, 10, 46, 84, 141, 149,
      157, 159, 160, 161, 162,
      163, 164, 165, 166, 167,
      218, 252, 259
Maldives 210
malt 102
Maluku, Indonesia. See Amboina
mango. See fruit
manilloes 156
mansion house. See house
maps 9, 31, 160, 165, 167, 240,
      252
Marcar, Ahmad 90, 91, 97, 104
Marine Coffee House. See
      coffeehouse
mariner 19, 20, 28, 45, 82, 101,
      125, 133, 227, 232

Marine Square. *See* Wapping
Maritan, off Madagascar 178, 186
Mark Lane. *See* London
marriage 17, 19, 76, 108, 116, 119, 120, 121, 122, 129, 135, 149
  civil 19
  licence 120
  licence allegation 262
  portion 120
Marsden, William 159, 162, 270
Marshall, Dr Thomas, Rector of Lincoln College, Oxford 167, 265, 266
Marshalsea, Southwark 151
Mary of Modena, second wife of James II 108, 145
Mary Stuart, daughter of James II, wife of William of Orange 108
Masfen, Philadelphia, sister of Robert Masfen, married Mr Lesley and Charles Sherer 125
Masfen, Robert 66, 82, 83, 86, 87, 88, 89, 90, 91, 93, 94, 106, 113, 115, 116, 118, 125, 126, 130, 131, 132, 155
Master, Streynsham 59, 64
masula 37
Masulipatnam, India 41, 48, 50, 63
mathematics 46
mats 102
Matthews, Captain Sir George, owner of the *London* and *Little London* 206
Mauritius 175, 178, 180, 230
May, Charles, of the *Worcester* 188, 189
Mears, Jacob 235, 236
Mears, Samuel 217

Mecca 226, 227
medicine 102, 145, 186, 251
  Ceylonese 61, 83
  Cordial Julep 251
  Electuary 251
  Elixir Proprietatis 251
  Histerick Water 251
  Jesuit Bark 251
  Lung Potion 251
  quinine 250, 251
Memoirs of ... George Psalma-nanzar 168
merchant 13, 14, 20, 21, 30, 44, 45, 54, 55, 60, 76, 88, 113, 120, 125, 129, 132, 133, 137, 142, 149, 159, 175, 183, 198, 212, 224, 232
  Dutch 141
  free 55, 60
  Scandinavian timber 111
merchants' accounts 46, 104
Mergui, Myanmar 105
mermaid 186
merman 161
Middleton, Ellen née, aunt of Thomas Bowrey 19, 20
Middleton, Hannah, cousin of Thomas Bowrey 9, 208
Middleton, Sollomon of the *Rising Sun* 198
Middleton, William, cousin of Thomas Bowrey 20, 122
Mile End Lane. *See* London
milk 102
Million, Henry 125
Mint, Royal 96, 221, 222, 224
missionary 158
Mocha 227, 228
Moghal, Grand. *See* Aurungzeb
monkey 84
monsoon 31, 32, 33, 39, 60, 70, 85, 86, 190
Moorfields. *See* London

Morocco, North Africa 157
Morregh, of the *Resolution* 191
mosquito 250
mourning 58, 118
Mozambique, East Africa 180, 185, 198, 227, 231
Mughal. *See* Moghal
mule 233
Muscat, Oman 70, 230, 297, 312
musk 80, 84, 90, 96, 98, 99, 107
  Chinese 96
muskets. *See* guns
Muslims xx, 52
muslin. *See* textiles
mutiny 67, 68, 132, 150, 195
mutton. *See* food

N
naik 41, 42, 43
Narai, King of Siam 62
Narasapuram. *See* Naraspore
Narasaput. *See* Naraspore
Naraspore, Andhra Pradesh, India 81, 87
Narsa, Sancho, shipbuilder of Madapollam 74, 75, 79, 81, 83, 91
national debt 241, 243
National Library of Singapore 165
navigation 21, 46, 51, 60, 74, 122, 208
  navigational instruments 82
navy 14, 17, 18, 20, 21, 24, 30, 177, 197, 223, 227
  Commonwealth Navy 14, 20, 51
  Royal Navy xiv, 31, 135, 140, 194, 197, 227, 230, 231
Newcastle 200, 213
New East India Company. *See* East India Company
Newgate gaol 151, 153, 163

New Light on the Mysterious Tragedy of the Worcester 6, 187
Newman, Captain Charles of the *Tankerville* 198
Newport, Glasgow 177
newspaper 3, 177, 215
  Post Man 215
  Scottish 204
New Testament. *See* Bible
Newton, Isaac, Warden, then Master, of the Royal Mint 221, 222, 223, 224
New York, America 5, 226, 232
Nicholson, Captain 99
Nicobar Islands, Indian Ocean 78, 85, 106
Nine Years' War. *See* war
Noden, Joseph, Thomas Bowrey's servant 2, 245
North Africa. *See* Africa
North Sea 14, 109
Norwich 40
notebooks 160
nutmeg. *See* spices

O
Odisha, India 53
oil. *See* food
Old East India Company. *See* East India Company
onion. *See* food
opium 93
oranges. *See* fruit
Orang-Outang 252
orang-utan 84
Ord, Tryphona. *See* Wheeler, Tryphona
Orp, John of the Prosperous 173
Osborne, Peregrine, Marquess of Carmarthen, vice-admiral and Tory politician 230

Ostend, Belgium 141, 142
oud 63, 307
Oxford University 145, 149, 160, 167

P
Pacific Ocean 143, 176
Padang. See Pattantecar
paddy 91, 94, 102
pagoda xvii, 39
  coin 42, 77, 78, 79, 83, 85, 87, 88, 98, 103
  temple 39
palanquin 87, 102
palisade 41
Panama 176
  Canal 176
pans 102, 190
panther 57
Papal Bull 43
papaya. See fruit
Papers of Captain Thomas Bow-
      rey xix, 4, 5, 6, 7, 8, 10,
      30, 43, 49, 64, 66, 67, 74,
      89, 94, 113, 127, 133,
      147, 148, 154, 156, 160,
      168, 187, 191, 194, 196,
      201, 218, 220, 221, 222,
      230, 241, 248, 254, 257,
      258
Papers of Thomas Bowrey, The
      5, 139
Parangipettai, India. See Porto
      Novo
Parliament 3, 14, 15, 16, 17, 18,
      108, 110, 124, 128, 133,
      169, 202, 205, 207, 224,
      235, 239, 252
  acts of 47, 124, 217, 252
  House of Commons xxi, 127, 169,
      171, 235, 239
  Member of 207

  Rump 17, 18
  Speaker 239
passenger, ship's 95, 107, 141,
      152
Passir, Indonesia 78
Patagonia 240, 241
Pattantecar, Borneo 144
pay 14, 21, 31, 40, 45, 55, 67,
      80, 89, 97, 124, 129, 131,
      132, 133, 137, 153, 157,
      158, 171, 214, 223, 225,
      231, 245, 246, 249, 251
Pazhaverkadu, India. See Pulicut
peas. See food
Peddapalli, India. See Pettipolee
Penang, Malaysia 159, 166, 312
Pennsylvania, America 237
Penn, William, founder of Penn-
      sylvania 237
pepper. See
Pepys, Samuel 17, 18, 25, 208,
      263, 264
perfume 55, 80
Perkins, Daniel of the Propserous
      173, 174
Pernambuco, Brazil 153
Persia 54, 55, 105, 106, 290
Persian. See language
Persian Gulf 8, 54, 228
Pettipolee, India 50, 76
Philippines 55, 143
Phipenny, Israel of the Speedy
      Return 180, 205
Phuket, Thailand. See Junk Ceylon
pickle. See food
pictures 221
  frame lacquered 221
Pigafetta, Antonio 159
pigs 101, 146
pilot 252
piracy 48, 56, 63, 104, 151, 153,
      169, 174, 204, 215, 218,
      225, 226, 227, 231, 232,
      233, 234, 238, 259

pirate 15, 105, 143, 151, 157, 173, 174, 175, 178, 179, 186, 187, 226, 227, 231, 232
  Barbary 157, 170
  buccaneer 303
  Caribbean 171, 176, 226, 233
  English 174
  European 226
plague. See sickness
plantains. See fruit
plasterer 102
plate 31, 82, 102, 161, 167, 208, 247
  pewter 208
Plymouth, Devon 17, 24, 196
Poach, Captain 113
poison 76
porcelain 44, 99, 142, 212, 221
  ballast 221
  bowl 87
  Chinese 142, 221
  tableware 99
  tea cup 87
pork. See food
Porto Novo, India 49, 77, 82, 87, 90, 91, 92, 93, 94, 95, 96, 97, 98, 100, 101, 102, 103, 104, 250
Port Royal, Jamaica 233
Portsmouth, Devon 25, 113, 133, 134, 135, 137, 205, 209, 220
Portuguese 33, 40, 43, 44, 48, 50, 59, 63, 71, 93, 100, 144, 158
Post Man. See newspaper
pots 102, 147, 208
poultry 69, 101
Powell, Gabriell 113, 139
power of attorney 30, 106, 125, 130, 131, 219, 269
Practical Navigation 252
Prickman, Samuel 82

Prince's Square, Wapping 110
privateer 24, 196, 227, 232
prize fund 219
Protectorate 21
provenance 7, 258
provisions, provisioning 17, 18, 42, 68, 77, 101, 136, 137, 139, 152, 155, 156, 173, 186, 226, 233
Prussia 235, 236
  King of 236
Prussian Gold Coast. See Gold Coast
Psalmanazar, George 168
Pudding Lane. See London
Pulicat, India xvii, 41, 103, 267
Puritans 247
purser 59, 60, 208
Pym, James, secretary of the South Sea Company 257

Q
Quaker House Library xiii, 5
Quakers xiii, 5, 7, 237, 245, 261, 276
Queda, Malaysia 62, 63, 97
Queen's Head Alley, Wapping 19, 20
Quilon, India 187, 188
quilts 123

R
Raffles, Stamford 166
Rajapore, India 67, 179
Rajapur. See Rajapore
Rajasthan, India 47
Ramsden, Mr 76
Rangoon, Burma 6
ransom 42, 132, 157
Ranton, Richard of the Prosperous 173

Ratcliffe, see London 28
Recife, Brazil. *See* Pernambuco
Red Sea 54, 55, 58, 227, 228
refugee 27, 28, 29
rent 7, 122, 147, 221, 245, 246,
    253, 269
respiratory disease. *See* sickness
Restoration of the monarchy 16
Reunion. *See* Isle Bourbon
Review, The 239
revolt 58, 73
Reynolds, John of the *Worcester*
    205
rheumatic illness. *See* sickness
Rhine-Meuse-Scheldt Delta,
    Holland 141
Rhode Island, America 151
rice. *See* food
Richards, Arthur 95
Richmond, Surrey 207
ring 118, 146, 218
  diamond 218
Rio de Janerio, Brazil 241
rivers 8, 26, 31, 41, 48, 52, 53,
    60, 79, 266
  Barking Creek 30
  Cooum 41
  Ennore Creek 86, 266
  Ganges 59, 60
  Haraspore 52
  Hooghly 8, 53, 59, 60, 61, 79, 266
  Humber 15
  Krishna 48
  Medway 30
  Thames 15, 17, 18, 19, 27, 30, 31,
      37, 42, 109, 117, 121, 122,
      133, 136, 182, 193, 201, 202,
      208
    estuary 18, 27, 122
  Woolwich Reach 30
robbery 151, 153, 204
Robinson, Captain 123, 130
Robinson Crusoe 237, 240
Robison, Andrew of the

    Worcester 204
Rodrigues, Mr 99
Roffey, Captain Caryl 143
Rogers, Woodes 240, 275
Rolls, John, business partner of
      Thomas Bowrey 132, 137,
      138
Roman Catholic Church xv
Roman script 164
rose water 102
Rossey. *See* Roffey
Rotterdam, Holland 141, 142
Rowley, Captain Samuel of the
      Rising Sun 194
Royal African Company 124,
      151, 153, 269
Royal Cockpit. *See* Cockpit-in-
      Court
Royal Navy. *See* navy
Rumi 164, 308
Russell, John 160, 251, 254

S

sacrarium 197
sailors 24, 25, 106, 231
salary. *See* pay
Salateers. *See* pirates
Salisbury, Ambrose 50
salmon. *See* food
salt 52, 76, 80, 102, 313
  production of 52
saltpetre 31, 190
Sambalpur, India 52
Sandown Castle, Kent 143
San Thome 41
Sarawak, Borneo, Indonesia 90
sati 47
Saunders, Daniel, of the
      Propserous 173, 174
Say, Captain Edward, of Mile End
      122
Scheveningen, Holland 24, 142

Battle of 24

School of Oriental and African
Studies, University of
London xiii, 162

scissors 57

Scotland xix, 44, 118, 175, 176,
177, 178, 181, 200, 201,
204, 205, 213, 216, 217,
218

Bank of Scotland 118

Company of, Trading to Africa and
the Indies 176

privy council 205

Queen's Commissioners for 217

Scots Company. *See* Scotland

Seaman, James, of the *Hannibal*
152

Searle, Andrew, junior 248, 249

Searle, Captain Andrew 248, 249

seers 102

Selkirk, Alexander 240

Seller, Jeremiah 252

Seller, John 252

servant 2, 6, 30, 34, 61, 82, 96,
102, 116, 132, 150, 202,
245

Shaxton, Captain 67, 68

sheep 52

Sheppard, Samuel 231

Sheppey, Isle of 109

Sherard, Dr James, apothecary
251, 276

Sherer, Charles, second husband
of Philadelphia Masfen
125, 126, 132, 144, 151,
190, 203

Shetland Isles, Scotland 212

shipbuilding, Indian 52

ships

Abingdon 211, 287, 296, 297, 298

Adventure 54, 74, 76, 77, 78, 79,
80, 81, 82, 83, 85, 98, 99, 151

ketch 74

Alexander Galley 191

Annandale 201, 202, 203, 216

Anne Frigate 155, 156

Anne Galley 193

Antelope 25

Arrabella 193

Arrivall 59

Aurengzeb 188, 189

Beaufort 104

Bengal Merchant 10, 106, 107, 108,
110, 112, 113, 149

Berkeley Castle 73, 149

Black Boy 191

Boa Vista 87

Borneo Merchant 79, 81, 82, 83, 84,
85, 86, 87, 88, 90, 91, 93, 94,
96, 98, 99, 100, 104

Chambers Frigate 220

Charles 31, 32, 34

Coast Frigate 150

Conimeer 88

Constant Friend 170, 171

Constant Warwick 14

country 53, 55, 60, 100

Defence 93

Defiance 180

Delagoa, sloop of the *Worcester*
185, 187, 188, 204

Dispatch 70, 71, 72

Dragon sloop 115

Drake 24

Duchess 240

Duck yacht 117, 122, 137, 139, 140,
141, 142, 249

Duke 240

Duke of Gloucester 138, 139

Eagle 151, 152, 153

Eaglet 24

Ekins Frigate 155, 156

Fancy 227

Francis 104, 106, 130

Frederick 170

Ganges 59

Ganj-i-sawai 227

George sloop 115

Gosfreight 148
Hannibal 151, 152, 153, 163
Home Frigate 148
Hope 24
Horsham 193
Hungerford 123, 130, 231, 248
Hunter fire-ship Mediterranean 24
Hunter frigate Bombay 70
John & Elizabeth 220
John Galley 155, 156, 170
Josiah 211
Linnet, sloop of the *Prosperous*
    174, 175
Little Charles. See Charles
Little London 206
London 27, 170, 187, 200, 206
Loyall Adventure 98
Loyal Merchant 34
Macclesfield 198
Mansel 148
Marianna 191
Marlborough 191
Mary Galley 5, 7, 46, 198, 207,
    208, 209, 210, 211, 212, 213,
    214, 225
  investors 207, 208
  launch dinner 208
Maynard 123
Pearl 84, 105
Prosperous ix, 169, 171, 172, 173,
    174, 175, 179, 190, 206, 271
  investors in 172
Rainbow 150
Raper (Rapier) Galley 180, 191,
    205
Redbridge 123
Resolution 138, 161, 190, 200
Rising Sun 193, 194, 195, 196, 197,
    198, 200, 212, 231
Rochester 193
Roe ketch 14, 15, 18
Royal James 99
Royal Navy xiv, 31, 135, 140, 194,
    197, 227, 230, 231

Sancta Cruz 59
Scipio 155, 156
Seamour 123
Shapir 99
Shrewsbury 95, 96
Speedwell 201
Speedy Return 175, 177, 178, 179,
    180, 181, 201, 204, 205, 215
square-rigged 76, 77
St George Galley ix, 127, 128, 129,
    132, 133, 139, 148, 149, 154,
    169, 220, 231, 245, 269
  investors in 129, 130, 132, 134,
    135, 136, 137
Swedish 134
Tankerville 198
tax on tonnage 124
Tonqueen Merchant 229
Trumball Galley 191
Tuscan Galley 148
Unity 24
Williamson 69
Windsor Frigate 207
Woolwich 30, 196
Worcester ix, 6, 154, 169, 171, 175,
    180, 181, 182, 183, 184, 185,
    186, 187, 188, 189, 190, 192,
    193, 199, 200, 201, 202, 203,
    204, 206, 208, 213, 214, 215,
    216, 217, 218, 219, 220, 225,
    229, 231, 233, 245, 254, 259,
    272
shipwreck 20, 104, 132, 226
shipwright 19
shipyard 19
shop 273
  China House 221, 244
shopkeeper 222
shot, iron 172
shrimp. *See* food
Siam 56, 77, 106, 267
Siamese 56, 62, 105, 106
sickness
  ague 82, 250, 251

cancer 246
cholera 45, 250
dysentery 34
fever 1, 23, 82, 83, 205, 246, 250
flux 34
heart attack 246
malaria 45, 82, 83, 250
plague 21, 22, 23, 30, 66, 251
rheumatic illness 246
smallpox 1
stroke 246
typhoid 45, 250
Siddi 308
signalling flags 83
silk. *See* textiles
silver xvii, 1, 2, 39, 49, 55, 56,
        101, 117, 119, 123, 126,
        129, 138, 146, 157, 178,
        186, 208, 221, 222, 223,
        224, 247
Simpson, John of the *Worcester*
        205, 206, 220
Singala. *See* Ceylon
Singapore 165, 166, 284, 289,
        291, 296, 312
slave, slavery 73, 103, 125, 170,
        227, 232, 233, 234, 235,
        237
  abolitionist 237
  East African 234
  sugar plantations 125
  triangular trade 75, 233
  West African 170
Sloane, Hans 8, 9
  Additional Manuscripts 9
sloop 84, 87, 88, 115, 173, 174,
        175, 185, 188
smallpox. *See* sickness
Smith, Captain Samuel, master
        of the *Charles*, then Chief
        Engineer and Master
        Controller of Ordinance at
        Bombay 30, 31, 71, 264
Smith, Elizabeth. *See* Bowrey

Smith, Henry, brother of Samuel
        66, 69, 72, 149, 151, 152,
        153, 156, 162, 163, 218,
        231
Smith, J Irvine 259
Society of Friends. *See* Quakers
soldier 57, 152
sole. *See* food
Solent 134
Sonsbeeck 195, 196
Sotherby's, auctioneers 5
South America. *See* America
South Atlantic 29
South Leith Church. *See* Leith
South Sea Company 239, 242,
        243, 252, 257
  Bubble 243
South Seas 143, 285, 313
Southwark, Surrey 7, 118, 207,
        221, 245
Spain 44, 177
Spalding, Augustine 159
Spanish xvii, 3, 13, 15, 20, 84,
        139, 177, 196, 226, 227,
        235, 239, 240, 241
  dollar 84
  shipping 226
Spanish Succession, War of.
        See war
spa water 251
Speaker of the House of Com-
        mons. *See* parliament
Spencer, John and Thomas 155,
        156
Spice Islands, Indonesia 44, 151
spices 44, 151
  cinnamon 43, 187, 188
  cloves 43
  ginger 188
  long pepper 77, 80
  mace 43, 89, 306
  nutmeg 43, 147
  pepper 44, 48, 54, 55, 58, 63, 77,
        78, 80, 84, 85, 86, 87, 94, 144,

147, 186, 187, 188, 200
turmeric 188
spire. *See* glass
spirits 81, 172
Spitalfields, London 100
  silk 100
Spithead, Devon 152, 209
Spivey, John of the *Constant
      Friend* 171
spoon 82, 152
  pewter 152
sprouts. *See* food
Sri Lanka. *See* Ceylon
Stair Society 259
St Alfege parish church,
      Greenwich 121
St Dunstan and All Saints parish
      church 262, 263, 275
St Dunstan's Hill. *See* London
steel 57
Stepney, Middlesex 17, 20, 22,
      25, 253, 261, 262, 263
St Helena, island in Atlantic 31,
      113, 313
St John parish church, Wapping,
      originally Wapping Chapel
      160, 254
St Katherine by the Tower parish
      church 247
St Lawrence, Madagascar 171
St Lo, George 252
St Margaret parish church, Lee,
      Kent 121, 254, 255
St Mary Magdalen parish church,
      Old Fish Ship, City of
      London 120
St Mary parish church,
      Whitechapel 23
St Mary's Isle. *See* Madagascar
storm vii, 70, 71, 91, 99, 182,
      189, 192, 193, 194, 211
St Paul's Cathedral 28, 110
Straits of Magellan 241, 242
strawberry. *See* food

stroke. *See* sickness
St Thomas, San Thome 41
Stuart, James Francis Edward, son
      of James II and Mary of
      Modena 109, 110, 145
Studds, Thomas, cousin of
      Thomas Bowrey 9, 46,
      171, 208, 252, 257
sugar 52, 57, 82, 102, 125, 202,
      233
  candy 102
  plantation 125
suicide 223
Sukadana, Borneo 144
Sumatra, Indonesia 44, 57, 58,
      62, 100, 211
supercargo 129, 156, 171, 172,
      177, 182, 194, 200, 203,
      210, 231
Surat, India 31, 32, 33, 54, 55,
      69, 70, 71, 72, 74, 150,
      171, 174, 175, 179
surgeon 7, 59, 76, 152, 178, 188,
      189, 204, 215
  of the Worcester 188, 189, 204, 215
surveying 46
Swally, India 32, 150
Sweden 17, 44
Sweet, Richard 125
Swinbrook, Oxfordshire 3
sword 73, 172, 186, 252
  blade 172, 186
Syal, Sultana Taj ul-Alam Safia-
      tuddin 58
Syam. *See* Siam

T
tailor 102, 117, 124, 269
Taiwan. *See* Formosa
tallow 82
Tamil 100
Tangiers, Morocco 25

Tanintharyi, Myanmar. *See* Tenasserim
tanner 37
tart. *See* food
Tasman, Abel 240
tassels, silk 99
Tatnell, James, of the *Hannibal* 152
tavern 25, 141, 142, 222
tax
  beer 124
Taylor, Captain 25
tea. *See also* beverages
  cannister 87
  tea cup 87
teak 75
Tellicherry, India 188
Temple, Lieutenant-Colonel Sir Richard Carnac 5, 6, 7, 8, 9, 10, 43, 187
Tenasserim, Myanmar 78
tent 173
Termonde, Holland 142
terrace 38
textiles 41, 44, 48, 49, 50, 52, 54, 56, 57, 76, 78, 80, 82, 85, 87, 88, 89, 97, 100, 123, 130, 138, 156, 191, 198, 221
  bedlinen, embroidered 221
  chintz 49
    painted 100
  cotton 48, 49, 53, 78, 89
  dyed 49, 101
  longcloth 53, 78, 85
  muslin 53, 123
  sarassa 89
  sarong 89
  silk 55, 65, 71, 76, 78, 80, 89, 99, 100, 117, 119, 121, 146, 172
    tassels 99
  Tonkin silk 65
  woollen cloth 172
Thailand. *See* Siam

Thalassery. *See* Tellicherry
therapeutic waters 145
Three Cranes Wharf. *See* London
tidal bore 59
tigers 84
timber merchants, Scandinavian. *See* merchant
tin 56, 57
tobacco 50, 62
toddy 102, 115
toddy tree 115
Tolson, Captain Joseph of the *Mary Galley* 208
Tolson, Richard owner of the *Mary Galley* 208
Tom, Peter of the *Rising Sun* 194, 196
tools 83, 233
Torbay, Devon 109
Tower of London 26, 27, 28, 29, 127
  gunpowder 27
toys 99, 221
  Japanese 99
trade xvii, xx, xxi, 14, 18, 20, 31, 43, 44, 45, 46, 48, 49, 53, 54, 55, 56, 57, 62, 72, 74, 75, 76, 78, 80, 81, 87, 89, 95, 100, 103, 111, 113, 118, 122, 124, 125, 126, 127, 128, 129, 138, 139, 141, 142, 143, 144, 156, 158, 163, 164, 169, 170, 172, 173, 176, 177, 178, 184, 186, 188, 197, 209, 212, 214, 216, 220, 221, 224, 228, 231, 232, 233, 234, 235, 237, 239, 241, 242, 244, 252
travel 15, 31, 95, 104, 147, 168, 195, 252
trekschiat 141, 142
Trial of Captain Green, The 259
Trinity House 119, 268

Younger Brother 119
Tristan da Cunha 211
trout. *See* food
Tunbridge Wells, Kent 123, 145,
    154, 197, 200, 203, 207,
    251, 270
turmeric. *See* spice
turtle 101
typhoid. *See* sickness
Tyso, Edward 252

U
ulak 266
Union of Scotland and England
    217
United East India Company.
    See East India Company

V
Valdivia, Chile 241, 242
valence 123
Vasco da Gama 43
veal. *See* food
vegetables. *See* food
Victoria and Albert Museum 4
vinegar. *See* food
Visakhapatnam, India. *See*
    Vizagapatam
Vizagapatam, India 76, 84, 85
VOC. *See* Dutch United East India
    Company

W
wages. *See* pay
Wales 80, 147, 166
Wall, Hellin. *See* Bowrey
Walton, William, neighbour
    and business partner of
    Thomas Bowrey 129, 134
Wapping Dock 19

Wapping, Middlesex 2, 13, 15,
    16, 19, 22, 24, 25, 26, 27,
    28, 29, 35, 37, 52, 99,
    110, 111, 116, 117, 119,
    122, 127, 128, 154, 160,
    172, 182, 197, 237, 251,
    254, 262, 263, 267,
    268
  Marine Square 2, 110, 221
  Well Close Square, also Marine
    Square 110, 111, 112, 119,
    127, 129, 248
Wapping Rose Garden 19
war 20, 24, 139, 196, 227, 229,
    235, 239
  Nine Years 139, 227
  Second Dutch 229
  Spanish Succession 196, 235, 239
Ward, Charles, Deputy Governor
    of Bombay 150
warehouse 136
warehouseman 76
Warham, Thomas cook for the
    Mary Galley launch dinner
    208
washer-man 102
water 5, 19, 33, 36, 43, 51, 59,
    60, 62, 82, 102, 145, 156,
    173, 174, 185, 186, 189,
    196, 200, 250, 251
watermen 19, 26
water woman 102
wax 102
wealth 17, 80, 120, 176, 221,
    230, 232, 244, 252
Webber, John 169
weights & measures xvii, xviii
Well Close Square. *See* Wapping
Wellcome Trust 259, 276
Wells, Richard builder of the
    Mary Galley 208
Weltdon, Anthony 105
West Africa. *See* Africa
West End. *See* London

West Indies 14, 103, 218, 226, 227
Westminster Abbey 110
whalebone 184
  baleen 87, 89, 184
whaling 183, 184, 185, 231
wheat 52, 102
Wheeler, James, Thomas Bowrey's business partner 74, 76, 115
Wheeler, Tryphona, wife of James Wheeler 76
wheelwright 37
Whitechapel, Middlesex 22, 23, 263
Whitehall 109
widows 7, 23, 30, 34, 46, 47, 48, 52, 71, 107, 120, 125, 248, 252, 253, 257, 261
  burning. See sati
wig 39
  periwig 126
Wigmore, Thomas 131
Wilkinson, of the Resolution 191
will xvi, 9, 16, 20, 30, 120, 130, 197, 247, 252, 253, 254, 257
William of Orange, William III, King 184, 224, 229
Wilson, Christopher 98
wine. See beverages
Winterbottom, Anna 166
witness statements 109, 153
women 20, 39, 40, 48, 51, 58, 62, 248
woollen broadcloth 49
Wootton, Isle of Wight 256
writing desk. See escritoire
writing style 258
Württembergische Landesbibliothek (State Library of Württemberg) xiii
Wybergh, Thomas, commander of the Rising Sun 194, 195, 196, 197, 198, 199

X
xebeck 157

Y
Yale University xiii, 5, 55, 276
Yang Lin 159
Yule, Elihu 5, 6, 55, 76, 262

Z
Zuider Zee, Holland 213